THE ANCIENT MYSTERIES REVEALED

Today, many people are dissatisfied with organized religion and distrust any establishment or system of doctrine. This is one of the reasons people are drawn to Wicca as an alternative religious or spiritual path. Now whether you're simply curious about Wicca, or seriously devoted to its study and practice, you can uncover the core concepts of this rapidly growing Nature-based religion.

The Wiccan Mysteries is a complete resource that explains every aspect of the Old Religion, revealing the Wiccan beliefs regarding reincarnation, the Gods, ethics, and more. Uncover the pre-Christian religious beliefs of Neolithic and Bronze-Age Europe, spiritual traditions that have been preserved within contemporary Wicca. Trace the origins of time-honored symbols and rituals back to the ancient Mystery Traditions of Southern Europe, Mesopotamia, and Egypt.

Here is material that was once exclusively taught only within the initiate levels of the older Wiccan traditions. Explore the inner meanings of the Charge of the Goddess and the other sacred writings of the Craft. Gain a fuller appreciation of the inner meanings and symbolism of Wiccan rites and traditional practices. Learn time-honored techniques to create your own astral temple, properly consecrate ritual tools, or work with a magickal familiar. *The Wiccan Mysteries* is an indispensible guide to understanding the essential teachings of the Wiccan religion.

OTHER BOOKS BY THE AUTHOR

The Book of the Holy Strega (Nemi Enterprises, 1981)

The Book of Ways, Vols. I & II (Nemi Enterprises, 1982)

Whispers, the Teachers of Old Italy
  (Moon Dragon Publishing, 1991)

Teachings of the Holy Strega (Moon Dragon Publishing, 1991)

Ways of the Strega (Llewellyn Publications, 1995)

ABOUT THE AUTHOR

Trained in the Family Tradition of Italian Witchcraft as well as Gardnerian Wicca, Brittic Wicca, and the Pictish-Gaelic Tradition, Raven Grimassi has been a teacher and practitioner for over twenty-five years. He is currently Directing Elder of the Aridian Tradition. It is his life's work to ensure survival of traditional material. He was the editor of *Raven's Call* magazine (1992–1995), a journal of pre-Christian European Religion, and has been a writer and editor for several other magazines. He lectures and teaches workshops and classes on the practices and natures of Wicca and Witchcraft, and has appeared on television and radio talk shows in the San Diego area.

TO WRITE TO THE AUTHOR

If you wish to contact the author or would like more information about this book, please write to the author in care of Llewellyn Worldwide, and we will forward your request. Both the author and publisher appreciate hearing from you and learning of your enjoyment of this book and how it has helped you. Llewellyn Worldwide cannot guarantee that every letter written to the author can be answered, but all will be forwarded. Please write to:

Llewellyn Worldwide Ltd.
P.O. Box 64383, Dept. K254–2,
St. Paul, MN 55164-0383, U.S.A.

Please enclose a self-addressed, stamped envelope for reply or $1.00 to cover costs. If outside the U.S.A., enclose international postal reply coupon.

THE
WICCAN
MYSTERIES

ANCIENT
ORIGINS & TEACHINGS

RAVEN GRIMASSI

1997
LLEWELLYN PUBLICATIONS
ST. PAUL, MINNESOTA 55164–0383, U.S.A.

FIRST EDITION
First Printing, 1997

Cover design by Lynne Menturweck
Cover art by William Giese
Illustrations by Shadowhawk and Lisa Novak
Interior design and editing by Connie Hill

Library of Congress Cataloging-in-Publication Data
Grimassi, Raven. 1951–
  Wiccan mysteries : ancient origins & teachings / Raven Grimassi.
    p.   cm. —
  Includes bibliographical references and index.
  ISBN 1–56718–254–2 (trade pbk.r)
  1. Witchcraft.   2. Witchcraft—History.   I. Title.
BF1566.G75   1997
133.4'3—dc21   97–11937
                                                                    CIP

The following publishers have generously given permission to use extended quotations from copyrighted works: From *Goddesses and Gods of Old Europe: 6500–3500 B.C. Myths and Cult Images New and Updated Edition*, by Marija Gimbutas. Copyright 1982 by Marija Gimbutas. Reprinted by permission from the publisher, University of California Press. From *Witchcraft Today* by Gerald Gardner. Copyright 1973 by Citadel Press. Published by arrangement with Carol Publishing Group. Reprinted by permission of the publisher, Carol Publishing Group. From *The Hero with a Thousand Faces*, by Joseph Campbell. Copyright 1973 by Joseph Campbell. Reprinted by permission from the publisher, Princeton University Press. From *The Witch's Way*, by Stewart and Janet Farrar. Copyright 1984 by Stewart and Janet Farrar. Reprinted by permission from the publisher, Robert Hale Ltd. From *Witchcraft for Tomorrow*, by Doreen Valiente, the poem "The Witches Creed." Copyright 1983 by Doreen Valiente. Reprinted by permission from the publisher, Robert Hale Ltd. From *Masks of God: Primitive Mythology*, by Joseph Campbell. Copyright 1959, 1969, renewed 1987 by Joseph Campbell. Reprinted by permission from the publisher, Viking Penguin, a division of Penguin Books USA Inc. From *Ecstasies: Deciphering the Witches' Sabbath*, by Carlo Ginzberg. Copyright 1991 by Carlo Ginzberg. Reprinted by permission from the publisher, Pantheon Books/Random House Inc. From *Roman and European Mythologies*, compiled by Yves Bonnefoy, translations by Wendy Doniger. Copyright 1992 by University of Chicago Press. Reprinted by permission from the publisher, University of Chicago Press.

Llewellyn Publications
A Division of Llewellyn Worldwide, Ltd.
St. Paul, Minnesota, 55164-0383, U.S.A.

DEDICATION

To my beautiful daughters, Michelle and Brieanna, whose unconditional love is the greatest mystery I've ever known.

ACKNOWLEDGMENTS

This was a difficult book to write, and my thanks go out to all who supported me during the course of creating the manuscript. First, I want to thank my friend Patrick, who has always been a good enough friend to tell me what I need to hear rather than what I want to hear. Special thanks to Jenny Gibbons for researching University archives, digging out facts from her own library, and for sharing her special knowledge of history with me. I want to express my appreciation to Diane, Leslie, Rick, Brian, and other friends for listening to me endlessly repeat my revelations as though they had never heard them before. Last, but certainly not least, to cyber friends and worthy adversaries on the Compuserve Wicca forum for helping me fine-tune my research.

CONTENTS

ILLUSTRATIONS

PREFACE

The purpose of this book is to restore the Wiccan Mysteries to their rightful place in the Community while providing a sense of the great antiquity of the Mystery Tradition within Wicca, the Old Religion. It is also my purpose to provide a historical basis for the many beliefs comprising Wicca. The vast majority of Wiccan Traditions have their foundation in the religion of the Celts. Unfortunately, very little of what the Celts believed and practiced can be proven historically. I believe that this has resulted in a certain lack of credibility concerning Wicca among many of the World Religions, and certainly within Academia as a whole. Sadly, there are those who label all Wiccan Traditions as *speculative modern reconstructions*, *revisionistic*, or *total fabrications* (including some Wiccans themselves).

This erroneous assessment is understandable among those who possess little, if any, understanding of the Mystery Tradition within the Old Religion, or the tenacity of secret societies in general. In an attempt to resolve some of these issues creating an obstacle for a wider acceptance of Wicca, I offer here a study of the antiquity upon which the Old Religion was established. Over the past twenty years I have studied and compiled an extensive database reflecting the theories, conclusions, and discoveries of many of the most widely acknowledged experts in the fields of mythology, archaeology, and European history. These include Mircea Eilade, Joseph Campell, Franz Cumont, Marija Gimbutas, Robert Graves, Michael Grant, Carlo Ginzberg and a host of others. Together with a study of the Inner Mystery Teachings of Wicca, I present here the occult legacy of pre-Christian European Paganism.

Many of the individual tenets that I have been able to connect to older civilizations can, if isolated, be dismissed as coincidental or perhaps even universal to humankind. However, when compiled together it becomes apparent that there are simply too many similarities to constitute anything other than the direct influence of one culture on another. As I will demonstrate in this book, this is the case concerning many of the Celtic Wiccan beliefs. Some people will regard my research as kicking the sacred cow, but if the reader is open-minded the evidence will speak for itself. I want to make it quite clear, however, that the outside origin of any specific belief does not diminish the integrity of the religion or culture in which it later resides.

The ancient beliefs and practices described in this book now reside within Wicca, and have been preserved by the Celtic peoples. I ask that the reader remember this while considering the many regions from which the Wiccan Mysteries migrated. There can be a great deal of pride in knowing that Celtic culture has helped to maintain the ancient Mysteries of Europe for us all throughout the centuries. In the final analysis it is unimportant who had what first, or who said what first; it is only important that the legacy survive.

This book has been written in a manner consistent with the tradition of training within the Mystery Tradition. Careful attention has been given to the progression of concepts and teachings, in order to form the appropriate mental pathways necessary to an understanding of the Mystery Teachings. By following the references to other chapters as aspects are revealed, the Mystery connections should become apparent. It is a common theme within the Mysteries that the adventurer is provided with a tool or magickal weapon to assist him or her in the Quest. I believe that you will find this book to be such a tool as you journey upon the Path of the Wiccan Mysteries. Read the book at least two or three times from cover to cover, and in doing so you will find things that will appear to have not been there before. Use the index to follow one particular theme or teaching, and make notes as you go along as to what themes are covered in other chapters. In the end you should be able to use the basic framework of this book to begin to unravel or develop a Mystery Tradition based upon any cultural tradition you care to practice.

Earliest known pentagram ring, originating from Crotona, Italy, circa 525 B.C.E. This drawing is taken from the book *Imagini degli Dei degli Antichi*, written by V. Catari in 1647. Catari called it the Pythagorean signet ring; it was said to have been worn by a mystical sect of Pythagoreans in southern Italy. The pentagram ring is a classic symbol worn by many modern Wiccans. It is interesting to note that Gerald Gardner's New Forest coven called themselves the Crotona Fellowship.

INTRODUCTION

Presented within these pages are the Inner Teachings of Wicca as a pre-Christian European Mystery Tradition. Here the reader will encounter the essential teachings of the Mysteries as perceived in the Old Religion of Europe. This is not a book of New Age philosophy, nor is it a presentation of individual adaptations within Wicca as a Religion. It is instead a book containing the ancient foundations of Wiccan belief and the esoteric concepts that empower Wicca as a System for spiritual development.

You cannot skim through this book and come away with an understanding of its teachings. The book must be read chapter by chapter in order to understand it in its totality. It will challenge you to expand your understanding, and perhaps at times even to re-examine your own perceptions. This is a book about the inner meanings of Wiccan rites, beliefs, and practices. You will not find cute little spells here, nor will you find patchwork rituals tossed together to create yet another Wiccan Tradition. What you will find instead are time-proven concepts and beliefs that have created, maintained, and carried Wiccan beliefs up into this modern era.

Wicca has changed a great deal since the days when Gerald Gardner first brought it to public attention in his book *Witchcraft Today* (The Citadel Press, 1954). Many people have come to Wicca from religions and teachings they could no

longer accept. Some came out of a sense of not belonging any-
where else, and some came out of a personal search for themselves. Because Wicca was more tolerant of other beliefs than
their former religion was, and because its structure allowed for
greater personal interpretations, the newcomers began to
change Wiccan concepts over the decades that followed
(1950–1990). Probably more than any other factor, aversion to
dogma had the greatest influence in the changes that reshaped
the old Wiccan Religion into modern Wicca.

Many of those who embraced Wicca were solitary practitioners who had little if any access to Initiate-level material. In
time they established their own systems and traditions based
upon what published books were available to them. In addition
they blended their own experiences as they practiced Wicca
from an essentially intuitive approach, following the guidelines
of various authors. Ironically the newcomers eventually out-
numbered the elders, and Wicca soon passed out of the hands
of Initiates and out into the public domain.

There were certainly gains to be had in this restructuring,
but things of great value were unknowingly tossed aside because
they were associated with dogma, rules, or sexual elements.
These were aspects that had caused personal pain in the
Seeker's former religion, and one by one Neo-Wiccans peeled
them away from the basic tenets of Wiccan Religion, particularly in the United States.

It is the purpose of this book to present the old Wiccan
Teachings once again, and to make available the basic initiate-
level teachings to which many solitary practitioners have never
had access. I believe that in reflecting back upon the wisdom of
our ancestors, and perhaps seeing things anew that have been
forgotten (perhaps initially misunderstood, or never before
encountered) that Neo-Wiccans can draw even greater sustenance from the spiritual stores of Wicca—The Old Religion.
For Wiccans "of the old school," this text can serve as a useful
reference guide and perhaps even provide some of the missing
pieces for those who practice eclectic traditions.

What you will encounter in this book is largely material that was once exclusively taught only in the Initiate levels of the old Wiccan Traditions. From this material you can gain a deeper understanding of the rituals and beliefs that are the foundation of the Wiccan Religion. It is my hope that this book will help establish an even greater appreciation for Wicca as a spiritual system. This text will also provide you with a complete overview of the basics of Wicca as a religion and spiritual path. Thus it is a book that can be shared with the curious and the experienced alike.

This book is first and foremost about the Mystery Teachings of Wicca. Second, it is a book about the origins of those mysteries. It is not a book about northern European religion or southern European religion, even though I will address them both a great deal. Neither is this a book about Wicca as a religion. Wicca is essentially a Celtic-oriented religion, but its Mystery Tradition is derived from several outside cultures. The focus for the origins of the Mysteries here is on *Old Europe* as defined by Professor Marija Gimbutas, author of *The Goddesses and Gods of Old Europe* and *The Language of the Goddess* (see chapter one). The focus for the Mystery Teachings is on the ancient experience of European cultures as they pertain to Wicca.

I began the examination of the Mystery origins in the region of Old Europe simply because that is where the oldest archaeological evidence for them is found, but please bear in mind that this book is not meant to exalt any culture above another with respect to who possessed what first. Despite the modern Western attitude that first means best, it does not mean so in this book. The purpose of this particular focus is simply to provide the reader with a sense of the rich heritage that was passed from one human community to another, and now resides within the Wiccan Mystery Tradition. Out of this, the reader may wish to further study the ancient cultures and deities from which these mysteries arose. Such an endeavor is sure to enrich the reader's own knowledge and understanding.

During the course of my research for this book I was astonished to find that the vast majority of studies into such fields as the origins of fairies and Wiccan deities were extremely ethnocentric. The insularity of many well-intentioned works left me stunned, as they bordered on an almost xenophobic approach to this field of research. As is generally the case when sitting in judgment of others, I found that I too was guilty of similar viewpoints. Therefore, I have tried to deal with the origins of each topic covered here in a verifiable historical/chronological order. I have attempted to edit out my own bias wherever recognized, and with the help of many friends (some almost too eager to oblige me) I believe I have been as successful as the human condition will allow.

It is difficult to write a book on the Wiccan Mysteries because mystery teachings are, by their very nature, something that someone experiences rather than reads about. It is also difficult to present a text of this nature to the Wiccan community at large, because such a work can be viewed as authoritative. Almost any approach must be taken with great care these days; many Wiccans come from a Christian background in which the mentality of the *One True Way* still evokes a "knee jerk" reaction to anything even closely related to it.

However, when I teach, I do speak with certainty and confidence in the things that I pass on. I say that this is how that is done, and this is how you go from point A to point B. If I am ambiguous in my own views, how can I instill a sense of confidence in someone who is just learning to trust in things not yet personally experienced? This is especially true concerning things of an occult nature. What I address here is what I believe to be factual and true—what my study, research, and personal experiences have led me to accept.

The time will certainly come for students of the Mysteries to question, and to adapt the teachings to their own views as they journey along. If the student becomes confused or puzzled, the teacher is there to say: "Well, according to the teachings, it's this way..." and then off they can go again on their own pursuit. In this sense, a teacher is a measuring stick by which the student can map out his or her own understanding of the mysteries. It is the spiritual sacrifice of a teacher to seemingly remain bound to the teachings of a tradition for the sake of the student. It is the purpose of a teacher to lead the student to their own realizations and to provide the tools by which the student may accomplish their own Quest.

Over the past twenty-five years I have studied, practiced, and taught the Ways of the Old Religion. I have worked with many Witches, Wiccans, and Neo-Pagans, and have been initiated into several different traditions. These include the Gardnerian/Alexandrian (English), Pictish-Gaelic, Brittic (Gaelic), and Strega (Italian) Traditions. I have danced in rituals, leaped the bonfires, cast spells, invoked the gods, and looked upward at the ancient moon in wonder. However, it is not my personal journey that I wish to share in this book, but rather what my research and experiences have revealed to me through the many years that I have studied and practiced. The Mystery Teachings contained within this book are drawn from a comparison of the inner teachings of those Traditions into which I have been initiated and trained.

I have had the good fortune to be initiated into different Craft Traditions representing northern, western, and southern Europe. Over the course of my studies it became apparent to me that the essential aspects of these Traditions appeared to be the same, despite different cultural origins. The myths and theologies, although employing different names and settings, were essentially the same. After several years of research and comparison, I became convinced that they all had a single common ancestor.

I first began researching Wiccan Mystery origins in a study of Celtic Britain. This led me to ancient Gaul, which in turn led me to the Romans. The study of the Romans took me to the Etruscans, and in turn to the Greeks which lead me to the ancient Minoans. The older a mystery teaching became, the further south I was drawn. Eventually I ended up in the Neolithic period of Old Europe. This is where I found the origins of many of the Wiccan symbols and religious concepts. In the end I believe I was able to unravel the twisted trail and to study the Mysteries relatively free of the many cultural influences that passed them on.

In this book you will find the teachings as I have come to understand them, both through my own experiences and the experiences of those who taught me. Here are the concepts and teachings that I found to be enlightening, connective, and transformational. I cannot compile everything known about each topic covered here within the confines of a single volume. However, should this work prove to be well received by the Wiccan community, then I will gladly produce an expanded volume on this subject. Until that time, I hope that you will find what I have written here to be of value to you in your own exploration of the Wiccan Mysteries.

ROOTS OF THE
WICCAN
MYSTERIES

When I first began to write about witchcraft I realized that it seemed to be a Stone Age cult which began by practicing hunting magic, and had found that the magic which would affect animals could be used to affect human beings, and to attempt to cause events to occur. I realized that the practice of magic had become a cult, which later grew into a religion, and that obviously at some later time foreign or exotic ideas had been introduced into the original simple folk magic; but I thought that these ideas had only come in at a comparatively later date, via the Greek and Roman Mysteries. That is still the simplest explanation; yet in real life one finds that seemingly simple ideas are apt to prove complicated on examination.

—Gerald Gardner, *The Meaning of Witchcraft*

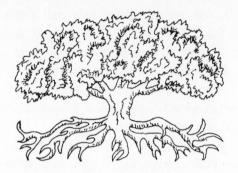

We cannot consider the Wiccan Mysteries without looking to the Celts, and to the Druids of the British Isles. The ancient lands of Ireland, Britain, Scotland, and Wales evoke images of mystical kingdoms and shrouded secrets, for here can be found the mysteries of the cauldron of Cerridwen and the teachings of transformation veiled in the story of Taliesin. Here too are the mystical Tuatha de Danann and many wondrous tales of mythic heroes such as Hu Gadarn and Cuhulainn. It is in such tales and myths that the principles of the Mystery Teachings can be encountered and unraveled.

However, the oldest known European Mystery Traditions (excluding the allegorical themes of Atlantis and Lemuria) actually originate from the ancient regions in and around Mesopotamia, Egypt, Greece, and Italy. In most cases these cultures predate the Celtic tradition by approximately a thousand years or more. In the Celtic lands the Druids taught a Mystery Tradition as well, which was a blend of indigenous beliefs and foreign influences. Many scholars today believe that the Druid cult was the surviving remnant of an earlier Indo-European priesthood. I will demonstrate in this book that the Mystery Tradition within Wiccan religion originated from the Neolithic Great Goddess culture of *Old Europe*, and not directly from Indo-European influences on Celtic religion in general.

In her book *The Goddesses and Gods of Old Europe* (University of California Press, 1982), Professor Marija Gimbutas describes Old Europe as a region encompassing Italy and Greece, and also extending into Czechoslovakia, southern Poland, and the western Ukraine (see map, page 5). Gimbutas states that here between 7000 and 3500 B.C. first dwelled the ancient matrifocal cult of the Great Goddess and her consort, the Horned God. She refers to the people of this ancient region as a pre-Indo-European culture: matrilinear, agricultural, peaceful, and sedentary.

Gimbutas goes on to speak of Old Europe and its unique aspects as a Neolithic culture. In the opening chapter she writes:

Between 7000 and 3500 B.C. the inhabitants of this region developed a much more complex social organization than their western and northern neighbors, forming settlements which often amounted to small townships, inevitably involving craft specialization and the creation of religious and governmental institutions. They independently discovered the possibility of utilizing copper and gold for ornaments and tools, and even appear to have evolved a rudimentary script. If one defines civilization as the ability of a given people to adjust to its environment and to develop adequate arts, technology, script and social relationships it is evident that Old Europe achieved a marked degree of success.

It is here in the Neolithic cult of the Great Goddess of Old Europe that the foundation of the ancient Wiccan Mysteries was created. Thus it is from here that we shall begin to relate the ancient secrets passed from one generation to the next. During the course of our exploration we will see the flow of Mystery Teachings as they pass from the Aegean into the Mediterranean regions. We will observe them as they enter Italy and merge with the Etruscan and Roman civilizations. From southern Europe we will trace their current westward, and then follow them up into northern Europe, for it is here that the Celts embraced the mysteries and incorporated them into their own belief system, which became what we now know as the Wiccan Mystery Tradition.

Old Europe, c. 7000–3500 B.C.
Replica produced with permission from *Goddesses & Gods of Old Europe*
by Marija Gimbutas (University of California Press, 1982).

In his book *The Mysteries of Britain* (Newcastle Publishing, 1993), Lewis Spence claims that the Druidic teachings among the Celts arose from a blending of the Neolithic Mediterranean culture with that of the native beliefs of early Britain. According to Spence, early Mediterranean voyagers of the New Stone Age and Bronze Age came to British shores and introduced the Cult of the Dead, common to ancient southern European beliefs of the period. With the commencement of the Iron Age, the island of Britain became isolated and thus Celtic beliefs transformed the imported teachings into a religion unique to the Celtic people.

The religion of Old Europe had spread west from southern Europe around 4500 B.C., as attested by the appearance of icons in Spain and France of the style common to the old matrifocal cult of the Aegean/Mediterranean region. By the year 3000 B.C. people from the Mediterranean, Spain, and Brittany settled in the hills of southern England, carrying with them the religion of Old Europe.

The Cult of the Dead, associated with spirits of the dead, which celebrated festivals in October and November, still exists from ancient times in Italy and the island of Sicily, just as it does in England. Historian John Morris (University College, London) in his book *The Age of Arthur* (chapter 8: Pagan Ireland) tells us that people from Sicily and southern Italy settled in Ireland in the third millennium B.C., and introduced burial tombs ultimately derived from the rock-cut tombs of Sicily and Italy. Morris says that these are the "people of Partholon" mentioned in Irish myth.

Sometime between 600–500 B.C. the Celts invaded England and encountered the former Mediterranean Cult of the Dead. Spence claims that the Celts at first feared the Cult, and were especially afraid of the *sidhe* (fairies) who were actually spirits of the dead. Another interesting Old European connection is that the earlier Etruscans (1000 B.C.) in northern Italy believed in a fairy race called the *Lasa* who were also associated with the dead (known later by the Romans as ancestral spirits called Lare). The similarities in appearance and lore are much too close for mere coincidence, as we shall see in chapter eleven.

Spence speculates that the Druids were actually a surviving priesthood from the Mediterranean Cult of the Dead, whom the Celts eventually came to respect and honor after their occupation of Britain:

> The long barrow men were traders, voyaging from Spain to Britain, at a period generally placed about 2000 B.C., and that they embraced the Cult of the Dead is proven by their burial customs. Other races followed them, but although their religious beliefs have left certain traces, the aboriginal Cult of the Dead remained the official faith, and absorbed all others of later introduction, the Keltic people embracing its principles and grafting their mythology upon it to a great extent...(Druidism) arose out of a Cult of the Dead which had been taking form during the Old Stone Age...

Thus the Druids became the Priesthood of the island, preserving the ancient traditions that had merged into a new and unique

Celtic religion. We must note however that Spence, through no fault of his own, is in error concerning the time of the long barrow men, having relied upon the faulty scientific evidence available to him at the time (the date is more likely 4000 B.C.).

As far as is known, the Celts had no temples prior to the Gallo-Roman period. They performed their ceremonies in forest sanctuaries under the guidance of the Druids who had become their religious leaders. The name Druid means "knowing the oak tree" or "finding the oak tree" and is obviously associated with the practice of worshipping in the woods. After the influence of the Romans, the Celts erected Pagan temples, many of which have been uncovered by archaeologists in Britain as well as in Gaul.

The Celts were the first defined people to form a distinctive culture in the European territories north of the Alps. Prior to the middle of the first millennium they were completely unknown to the civilized Mediterranean world. By the fourth century B.C. they were classified by the Greeks as being among the most numerous of the barbarian people in the then-known world (the others being Scythians and Persians).

It is possible to trace the origins of the Celtic tribes as far back as the Bronze Age Tumulus culture, which reached its peak around 1200 B.C. However, the Celts do not appear as a distinct and identifiable people until the time of the Hallstatt period (seventh–sixth centuries B.C.). During the Hallstatt period the Celts expanded through France, the British Isles, and eastward from central Europe. Celtic bands also later entered Italy, Romania, Thrace, and Macedonia. Here they attacked Etruscan, Roman, and Greek territories, and were eventually driven back across the Alpine foothills by the Roman legions.

From the middle of the first century B.C. the Celts were caught between the expanding Roman Empire along the Rhine and Danube and the Germanic invaders from the south. By the end of the century the Celts had lost their command on the continent and were later contained by the Romans who moved on to invade Britain (first around 56 B.C. under Julius Caesar). Eventually their culture was transformed by centuries of Roman occupation, and later by the Roman Catholic Church. The ancient Pagan traditions were driven into an *underground* society where they survived within the Old Religion of Wicca (as well as in many popular folk customs).

The history of the Old Religion extends far back into the dim past of the hunter-gatherer's emergence into an agricultural community. That is to say that at this point it becomes more recognizable to us. The roots of Wicca as an expressive religion date back into the Ice Age when humans were painting and carving scenes upon the walls of caves. Some scenes portrayed hunting themes and others appear as ceremonial in nature if not supernatural in concept. As we continue to explore the history of the Old Religion here, please note that where I do not present dates or reference a source, I am speaking about the oral history of the Mystery Tradition.

When the hunter-gatherer, forest-dwelling humans began to emerge into an agricultural society they brought with them the ancient deity forms of the wilderness. The stag-horned god of the forest was transformed into the goat-horned god of the pasture. This was due in a large part to the necessity of domesticating animals within an agricultural society. The god of the forest then becomes the god of the harvest.

The focus of the early cult, however, was not on deity in a masculine form but rather in a feminine form. The early ancestors of Wiccans worshipped the Great Goddess, who personified the mysteries of women. As the Great Mother, she reflected the mysterious and powerful nature of women to bleed for days without growing weak, and to give birth to another human being. Not only was this power a mystery to early men, it was also a mystery to the women themselves. Out of the need to understand (and in some ways to control) these abilities, the women isolated themselves from the men and formed female societies.

Some very convincing modern studies seem to indicate that it was the women who first established the taboo system. In some respects this was simply to escape sexual attention from the males, but it was also in order to be present to one another during times of menstruation and child birth. Women passed on the knowledge of herbs to soothe pain and reduce bleeding along with other "secrets" to which the men were not privileged. Under patriarchal rule the taboos remained in place, but took on different associations than were originally intended.

Men naturally feared what they could not understand, and perceived the taboo system not as a time for women to be alone together, but as a situation that men had to avoid. Thus for men the process of menstruation and childbirth became confused with fear and dread. All they knew was that these times excluded the pleasures of sexual intercourse and caused physical pain for the women. Out of the imaginings common to human nature when forced segregation takes place, negative images began to develop. These negative images evolved over the centuries into a mentality that erroneously viewed menstruating women as unclean and contaminating.

It was due in part to this mentality that men moved away from the spirituality of the Goddess Cult into that of the warrior/hunter cult. Because they could not breast-feed, menstruate, or give birth (and their role in impregnation was as yet not fully realized), men sought an understanding of their own relevance. This was, however, a slow process and many men remained within the matrifocal religion serving as priests. The majority of these men were elders and lamed hunters who, left behind during the hunting and fighting, were taught by the female shamans. Out of this body of men arose what became the priesthood of Wicca. In time there occurred a rift among the male societies and they eventually separated into solar- and lunar-oriented cults. As men rose to power, they challenged the structure of matrilinear descent and the supremacy of matrifocal religious concepts.

The Great Mother image remained a powerful force even after the shift from matrifocal religion to patriarchal religion. The Catholic Church maintained her divinity in the form of Mary, the mother of God. Even the church itself came to be known as the Holy Mother Church. The need for a nurturing Source to be close at hand (and to serve as in matrilineal times) was never driven from the psyche of men. The mother figure is the strongest and most lasting image within the human experience.

It was largely women who established human culture and brought humankind out of the hunter-gatherer era and into that of an agricultural society (see chapter thirteen). The image of the

Great Mother Goddess was the outward symbol of the concerns and needs of the human community. But she also embodied the fears of early peoples and thus she was also known as the "Mother Terrible," the destroyer of life, wherein she represented death. Like her symbol the moon, the goddess transformed herself into different guises and different reflections of light and dark.

Villages reliant on cultivated plants and domesticated animals first appeared in southeastern Europe as early as the seventh millennium. Carved stone images of the Great Mother Goddess appear in the Neolithic art of Old Europe around 6500 B.C. along with stone images of male horned deities. The vast numbers of statues and images uncovered by archaeologists indicate a widespread matrifocal cult among the peoples of Old Europe. This ancient cult contained the origins of Wiccan religious beliefs.

When the word "Wicca" first became known to the public at large, it was used to refer to the old pre-Christian European Religion. Today, the meaning has changed to include a more open view of Neo-Pagan and New Age concepts. The Old Religion of Wicca was originally a fertility cult that worshipped a Goddess and a God. It had, at a certain stage of development, a hierarchy that was comprised of a High Priestess and a High Priest, assisted by Priestesses and Priests. In essence Wicca was a Nature religion focusing on the energies that flowed over the earth with the changing of the seasons.

In this chapter we will examine the basics of the Old Religion, presenting a view of what the Old Religion once was, and what it is today. I think that it is important to recall our heritage, and to discern our present condition, lest we forget who we were and therefore who we are today. We must not forget that the Old Religion was founded upon the Laws of Nature, and has within its own structure certain laws and ways, patterned after those of Nature. The Mystery Tradition within the Old Religion is a *system* through which individuals can learn to evolve spiritually through an understanding of the metaphysical laws reflected in the ways of Nature.

The cultural roots of the Old Religion go back to the early tribal days of humankind. In their attempts to understand the world around them, these primitive people took the first steps toward religion. In the great forces of Nature, such as storms and earthquakes, they saw the actions of Beings greater than themselves, which they later called Gods. From this human tendency to personify things arose a host of spirits and deities. Craft legends are full of stories in which the Gods interact with humankind. Even the most common esoteric myths tell of such encounters. It seems likely that early humankind did indeed encounter a superior race of Beings (whether Gods or people from an earlier advanced society) who impressed them enough to inspire the resulting forms of ritual worship. There are certainly enough unsolved mysteries (such as Stonehenge, the Nazcar plains, and the statues at Easter Island) to give one cause for deeper thought.

In the Old Ways, the legends tell of the great Gods who watched over their followers, and delivered them safely from the Fall of Humankind through the First and Second Ages. These ages reflect the legends of Lemuria and Atlantis. It was not only the Gods, however, who cared for and guided humankind, but the early shamans of the tribes. The first shamans were most likely women who, during the daily course of food gathering and preparation, came to learn the secrets of herbalism.

Prior to the advent of agriculture, humans depended upon animal life and, therefore, on the tribal hunters. Legends tell of the bravest hunters who dressed in animal disguise (skins and horns) in order to get close to the herds. In time the image of this horned hero became the image of the God who provided animals for the tribes. As previously noted, eventually the horned heroes (usually through injury) no longer went on the hunts and due to their special status within the clan were given magickal and religious training by the female shamans. Out of this arose the role of the Priestess and her Priest. Originally, the women directed the religious/spiritual ways of the tribe and men were excluded from any major roles. Women appeared magickal to men because of their ability to produce offspring, and therefore men easily accepted female domination. It wasn't until men realized their role in procreation that they pushed for a greater role in religious matters. This resulted in a partnership relationship between the genders, as opposed to the earlier dominance relationship. Later, as men were increasingly forced to become warriors as well as hunters, they grew in importance and gained more control over all tribal concerns (see chapter fourteen).

The existing matrifocal society (that the hunter/warrior cult eventually usurped) had long been established over many centuries. Its Great Mother Goddess was the earliest of deity forms created by humankind. Of this early cult Marija Gimbutas writes:

> *The Goddess-centered art with its striking absence of images of warfare and male domination, reflects a social order in which women as heads of clans or queen-priestesses played a central part.*
>
> —Marija Gimbutas, *The Language of the Goddess*

Gimbutas states that the Great Goddess cult of Old Europe was brought to a gradual decline beginning perhaps as early as 4300 B.C. and ending its solitary reign sometime around 2500 B.C. (due to the patriarchal expansion of the Indo-Europeans). From 2500 B.C. on, the religion of Europe functioned as a blend of matrifocal European beliefs and Indo-European patriarchal practices (in most regions other than central Europe, where Gimbutas states that the Great Goddess cult was obliterated).

She also writes that in southern and western Europe resistance held out much longer, a possible explanation for why so many of the old European mystery teachings were retained by such traditions as the Strega of Italy (a witch cult that still exists today):

> *The Aegean and Mediterranean regions and western Europe escaped the process the longest; there, especially in the islands of Thera, Crete, Malta and Sardinia, Old European culture flourished in an enviably peaceful and creative civilization until 1500 B.C., a thousand to 1500 years after central Europe had been thoroughly transformed. Nevertheless, the Goddess religion and its symbols survived as an undercurrent in many areas.*
>
> Ibid.

The author also speaks of a balanced "non-patriarchal and non-matriarchal social system" that continued to be reflected in elements of Etruscan and Roman religion. When we consider that the Etruscans came to power around 1000 B.C. in Italy, it appears that they either maintained or inherited much of the Old European religion, passing it along to the Romans who embraced many Etruscan concepts. The ancient Greek historian Theopompus (fourth century B.C.) wrote that Etruscan women were socially equal to the men, literate, "far too permissive" sexually, and possessed a general love of pleasure.

Rome went on to eventually conquer almost all of the known world in its time. The occupying Roman soldiers spread the Italian Paganism of their own rural villages into all the lands they conquered or occupied (as opposed to the Roman state religion, to which historically the common people gave only "lip service" at best). This accounts for many of the similarities between northern and southern European Pagan beliefs and practices. In A.D. 43 the Romans officially invaded Britain (as opposed to Caesar's earlier venture) and held power over the isle until around the middle of the fifth century A.D. (A.D. 410 by British accounts). So great was the influence of almost 400 years of Roman occupation that Celtic culture, religious art and architecture were unalterably changed. See chapters three and eleven for further information.

Gerald Gardner, in chapter six of his book *The Meaning of Witchcraft* (Weiser, 1976), addresses the Roman Mystery Tradition and the Villa of the Mysteries in Pompeii, in context with the initiation ceremonies of Celtic Wicca: Here he states:

> *Now, this could mean that the real witch secrets came to Britain by means of the Mysteries, that is to say prior to, say 100 A.D., and that the British witches were only village wise women...In those days religious ideas were freely exchanged and freely adopted; but it is possible that certain ideas and practices came to Britain via the Mysteries brought by the Romans.*

In fairness to Gardner's intent here, he did not feel that this possibility represented the whole truth of it, and he firmly believed in Wicca as the survival of western European Paganism (which he was unaware had earlier crossed over from southern Europe). In order to understand the origins of pre-Christian Wicca we must look back into ancient history and human civilization.

As humans began to construct cities and empires, the religious views of the Solar and Lunar philosophies began to grow apart. The controlling, rule-making, dominating aspects of the Solar philosophies appeared better able to quickly conquer and subdue enemies than could the influencing, intuitive, and cooperative aspects of the Lunar. This, in time, led to the forming of two separate Pagan religions. However, since it was the men who held political and military power, and the men who presided over Solar Rites, the Lunar Cults were eventually outlawed for fear of undermining the strength of the Solar Cult.

The Lunar Cults began to practice their rites in secret, away from the cities. Forests and mountains became the temples of Lunar cultists. Despite the dominance of the Solar-oriented men in power, the hearts of the people were with the Lunar Way (with the Goddess). Secret cults sprang up such as the Italian Benandanti who fought against evil spirits, carrying staffs of fennel stalks into the fray as they defended the crops of the harvest. Other societies came forward to protect and preserve the Old Ways as well (such as the Society of Diana).

The Witch Cult and other Mystery Traditions flourished up until the fourth century A.D. when early Christians looted and destroyed Pagan temples and prevented the rites from being performed. In A.D. 324 the Emperor Constantine decreed that Christianity should become the official religion of the Roman Empire. Pagan temples were destroyed or converted into Christian churches. Gradually through the years Pagan customs were absorbed by Christianity, and the Old Religion began to withdraw from the populace, existing only within the shadows. Only small groups of people gathered at the ancient sites to perform the seasonal rites, for the majority feared the Christian zealots, yet village and townsfolk still sought out the local witch for healing and magickal help.

In Southern Europe certain regions still held strongly to the Old Religion. Tuscany, in the north of Italy, was probably the strongest center of Paganism, followed closely by the region of

Benevento, in lower central Italy. In time, however, even these strongholds fell to the power of the Christian Church. In A.D. 662 a Christian priest named Barbatus was sent to Benevento to convert its Pagans. The ruler of that region was a man named Romualdus, and Barbatus tried unsuccessfully to convert him. The Emperor Constans II laid siege to Benevento, threatening to slay the entire city. Barbatus obtained the Emperor's promise to spare the city if they would renounce their Paganism. Romualdus agreed to this, so long as the city was spared. In A.D. 663 Constans lifted the siege, and Barbatus was chosen as the Bishop of Benevento. The Pagan sites of worship were destroyed, and Christianity officially replaced Paganism.

In northern and western Europe the Old Religion came under intense persecution. The old local Pagan gods were still worshipped in small villages, and most settlements had a local wise woman or wise man who was knowledgeable in herbs and charms. The church violently attacked these individuals, labeling them as agents of Satan and employing Biblical verse against them, resulting in death sentences for the practice of Witchcraft.

All survivals of Pagan belief, worship, and practice were condemned as demonic and were suppressed by Christian theology and law. The *Synod of Rome* in A.D. 743 outlawed any offerings or sacrifices to Pagan Gods or spirits. The *Synod of Paris* in A.D. 829 issued a decree advocating the death of witches, sorcerers, etc. , citing the Biblical passages of Leviticus 20:6 and Exodus 22:18. The earliest trial carrying the death penalty occurred in 1022 in Orleans, France. Executions of witches occurred as early as the 1100s, but the practice did not become acceptable until the 1300s. The first execution in Ireland was that of Dame Alice Kyteler in A.D. 1324. The first public trial, in France, appears to have occurred in 1335, involving one Anne-Marie de Georgel.

One of the earliest examples of secular legislation against witchcraft was instigated by the twelfth-century Normal King of the Two Sicilies, Roger II. He stated that the concoction of love potions, whether they worked or not, was a crime. In 1181 the Doge Orlo Malipieri of Venice also passed laws punishing potions and magick.

Although Witchcraft was officially a punishable crime throughout the thirteenth century, the witch mania of northern Europe did not sweep southern Europe until the early fifteenth century.

Papal Bulls, like the one issued by Innocent VIII in 1484, turned the persecution of witches into an uncontrolled epidemic. In the first year of its publication forty-one people were burned in Como, Italy, after the zealous investigations of the Dominican Inquisitors. In 1510, 140 witches were burned at Brescia and 300 more at Como three years later. At Valcanonia seventy people were burned and the Inquisitor claimed to have another 5,000 under suspicion. Germany saw over 6,000 executions and northern European figures as a whole are estimated at 50,000 over the course of the Persecution. France and England had less than 2,000 executions, while eastern Europe totaled approximately 17,000.

In England in 1951, the last of the laws against Witchcraft were repealed by Parliament. Soon after this, a revival of the Cult arose in Great Britain. In 1954 and 1959, Gerald Gardner published his books, *Witchcraft Today* and *The Meaning of Witchcraft* (Macmillan, 1922), which revealed much of the true nature of the Cult. Gardner himself was an English witch, and did much to change the Christian-made image of Witchcraft. Oddly enough, the rites that Gardner revealed contain Italian aspects of Witchcraft. The Italian name Aradia appears in the English System, along with the original Italian script for *The Charge of the Goddess*.

Two men whose research had a great deal of influence on Gerald Gardner were Charles Leland and James Frazer. Leland studied and researched Italian Witchcraft in the late 1800s and Frazer was famous in his day for his research on the relationship between magick and religion. Both men were published authors; Leland wrote *Aradia—Gospel of the Witches* and also *Etruscan Magic & Occult Remedies* (University Books, 1963 edition), and Frazer wrote *The Golden Bough* (Macmillan, 1922) which for many years was a standard classic in the field.

Many of the elements of Wicca, as Gerald Gardner related them, can be found in the earlier works of Leland and Frazer. The well-known *Charge of the Goddess*, for example, clearly originates from the Italian text found in Leland's *Aradia—Gospel of the Witch-es* written almost half a century earlier than the Gardnerian version. The ceremonial practice of witches gathering in the nude (skyclad), worshipping a God and Goddess, and practicing magick also precedes Gardner's writings and is mentioned in *Aradia—Gospel of the Witches* (published in 1890). This I have covered in depth in my book *Ways of the Strega* (Llewellyn, 1995), presenting an abundance of supporting historical documentation.

During the 1950s and 1960s Wicca grew and expanded across parts of Europe and into the United States and Australia. Many Wiccan and Neo-Pagan magazines were established, creating a network for the Pagan community. Two of the earliest most successful periodicals were *Green Egg* and *Circle Network News*, which are still important publications today. Others such as *The Crystal Well*, *Harvest*, and *The Shadow's Edge* were leading journals in their own time. The Wiccan Pagan Press Alliance (WPPA) now serves as a network and support system for writers and magazines in the Pagan community.

During the late 1960s Wicca offered an alternative spirituality to a new generation, and many of those who were involved in the Hippie Movement came to Wicca. Wicca was less strict and dogmatic than the Judaic-Christian systems still prevalent in the 1960s. This had a great deal of appeal to a generation that was already questioning society and its supporting structures.

Wicca also drew to itself those who had suffered emotional pain from the Establishment and the Church, due to alternative lifestyles or unconventional views. Following the Hippie Movement that taught love and individuality came the New Age Movement. This movement introduced the use of crystals, brain wave frequencies, aliens, and just about everything else into the picture. Perhaps more than any other message, the New Age emphasized a focus on the Self. This was not the same teaching of individuality as in the 1960s; it was something much more extensive and pervasive.

The decade of the 1980s saw perhaps the most significant changes to date. New Age philosophy had sprouted within Wicca and found fertile ground in the open-minded nature of its practitioners. In a very short time many Wiccan beliefs were modified and altered to accommodate a new generation. This decade saw also an abundance of books produced on Wicca and other related topics. New traditions were springing up here and there, and everyone had a different idea or a newer approach. This decade shifted the focus away from the old established Wiccan traditions and toward modern eclectic systems.

Here in the decade of the 1990s we have seen the rise in popularity of computer bulletin boards carried on such services as Compuserve and America OnLine (AOL). These services provide a forum for Wiccans and Neo-Pagans to discuss a variety of topics and to ask and answer questions. Some subscribers have formed *Cyber Covens*, holding rituals on-line over the computer's modem. I personally have some mixed feelings about the whole thing, but it is interesting to observe the modern evolution of Wicca.

Due to some of the changes and modifications within modern Wicca, many of the older practitioners have begun to use the term *Witch* rather than *Wiccan* to describe themselves. This phenomenon is especially curious when one considers that not that long ago many of these same people preferred using the term *Wiccan* because of the public's misunderstanding of what a Witch is. The use now of this term seems to indicate a desire to be identified as a practitioner of an older, more traditional belief system. Wicca today seems more inclusive of self-styled traditions heavily reliant on eclectic material. When someone calls oneself a Wiccan today, it can mean that they may include any number of beliefs or practices that another Wiccan may or may not embrace as well.

When I consider Wicca today as a New Age religion, compared to Wicca even just a few decades ago, I am left with several impressions. Wicca is like a tree, and it seems to me that the old Wiccan ways represent the roots. Neo-Wiccan traditions are like the blossoms that appear anew in the spring, and perhaps this New Age is yet another spring season. The fragrance of the flowers differs from the fragrance of the old wooden tree on which they grow. Perhaps the fragrance of the flowers may be the emanation of the tree's spirit, the essence of what the tree produces.

For a tree to flourish and continue to produce flower and seed, it needs a sound root system from which to nourish new growth. It is easy to delight in the flowers and to neglect the care of the plant as a whole. The roots of a plant sustain it in times of adverse conditions. In many cases the plant can seemingly disappear, but the roots beneath it will re-establish the plant again under the right conditions. I am concerned that the main focus today within the Wiccan community is on producing beautiful flowers, and that the knowledge of the tree as a whole is becoming lost.

If we can join together now in a balance of old ways and new ways, we can ensure that the wisdom and knowledge of our ancestors survive along with what we ourselves have to pass on to our own descendants. We are the ancient Wiccans of Tomorrow, and I hope that our courage and dedication to this ancient religion earns us the same respect among our descendants, as we ourselves hold for those brave men and women who endured the Inquisition.

What was it that these Wiccans of old guarded with their lives? Was it a collection of spells and rituals? Was it merely a comfortable set of pre-Christian beliefs that they preferred to hold on to? No, it was instead a mentality and a spirituality that they protected. It was the tools and the keys to understanding, by which the mysteries could be accessed, that carried more importance than their own lives. They were protecting the roots of the tree.

A teacher of mine once said that if we have nothing worth dying for, then we have nothing worth living for. Would we risk our lives today to protect our own Book of Shadows if conditions such the Inquisition still existed? Do we understand what it really was that held so much importance to our Wiccan ancestors? There is an old story of a group of witches who walked out into the sea and met their death rather than be taken by the Inquisition. As they walked out into the water, they chanted the sacred names of the goddess until the last of their voices was silenced beneath the sea. These were witches who understood the mysteries.

Wicca is like a tree with its branches outstretched, providing shelter and nourishment to all who seek refuge in its shade. Spring brings new growth that appears upon the boughs, and from the old wood of the tree there issues forth its fruit. Laying hidden beneath it all are the roots that hold the tree upright in its place. If the roots are fed, then the tree flourishes. If the roots receive nothing, then the tree withers and falls in the course of time. The roots of the tree we today call Wicca are in need of our attention. Let us turn back then and tend the ancient garden.

CIVILIZATION TIMELINE

DATES	EVENTS
6500 B.C.	– Early Neolithic period in southern Italy.
6000 B.C.	– Early Neolithic period in Iberia.
5300 B.C.	– Early Neolithic period in central Europe.
5000 B.C.	– Early Neolithic period in northern Italy.
4500 B.C.	– Early Neolithic period in Britain.
4000 B.C.	– Long Barrows.
3500 B.C.	– Sumerian Civilization.
3000 B.C.	– Egyptian Civilization.
2500 B.C.	– Minoan Civilization.
2000 B.C.	– Greek Civilization.
1000 B.C.	– Etruscan Civilization.
753 B.C.	– Roman Civilization (Founding of Rome).
700 B.C.	– Appearance of the Celts.
600 B.C.	– Greek colonies in Italy influence Etruscans.
500 B.C.	– Celts invade Britain.
400 B.C.	– Celts invade northern Italy.
300 B.C.	– Celts invade Greece.
100 B.C.	– Etruscans absorbed by Rome. Celts driven out of Italy.
50 B.C.	– Roman Invasion of Gaul.
43 A.D.	– Roman Invasion of Britain.
150 A.D.	– Celts conquered by the Romans. Britain and Gaul under Roman rule.
410 A.D.	– Roman withdrawal from Britain.

CHAPTER
TWO

PRINCIPLES AND BELIEFS

The problem of mankind today, therefore, is precisely the opposite to that of men in the comparatively stable periods of those great coordinating mythologies which are now known as lies. Then all meaning was in the group, in the great anonymous forms, none in the self-expressive individual; today no meaning is in the group—none in the world: all is in the individual. But there the meaning is absolutely unconscious. One does not know toward what one moves. One does not know by what one is propelled. The lines of communication between the conscious and the unconscious zones of the human psyche have all been cut, and we have been split in two.

—Joseph Campbell,
The Hero with a Thousand Faces

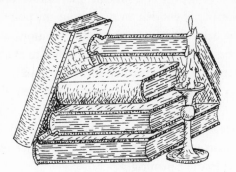

Wicca, as a religion, first came to public attention with the publication of Gerald Gardner's book *Witchcraft Today* in 1954. This was followed by his book *The Meaning of Witchcraft* published in 1959. At that time Wicca was viewed as an ancient European fertility cult that had survived in the form of an underground cult, persecuted by the Christian church during the Middle Ages.

With the advent of such authors as Scott Cunningham, Wicca took on elements of New Age philosophy. The decade of the 1980s saw many changes and adaptations within the Wiccan religion. Self-Initiation began to replace Initiation at the hands of experienced practitioners. Tenets of belief were deleted or modified to suit personal needs, tastes, and politics. Wicca became two almost separate religions, *split in two*: Elder Wicca and Neo-Wicca.

There is an old story that the original Tarot decks contained two Fool cards, seemingly identical in appearance—one at the beginning of the major Arcana and the other at the end. Upon closer inspection however, the second Fool card depicted a latched traveler's bag slung over the character's shoulder. The bag itself appeared full, whereas in the first card the bag was empty and unlatched. Both cards represent the spiritual seeker or traveler. As the story is told, the second card's bag was filled with the experiences of all the major Arcana cards proceeding it.

The message of the two Fool cards is that there are two paths an individual may follow. He or she may strike out alone and encounter the experiences that await without any point of reference from which to deal with them (acting upon intuition), as in the symbolism of the first card. The second approach is to journey forth on one's Quest carrying the knowledge gathered from the experiences of others, drawing on them for reference as needed. Both types of characters appear to be the same on first encounter, but the difference is made clear by what they carry along with them. We will now examine these two approaches to Wiccan spirituality, both of which have true value in their own right.

Elder Wiccans believe in following the teachings of those who came before them, as well as incorporating their own understanding into a spiritual map. Joseph Campbell wrote, in his book *The Hero with a Thousand Faces* (Princeton Univ. Press, 1968), the following passage which reflects Elder Wiccan mentality:

> *...letting the ancient meaning become apparent of itself. The old teachers knew what they were saying. Once we have learned to read again their symbolic language, it requires no more than the talent of an anthologist to let their teaching be heard. But first we must learn the grammar of the symbols....*

Thus Elder Wiccans adhere to the old ways and remain receptive to those who speak with seeming authority, listening and learning from any who will teach from experience. There will always be time for careful discernment after the words have been well considered.

Neo-Wiccans tend to reject dogma and structure within the religion and have a general mistrust of anyone who claims to be an authority. They believe in following their own intuition and their own personal code of ethics and morality. Neo-Wiccans look within, perceiving themselves to be both student and teacher at the same time. Elder Wiccans look to Nature as the *spiritual blueprint*, and see within Her the existence of definite rules, laws, and ways that serve as teachers. This is probably the main difference between the Old Ways and the New Ways; Elder Wiccans consider the established Ways to be the keys to understanding, Neo-Wiccans consider the established Ways to be restrictive barriers to the development of their own spirituality.

The focus on the Self (as in New Age philosophy) was not a view originally held within traditional Wicca. Wiccan beliefs and practices arose from a sense of community within the early clans. Myths and legends were created in order to preserve the knowledge of Wiccan spirituality for the benefit of those who were to follow. To "go it alone" was not a traditional Wiccan value. To follow the well-worn Path to its end, and then proceed to find one's way, was a traditional Wiccan value. To gain an understanding of the traditional role of the Self within Wicca, I direct the reader to chapter twelve. Chapters five, six, thirteen, and fourteen also address the issue of the individual's personal path within the Wiccan religious structure.

Neo-Wicca began as seekers from other religions came to the Old Religion in search of a spiritual path more suited to their individual needs. This was largely due to the New Age philosophy influencing Wicca, which basically promoted: *Do your own thing, no pre-set rules, do whatever feels right.* As the base of solitaries grew, their only source of information came from whatever books were available to them. They accepted those teachings with which they were in agreement, and tossed out those that they found to be uncomfortable. Some eventually formed groups (covens) and went on to gain personal experience through their involvement in ritual work and Goddess worship. Out of this arose many eclectic Wiccan traditions.

Wicca, as Gerald Gardner taught it, was a Nature religion with a focus on a Fertility Goddess and God. In this pantheon there were also various nature spirits such as Elementals, along with a company of powerful entities called *The Watchers*. These entities guarded the ritual portals known as *The Watchtowers*, which stood at the cardinal points of the ritual circle. The Goddess of Wicca was also called *The Great Goddess* and was considered to be the Mother of all Gods. The Goddess was also associated with the moon and thus she was sometimes called the *Queen of Heaven*. She reigned with a male consort called *The Horned One* who was a nature god and was also associated with the sun. In this association he bore the aspect of a Father God or *Lord of the Heavens.*

Traditional Wiccan beliefs include the teaching of reincarnation, through which a soul experiences many lifetimes, evolving as a spiritual being. Each life experience contains lessons that prepare the soul for a future existence in a higher nonphysical dimension. In Wiccan theology this realm is sometimes referred to as *the Summerland.* In this spiritual realm (associated with the moon) the Wiccan experiences the pleasures of rest and renewal in a Pagan paradise.

As this chapter continues we will take an in-depth look at the Philosophy of Wicca and also examine each of the tenets of belief. This book is, for the most part, concerned with the esoteric teachings of Wicca. Therefore its focus is more on the old Initiate concepts than on New Age philosophy. We will not exclude the modern ways of Wicca but we will focus more on the time-proven practices and tenets of Elder Wiccan belief that have preserved the Mystery Teachings. We will begin now with an overview of traditional Wiccan concepts.

PHILOSOPHY OF THE OLD RELIGION

The basic philosophy of the Old Religion is based on the ways of Nature, and humankind's understanding of spirituality as revealed in the sense of a healthy community. It is within the supporting structure of codes of conduct, common courtesy, and respect for others that the essence of our spirituality can be discerned.

Essentially, the philosophy of Wicca emanates from the ancient view that everything was created by the Great Gods (from the same procreative source) and that everything bears the "divine spark" of its creator. In Creation it is taught that there are four "Kingdoms": Mineral, Plant, Animal, and Human. Each of these is an expression or manifestation of Divine Consciousness. Individual souls pass through these Worlds, gaining knowledge and experience, moving toward reunion with the Source of All Things. In a certain sense it

can be said that souls experiencing the physical plane are like conscious probes sent out by the Divine Creator. Likewise, it can be
said that souls are like brain cells in the mind of the Divine Creator,
individual entities and yet part of the whole.

Built into the physical creation is the Law of Cause and Effect
(the spiritual counterpart of which is "Karma"), which serves to
keep everything in balanced motion. Karma causes the soul to
experience those levels of positive or negative energies that the
soul itself projects on other souls. Thus through many lifetimes
upon earth the soul is tempered and shaped so that it will be functional within the Spiritual Worlds in which it must someday dwell.
According to ancient belief the soul may physically incarnate
many times until it is able to free itself from the Cycle of Rebirth.

Behind the "scenes" of physical existence, there dwell the
forces that animate the world. The ancients expressed these forces
as the Elemental Kingdoms, of which there are four: Earth, Air,
Fire, and Water. Within these Forces or Kingdoms the ancients
viewed the active agents as conscious spirits. To the spirits of earth
they assigned the term "Gnomes," to those of Air "Sylphs," to Fire
"Salamanders," and to those of Water "Undines." Everything in
Nature was created and is maintained by one or more of these Elements (and their agents). This is why the Elementals are summoned in ritual or in magic, so that something may be created or
established (although in this case we become the "Creator" directing manifestation).

All forms of life are respected in the Old Religion. Everything
is of equal importance. The only difference is that things are merely at different levels of evolution within the Four Kingdoms.
Humans are no more important than animals, nor are animals more
important than plants, and so on. Life is *life*, no matter what physical form it may dwell in at the time. We are all part of the same creation and everything is connected and linked together.

Nature is considered to be the Great Teacher. The Mystery
Teachings tell us that the Divine Source placed into the fabric of
Creation a reflection of what created it. Therefore, the laws of
Nature are reflections of Divine Laws or principles, which operate

in a dimension behind and above those of physical Nature. Thus the ancients coined the phrase "as above, so below."

Studying the ways of Nature gives us a glimpse (crude though it may be) of the Divine Ways, and from these we see the returning of the seasons (reincarnation) and the laws of cause and effect (Karma) concerning the use (and misuse) of the earth's land, air, resources, and living creatures. This is one of the purposes of seasonal ritual, for these rites saturate us and harmonize us with the focused essence of Nature at these given times. The more that we gather at the seasonal tides of Nature, the more we become like Nature. When we become like Her it is easier to understand Her.

When we look at the so-called Lower Kingdoms, we see cooperation among various insects such as ants or bees, and in many animals we find herds or packs, etc. (in this we come to know the Divine Way of the Group Soul). All souls will experience both the group and the self, in order to understand the need for self-limitation (as in compromise and cooperation). A group of creatures working together can better defend themselves and provide for their needs than can a solitary creature. In the Divine reflection of this principle, we find that a soul is enriched by giving of itself to another soul, and is isolated when it places itself above another.

We have all experienced the joyful feeling of making someone else feel good about something, and the selfish/guilty feeling of placing our own importance over that of a friend or loved one. We have all experienced the feeling of group acceptance and recognition, as well as the pain of rejection. Yet even when we find pleasure or joy on our own there is still the need to share it with another person in some manner. Out of this arises the teaching of service to others, for Wiccans have always been the local healers and counselors.

Connected to the teaching of the soul's relationship to another soul, we find that the ancients believed in a race of gods who oversaw and interacted with humankind. To the ancients a god could be any singular, seemingly self-directed force of Nature whose actions might manifest in such things as storms, earthquakes, rainbows, beautiful star-filled nights, and so on. As human awareness and intellect grew, so too did the concept of the gods.

Wiccans generally perceive their Gods as caring, benevolent Beings in a role not so unlike that of a loving human parent (although many Neo-Wiccans perceive the God and Goddess as metaphysical concepts instead of aspects of Divine Consciousness). A parent provides in certain ways for a child, but basically must teach the child to prepare for its own life. During the course of their relationship the child will not always understand the actions of its parents. Eventually the child will begin to question the authority of the parent. However, a relationship still exists and requires mutual understanding and communication in order for a loving spirit to thrive.

At times a child may feel that the parent is unjust or unkind, not really understanding that the parent must set limits and rules on the child's behavior for his or her own well-being. Rules and limits exist within Nature and are essential to the formation of mature reasoning and behavior ("as above, so below"). Yet, it is not the belief among Wiccans that the gods set obstacles or tragedies in the path of Humans, nor do the gods test one's faith or belief in them. It is the law of Karma, and the misfortune of random occurrence, that manifest what we perceive as the sorrows and struggles of life. It is the gods who stand with us and help us find the strength to continue forward.

One of the greatest tenets of belief in the Old Religion is that of accepting responsibilities for our own actions. We build or destroy our own lives, and we allow or disallow our own "lot in life." The Gods are there to help us but we must do the work. Even when random occurrence or Karma seems to break us down it is we who must push onward. Nature provides the keys to understanding this process so that we are not alone; these keys are found in the Wiccan Mysteries. In effect, the Mystery Teachings of Wicca help us to find our way by following the well-worn path that others have left behind.

Wiccans cannot turn everything over into the hands of the gods and say, "You take care of it now." We must be responsible for ourselves and our own actions (or lack thereof), for more often than not, it is we ourselves who brought the situation into manifestation. When we realize that, and act on it accordingly, then the gods join with us. It is the desire of our gods that we be happy in this life, and that we fulfill our goals and aspirations before our time on earth concludes.

In the Old Religion death is simply an exiting from one world to another. The physical body is much like a garment worn by the soul, and it is discarded when it is worn out or damaged beyond repair. Birth is an entrance of the soul into the world. And "as above, so below," it seems that the other Worlds contain their own versions of birth and death.

The teachings tell us that from this physical world, Wiccans pass into a spirit world known as the Summerland (or as the Realm of Luna). This is a metaphysical astral realm of meadows, lakes, and forests where it is always summer. It is a Pagan paradise filled with all the lovely creatures of ancient lore, and the gods themselves dwell there. Yet, the ultimate spiritual attainment of Wiccans is not the Summerland, but the original union they once shared with the Group Soul, dwelling in oneness with the Divine Source of All Things.

This union is not a place within an astral realm, as is the Summerland, but rather a state of being. This is one of the reasons for which we reincarnate, living our different lives as males and females, rich and poor, etc., shedding one personality after another, learning and growing, becoming aware of and compassionate toward all other souls. This type of spirituality creates a higher vibration within the soul, allowing the soul to escape the pull back into physical matter, which is inherent in a low vibrational rate.

Out of all that Wiccans perceive in the order of the physical world, there arises a basic code of conduct:

- If no one is harmed by your action (either physically, emotionally, or spiritually), then do as you Will to do in Life, in accordance with your Higher Self. Seek your identity and your purpose.

- When someone does something good for you, then repay the kindness by doing something good for another person, so that the seed that was planted will bear fruit.

- Keep your word and your oaths, when you give them.

- Do not kill anything, except when food or protection are required.

- Acknowledge and give due reverence to your gods, observing all of the sacred times and festivals.

- Belittle no one's beliefs, but simply offer what it is you believe to be true.

- Strive to live in peace with those who differ with you.

- Strive to be aware of those around you and seek compassion within yourself.

- Be true to your own understanding and strive to turn away from what is opposed within you.

- Help others according to their need and according to your ability to give of yourself.

- Respect Nature and strive to live in harmony with Her.

THE TENETS OF WICCAN BELIEF

In this section we will examine each of the main tenets of Wiccan belief. We will also take note of the parallels found in other world religions.

REINCARNATION

Reincarnation is the belief that a soul is reborn again into the physical world after death. This teaching is an important concept in Wicca, and in other religions such as Buddhism, Hinduism, Janism, and Sikhism. Among the ancient Greeks it was called *Palingenesis* (to have origin again) and was a common teaching in Orphism.

In the ancient southern European mystery cults it was taught that the soul survives bodily death and is later reincarnated in a human or other mammalian body, eventually obtaining release from the Cycle of Rebirth. The ancient Romans recorded that a similar teaching was also held by the Druids in northern Europe.

The Druids believed that the soul passed into the realm of Gwynvyd if the deeds of the individual were positive. If his or her deeds were evil in nature, then the soul passed into the realm of Abred. In Gwynvyd the soul enters into a state of bliss, and through Abred the soul incarnated into an animal form that best suited its nature at the time of death. In either case the Druids believed that the soul could return again into a human body in a new lifetime. See chapter six for further information.

THE SUMMERLAND

Wiccans perceive of an "Afterlife" realm known as the Summerland, in which souls rest and are renewed before they are born again into the physical world. Among the Celts this realm was generally known as *Tir nan og*, the Land of Undying Youth. In the well-known Wiccan verse called *The Charge*, it is referenced in the following passage:

> "...*for mine is the secret door which opens upon the Land of Youth, and mine is the cup of wine of life, and the cauldron of Cerridwen, which is the Holy Grail of Immortality.*"

This realm is much like others common in British/Celtic Mythology. In the legends of King Arthur we encounter the realm of the Isle of Apple Trees (known as Avalon) where dead kings and heroes dwell. Among the Druids a similar realm existed called the Isle of Sein or the Isle of Seven Sleeps (*Enez Sizun*). These all bear resemblance to the Wiccan Summerland.

In southern European Witchcraft there exists a realm called Luna which is very much like the Wiccan Summerland. It is a Pagan paradise filled with mythological creatures who inhabit beautiful woods and meadows. Here the souls of witches dwell for a time, encountering the Elders who have died before them, as well as the God and Goddess (see chapter six).

THE GOD AND GODDESS

The Source of All Things, also known as the Great Spirit, is generally personified in Wiccan belief as a Goddess and a God. Since Wicca is a Nature religion it focuses on a balance of Masculine and Feminine in its concept of Deity. There are, however, some traditions that conceive of Deity as a Goddess only, who contains the Masculine and Feminine polarities within Herself. An example of this would the Dianic Tradition. Many Neo-Wiccans perceive Deity in a more Eastern philosophy, seeing the Gods as detached metaphysical concepts connected to the cycles of Karma and rebirth.

The Goddess in Wiccan belief represents the Great Mother of the ancient matrifocal cults. She is also seen as a triple goddess known as the Maiden, Mother, and Crone. The God is the Horned God of the forests, the fertility aspect common in ancient pagan religion. In some Traditions he is portrayed with goat horns and in others with stag's horns (see chapter four for further information).

AS ABOVE, SO BELOW

This teaching addresses the issue of the physical dimension as the reflection of a higher nonphysical dimension. Everything that exists within the physical world was first an energy form within a higher dimension that eventually manifested in the world of physical matter. The physical expression of this form or concept becomes denser (in all respects) as it passes into the physical dimension and yet still reflects the basic concept of the higher principle.

In the Egyptian Mysteries it was taught that "that which is below is like that which is above, and that which is above is like that which is below" (Creation is of the nature of the Creator). This concept concerns not only the manifestation of physical matter but is also contained in the Laws of Nature/Principles of Physics. This is why within Wiccan theology Nature is viewed as the Great Teacher and why Wicca focuses on reverence for Nature. It is through our understanding of Nature and Her ways that we can understand the ways of the Creators who brought all into existence, for the nature of the Creators is reflected within their creations, just as the style of an artist can be detected within his or her art.

The Old Religion contains certain established *laws* and *ways* because it is based on the blueprint of Nature (which likewise reflects the nature of what created it, in other words the Divine Consciousness). Eastern philosophy has somewhat undermined this tenet of Wiccan belief, and today many Neo-Wiccans dismiss the old established structure and doctrine of the Mystery Teachings. They adhere more to the Eastern philosophy of Cosmic Principles, and where the Elder Wiccans embrace a conscious god and goddess, many Neo-Wiccans embrace metaphysical principles instead.

OCCULT DIMENSIONS

Wiccan occultism teaches that there are seven planes or dimensions that comprise existence. The highest dimension is the Ultimate Plane (unknowable from our human perspective). The lowest is the Physical Dimension. In essence these are the highest and lowest frequencies at which energy vibrates or resonates in a metaphysical sense.

The traditional order in which these dimensions are placed is as follows:

1. Ultimate

2. Divine

3. Spiritual

4. Mental

5. Astral

6. Elemental

7. Physical.

In reality they do not occupy space as we understand it, and their relationship to each other is not literally one above or below another. It can be said that they occupy the same space at the same time, but exist as different states of energy (see chapter seven for further discussion of this concept).

CAUSE AND EFFECT

Wiccans believe that both positive and negative energies return (in some related aspect) back to the originator of those energies. This is sometimes referred to as the Three-Fold Law. As a "law" the teaching says that "that which you do shall return to you three-fold" (three times as much). This is quite similar to the Eastern Mystical Systems that teach the concept of Karma. Neo-Wiccans view the Three-Fold Law as simply an "action and reaction" principle similar to the Laws of Physics. The Mystery Teachings of Elder Wicca associate it with the goddess known as Wyrd. See chapters six and seven for further information.

MAGICK

In Wiccan belief, Magick is the ability to bring about changes in accordance with personal will or desire. In effect it is actually the understanding of how the inner mechanism of Nature works (the so-called supernatural), as well as the understanding of how a person can enlist the aid of a spirit or a deity.

True magick is not superstition or folk magick, such as one encounters in the ascribed powers of herbs and natural charms. It is the understanding of metaphysical principles and how to employ them in order to make manifest one's wishes or needs. Very often magick requires the use of prepared tools and established states of consciousness. This topic is covered in greater depth in chapter nine.

ETHICS

Wiccans basically believe in a "live and let live," non-violent philosophy, and tend to be tolerant of the beliefs and lifestyles of others. There is a basic gentleness of spirit within most Wiccans and a striving toward peaceful coexistence with those around them. Yet there is also a focus on themselves and their personal needs, and Wiccans do not generally "turn the other cheek" when attacked.

Wiccans avoid certain acts not so much because they believe in some resulting punishment as they do out of a basic sense of right and wrong. It is wrong to steal, it is wrong to needlessly take a life, it is wrong to intentionally hurt someone. Sexual conduct is generally seen as a personal issue and in traditional Wicca there is no judgment on how one conducts their own affairs.

The popular text known as *The Wiccan Rede* best sums up Wiccan ethics. The Rede says: "An as it harm none, do what thou will." Some Wiccans interpret this to mean that a person can do anything they wish as long as no one is harmed by it, and thereby that person is free of any Karmic debt. This is not exactly the interpretation of the Rede within the Mystery Teaching.

To do as one wills to do actually means to find one's purpose (one's True Will) and to fulfill it. This is intended to be for the benefit of the person but not to the detriment of another person. In a higher sense this Wiccan tenet is related to Eastern Mysticism. It is the work of the neophyte to master his or her physical senses and to pass into nonattachment. Once the student has risen above the desires and needs of the flesh, then he or she can view the world with detachment and so discover their true Will or Purpose.

At this stage there is no greed, envy, or jealousy, and therefore the person can act through knowledge of his or her own pure will, which then naturally causes no harm to another because it is not centered on any relationship, personal prestige or any personal gain within a society. It is the true will of the divine nature within the person, acting in accord with its purpose in this lifetime.

RITUAL

Ritual is both a means of worship and a method of communicating to deities or spirits. It is a symbolic language that can gain access to other dimensions or states of consciousness. Ritual also allows us to step out of our mundane personalities and become something greater than ourselves.

In Wicca, rituals have been created to connect us with the energies of the seasonal shifts of our planet. These periods of energy flows are marked by the Solstices and Equinoxes. The other times of power exist at exactly the midpoints between these times of power and constitute the other four Sabbats.

Many Wiccan Traditions have different names for the ritual Sabbats, depending on their cultural influence. The Sabbats are commonly known as follows:

- Imbolg or Candlemas (February 2)

- Spring Equinox or Lady's Day (March 21)

- Bealtaine/Beltane or Roodmas (April 30)

- Midsummer or Summer Solstice (June 22)

- Lughnasadh or Lammas (July 31)

- Autumn Equinox (September 21)

- Samhain or Hallowmas (October 31)

- Yule or Winter Solstice (December 22)

See chapter ten for further information.

HERBALISM

The old teachings tell us that there dwells within all things a living consciousness called *Mana* or *Numen*. Just as humans are souls encased in a physical body, plants also bear a divine spark within them (as do stones, trees, and all inanimate objects). It is the power of a plant's Numen or Mana that is employed in magick and spell casting. The ancients created a table of correspondences for various plants ascribing certain natures to them.

The collective energy of Numen or Mana within a setting such as a forest or lake is responsible for the peaceful feeling we experience there. This is why many people enjoy camping and hiking. It is also what draws us to a particular area or influences us to choose a favorite place to sit or to park our car. In such cases we are responding to a harmonious emanation of Numen or Mana.

In ancient times, Nature spirits were associated with meadows and woods. The power of various herbs were believed to derive from contact with fairies and other supernatural creatures. Certain planetary bodies were also believed to empower various herbs, including the Sun and the Moon. The etheric metaphysical properties of the Moon were said to pass power into herbal plants. This was one of the reasons it was taught that herbs could only be gathered beneath the Full Moon. See chapter nine for further information.

FAMILIARS

It is an ancient teaching that a psychic rapport can be established between a human and an animal (or a spirit). Such a relationship is known as having a familiar spirit. This concept dates back to the early shamanistic days of animal totems associated with human clans. Each clan believed in a certain animal spirit that protected or aided the clan. This is not unlike some of the American Indian tribes who named themselves after various creatures (such as the Crow tribe).

The wearing of a feather or animal pelt was believed to empower a person with the qualities of the animal from which they came. The wearer of such an object would mimic the mannerisms of the animal in order to awaken the power dwelling within the feather or pelt, etc. He or she was then becoming familiar with the spirit of the animal, and once this power could be easily invoked then this person was said to possess a familiar spirit.

Eventually this concept was extended to include establishing a psychic link with a living creature. The living spirit of the creature could possess the shaman, or be sent off in spirit form to aid him or her in some magickal work. During the Middle Ages this was the most common relationship with a familiar, and is the basis for the classic image of a witch and her familiar as depicted in art.

DIVINATION

Divination is the ability to discern what the future holds in store for us. Actually, it allows us to foresee what is going to happen if all factors remain constant. The tools of divination allow us to view the patterns that are forming which will in turn result in the particular manifestation of a specific situation. Thus divination allows us to either prepare for what lies ahead or to take action to alter the patterns and thus avoid the situation.

Some people believe that the future is fixed in time and they subscribe to the theory of predestination. If this were so then everything would be on auto-pilot and no one would have the freedom of personal choice. We would all be just along for the ride, so to speak. Others believe that the major events of one's life such as marriage, children, injury, and death are predestined, but that in day-to-day life a person has free choice. The Mystery Teachings tell us that the basic energy pattern of our life is pre-established (as reflected in the art of astrology) but that we can alter it (as in the art of magick and the gift of free will) as needed.

In Elder Wiccan belief, the future is not already decided, but the pattern is established in the astral fabric and will manifest if nothing alters it. Everything that manifests in the physical dimension is first formed in the astral dimension. This is one of the keys to magick. Divination allows us to glimpse the astral pattern and see what has formed in the astral material. Astrology allows us an overview of what lies in store if nothing alters our course.

The most common tools employed in the divinatory arts are: Tarot cards, rune stones, psychometry, crystal visions, and the reading of signs and omens. Techniques such as palmistry and phrenology fall under the category of psychometry.

PERSONAL POWER

It is an ancient teaching that the human body contains zones of energy. These zones can be applied and accessed in order to generate personal power towards a magickal goal. In Eastern Mysticism these centers are called chakras, and it is taught that there are seven such zones of power within the human body. In Wicca the concept is the same, but the chakras are often referred to as personal power centers.

The first center is located at the crown of the head and is perceived as the *meeting place* between human and divine consciousness. The second is located in the center of the forehead just above and between the eyes. It is often referred to as *the third eye* because it is believed that the sum of the five human senses is amplified within the pineal gland, and that this produces a sixth sense of psychic sight or perception.

The third center is located at the throat area and is involved in the influence of tones and vibrations that in turn affect energy patterns. The fourth is located at the heart area and is concerned with feeling energy patterns, thus it is often associated with our feelings toward others and our feelings toward places and situations. The fifth center is located at the solar plexus and is the center through which the soul derives nourishment from etheric energy with the physical dimension.

The sixth center is located just below the navel and is known as the personal power center. It is here that we relate to our own power or lack thereof. This is often experienced as a feeling *in the pit of the stomach* when we are confronted with something challenging (like an important job interview). The seventh center is located in the genital area and is associated with energy in a pure form; in other words it is raw energy.

The rate at which these centers vibrate, and the degree of harmony existing between them, creates an energy field around the human body known as the aura. The aura is the energy representation of who and what we are. When we meet someone and feel an instant like or dislike for them, it is the energy of their aura to which we are responding (for further information see chapter eight).

CHAPTER
THREE

THE SACRED
WICCAN TEXTS

What we are today comes from our thoughts of yesterday, and our present thoughts build our life of tomorrow: Our life is the creation of our mind.

—Buddha

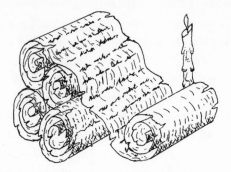

Presented in this chapter are the traditional verses of the Wiccan religion, along with a commentary on each. Wherever appropriate I have included either the mystery teachings or their associated references. I have also added the full text of the Mystery Teaching associated with the *Legend of the Descent*. All religions embrace a sacred text of one type or another. These can be ancient writings or modern works in which the essential nature of the religion's spirituality is expressed. In some cases, the texts themselves may not have been originally designed as a religious writing, but have inspired individuals to create a fellowship based on the principles expressed.

Within Wicca there are several texts that are now famous throughout the community. These have been presented to us in the writings of Gerald Gardner, Doreen Valiente, Janet and Stewart Farrar, Lady Sheba, and many others. They comprise some of the most beautiful and spiritual writings found in Wicca today. They are truly wonderful gifts to our community, and I am honored to be able to present them here in my book.

The Charge of the Goddess

Whenever you have need of anything, once in the month and better it be when the moon is full, then shall you assemble in some secret place and adore the spirit of me, who am Queen of all witches. There shall ye assemble, ye who are fain to learn all sorcery, yet have not won its deepest secrets; to these will I teach all things that are as yet unknown. And ye shall be free from slavery; and as a sign that ye be truly free, you shall be naked in your rites; and ye shall dance, sing, feast, make music and love, all in my praise. For mine is the ecstasy of the spirit, and mine also is joy on earth; for my law is love unto all beings. Keep pure your highest ideals; strive ever towards them, let nothing stop you or turn you aside. For mine is the secret door which opens upon the Land of Youth, and mine is the cup of the wine of life, and the Cauldron of Cerridwen, which is the Holy Vessel of Immortality. I am the gracious Goddess, who gives the gift of joy unto the heart of man. Upon earth, I give the knowledge of the spirit eternal; and beyond death, I give peace, and freedom, and reunion with those who have gone before. Nor do I demand sacrifice; for behold, I am the Mother of all living, and my love is poured out upon the earth.

I am the beauty of the green earth, and the white moon among the stars, and the mystery of the waters, and the desire of the heart of man. Call unto thy soul, arise, and come unto me. For I am the soul of Nature, who gives life to the Universe. From me all things proceed, and unto me all things must return; and before my face, beloved of Gods and of men, let thine innermost divine self be enfolded in the rapture of the infinite. Let my worship be within the heart that rejoiceth; for behold, all acts of love and pleasure are my rituals. Therefore, let there be beauty and strength, power and compassion, honor and humility, mirth and reverence within you. And thou who thinketh to seek for me, know thy seeking and yearning shall avail thee not unless thou knoweth the mystery; that if that which thy seekest thou findest

not within thee, thou wilt never find it without thee. For behold,
I have been with thee from the beginning; and I am that which
is attained at the end of desire.

—Stewart Farrar, *What Witches Do*

COMMENTARY

The Charge is one of the most powerful texts associated with the Lunar Mysteries within Wicca today. In the opening verses we are given a set of instructions designed to establish the necessary mentality through which the Goddess can impart her teachings to us. The ancient techniques of dancing, chanting, and Pagan merriment are listed and are to be performed in praise of the Goddess. From these practices arises the ecstasy of the spirit that merges us with the presence of the Goddess.

The Charge then depicts various aspects of the Goddess associated in many ways with the *Legend of the Descent*. She is the secret door that opens upon the Land of Youth, a reference to the portal through which one passes into rebirth or into Tir Nan Og (the Celtic realm where departed souls abide). The cup of the wine of life is a reference to the life-giving powers of the womb, and to the Blood Mysteries as well as the intoxicating elixirs generated by the female body through magickal stimulation of the endocrine glands (see chapters thirteen and fifteen). The Cauldron of Cerridwen is the vessel of rebirth, the mechanism of renewal in, and release from, the Underworld. The passages in this section again point to the Mystery Teachings of rebirth among one's clan, symbolized here in the Cauldron mythos. This lunar symbol, and its associations with the mysteries, are discussed in greater detail in chapters eleven and twelve.

The second half of the Charge describes the Goddess as reflected within Nature and the Cosmos. She is the beauty of the earth, the animating and maintaining factor. She is the mystical power of the Moon, and the forces inherent in the primordial waters from which Life itself issued forth. To open our spirits fully to the Goddess is to see her within ourselves (to become enfolded in the rapture of the infinite). *The Charge* concludes with the final mystery; if we cannot find what our spirit desires, already present within our own inner being, then an external quest will be fruitless as well, for the divine spark of the Goddess has been with us since our creation, and can only be embraced in a surrendering of the self to the Goddess (just as she herself surrendered to the Dark Lord and entered into the enlightenment of her Totality). Some Wiccans have interpreted the closing verse to mean that we already possess all of the answers within ourselves and we need only look to our own inner nature. What the Mystery Teachings refer to here is that we must look to the Divine Nature within ourselves, to the creative spark reflective of the Divine principles (operating within us and the ways of Nature). For us to say that we are the God or Goddess is like a skin cell on the palm declaring itself to be the hand.

The Myth of the Descent of the Goddess

Dea, our Lady and Goddess, would solve all mysteries, even the mystery of Death. And so she journeyed to the Underworld in her boat, upon the Sacred River of Descent. Then it came to pass that she entered before the first of the seven gates to the Underworld. And the Guardian challenged her, demanding one of her garments for passage, for nothing may be received except that something be given in return. And at each of the gates the goddess was required to pay the price of passage, for the guardians spoke to her: "Strip off your garments, and set aside your jewels, for nothing may you bring with you into this our realm."

So Dea surrendered her jewels and her clothing to the Guardians, and was bound as all living must be who seek to enter the realm of Death and the Mighty Ones. At the first gate she gave over her scepter, at the second her crown, at the third her necklace, at the fourth her ring, at the fifth her girdle, at the sixth her sandals, and at the seventh her gown. Dea stood naked and was presented before Dis, and such was her beauty that he himself knelt as she entered. He laid his crown and his sword at her feet saying: "Blessed are your feet which have brought you down this path." Then he arose and said to Dea: "Stay with me I pray, and receive my touch upon your heart."

And Dea replied to Dis: "But I love you not, for why do you cause all the things that I love, and take delight in, to fade and die?"

"My Lady" replied Dis "it is age and fate against which you speak. I am helpless, for age causes all things to whither, but when men die at the end of their time, I give them rest, peace and strength. For a time they dwell with the moon, and the spirits of the moon; then may they return to the realm of the living. But you are so lovely, and I ask you to return not, but abide with me here."

But she answered "No, for I do not love you." Then Dis said "If you refuse to embrace me, then you must kneel to death's scourge." The goddess answered him: "If it is to be, then it is fate, and better so!" So Dea knelt in submission before the hand of Death, and he scourged her with so tender a hand that she cried out "I know your pain, and the pain of love."

Dis raised her to her feet and said "Blessed are you, my Queen and my Lady." Then he gave to her the five kisses of initiation, saying: "Only thus may you attain to knowledge and to joy."

And he taught her all of his mysteries, and he gave her the necklace which is the circle of rebirth. And she taught him her mysteries of the sacred cup which is the cauldron of rebirth. They loved and joined in union with each other, and for a time Dea dwelled in the realm of Dis.

For there are three mysteries in the life of Man which are: Sex, Birth, and Death (and love controls them all). To fulfill love, you must return again at the same time and place as those who loved before. And you must meet, recognize, remember, and love them anew. But to be reborn you must die and be made ready for a new body. And to die you must be born, but without love you may not be born among your own.

But our Goddess is inclined to favor love, and joy and happiness. She guards and cherishes her hidden children in this life and the next. In death she reveals the way to her communion, and in life she teaches them the magic of the mystery of the Circle (which is set between the worlds of men and of the gods).

—from The Aridian Tradition,
Raven Grimassi, *Way of the Strega*

COMMENTARY

This text begins with the ancient Mystery Teaching that the Goddess was originally incomplete in the integration of her *totality*. In order to possess the knowledge of all things, she descended into matter and experienced decline and physical death (an ancient mythos in many religions). her journey to the Underworld is symbolic of her passage through the currents flowing between the worlds; *"And so she journeyed to the Underworld in her boat, upon the Sacred River of Descent."*

As the myth unfolds we encounter the theme of relinquishment, noted in the demand for payment by the Guardians at each gate. The seven gates which the Goddess encounters are symbolic of the seven planes (see chapter seven). A surrendering of the Self in order to obtain enlightenment is an ancient theme, found not only in the Mystery Tradition but also in such public religions as Christianity and Buddhism. The items required by the Guardians each represent an isolating or insulating aspect of Consciousness. In this myth is the blueprint for our own surrender to enlightenment, as seen in the drama of the Goddess.

At the first gate she relinquishes her scepter, which is a symbol of her personal power to extend influence outward over other things around her. The loss of such a state of Consciousness isolates one and brings the focus of the Universe directly upon his or her own existence. The second gate requires her crown, symbolic of her authority; in other words, what others will grant submission to in recognition of her power or worthiness. This may be seen in our own lives as a loss of status among our peers or within our community. This separates us from being able to identify ourselves with our careers or families, leaving only what we really are, stripped of external references within the society in which we exist. In other words, we are not what we do for a living, or what we provide for others. When we can no longer identify who we are with what we do, then what remains is who we truly are.

The Guardian of the third gate requires the necklace of the Goddess. This item is symbolic of her claim to personal value, her achievements and accomplishments. In modern society, wealth is viewed as a sign of personal power. It states that the individual is successful and influential according to the standards of the society in which the person operates. This is the cultivated self-image of the individual. Where an individual uses career or position as a buffer to shield the true Self from the perception of others, he or she is employing Self-Image as a shield against personal introspection.

At the fourth gate the Goddess removes her ring. The ring is symbolic of class level and personal labeling. In modern society the ring denotes relationships such as engagement and marriage. In ancient times it signified membership in organizations, orders, lodges, and various religious systems. To remove the ring is to stand alone without connection, association, or definition.

The Guardian of the fifth gate requires the Goddess to relinquish her girdle. The girdle symbolizes social status and the personal facades we establish. It is the recognition of our personal limitations and imperfections manifested in the construction of outward appearances. To relinquish the girdle is to open the Self to examination. In ancient Rome the girdle was worn by a woman as an outward symbol that she had now reached the stage of puberty. When the woman was to marry, her parents would tie a knot in the girdle which was later untied by her husband on the wedding night. A married woman continued to wear the girdle which her husband had knotted again after the wedding night. The knot was untied once more when the woman gave birth to her firstborn child, then her girdle was dedicated to Artemis and was no longer worn. In ancient times a virgin was a woman who had not yet given birth, and so she lost her virginity during labor. Therefore the girdle could no longer be worn in public.

At the sixth gate the Goddess removes her sandals. This represents the chosen path we walk, or the politics we adhere to. It is what allows us to move along the belief system we embrace. To remove the sandals is to let our personal views drop away. We stand alone without personal agenda, self-direction, or political position. Thus stripped of all our self-imposed limitations (although we do not think of them as such) we can only walk the way of our spirit. Spirit is not concerned with the affairs of physical existence. Its focus is on matters of the heart and soul.

At the seventh and last gate, the Goddess drops her gown as the final payment to the Guardians of the Portals. The gown is the mortal covering, the connection to linear existence. It is also the Self and its fragile veneer, covering the spirit in a mantle of self-expression. It is what isolates the spirit from the whole of spiritual experience. Once the gown is removed then the spirit may join in union with the Community of Spirits. This is reflected in the Wiccan practice of celebrating skyclad (nude) in the ritual circle.

At this point in the myth, the Goddess is brought to the Lord of the Underworld. She stands naked before him and so struck is he with her beauty that he kneels before her. Psychologically this is the meeting between the anima and the animus. It is the point at which life and death, increase and decline meet and renew the endless cycle. The Lord of the Underworld tempts her to remain with him and to embrace his realm of existence. This is the temptation to rest in slumber and avoid the labors of the day, for the seed to sleep beneath the soil and struggle not toward the light. The Goddess can end all strife and unite with her opposite, but on his terms.

In the myth the Goddess resists the Lord of the Underworld and protests against his role in the decline of life. Since she will not embrace him freely he compels her to accept his scourge. He teaches her that he is not responsible for decline and death; his is a role of comforting and transforming those who have crossed over. Thus the Goddess passes into an understanding of her polarity and incorporates it into her own Being. This is reflected in her proclamation of new-found love for the Dark Lord.

Next the legend relates that the Lord and Lady reveal their respective mysteries to each other. The Goddess receives the necklace of rebirth, symbolic of the connective link between the worlds, the inner mechanism. The Dark Lord receives the cauldron of rebirth, symbolic of the power manifest. In the myth we are told that they love and become one. Here we find the achievement of balance between the life and death. No longer are they enemies, but equal participants in a cycle of renewal. The three mysteries in the life of humankind are revealed: Sex becomes the gateway to life from the Underworld, Birth is the renewal, and Death is the transformation whereby old age becomes youth again. Just as a person must sleep in order for his or her body to be refreshed, so too must the soul rest and renew itself in the sleep of the Underworld.

The legend continues with the Mystery Teaching concerning reincarnation. Here we are told that we must meet, recognize, remember, and love anew. This teaching originates from the time of the early clans and is connected with the Slain God mythos. The sending of the willing sacrifice to convey the needs of the tribe before the Gods themselves is a very ancient concept. Once the sacrificial victim was dispatched the clan held magickal rites designed to ensure the rebirth of the soul among his or her own people. This is one of the reasons Hereditary Witch families are so concerned about blood lines.

The final passages in the legend address the issue of the enlightenment gained by the Goddess herself in the descent. To be one of her hidden children is to descend into the shadows and unite with her mythos. In so doing the soul is aligned with her renewal and unites with her in spiritual union (the way of her communion). In the last verses we find that the magick whereby we become aligned to the Goddess resides between the worlds. The Circle of Magick on this plane is the ritual circle wherein we celebrate the wheel of the year and the Lunar rites. Once properly cast the circle moves between the worlds and we are magickally aligned with the Goddess. *As above, so below*, the Circle of Magick upon the planes is the unfolding of the *Legend of the Descent* whereby we encounter the Dark Lord and inherit the legacy passed to her in this Realm of Shadows, the legacy of renewal and rebirth.

The Witches' Creed

Hear now the words of the witches,
The secrets we hid in the night,
When dark was our destiny's pathway,
That now we bring forth into light.

Mysterious water and fire,
The earth and the wide-ranging air,
By hidden quintessence we know them,
and will and keep silent and dare.

The birth and rebirth of all nature,
The passing of winter and spring,
We share with the life universal,
Rejoice in the magical ring.

Four times in the year the Great Sabbat
Returns, and the witches are seen
At Lammas and Candlemas dancing,
On May Eve and old Hallowe'en.

When day-time and night-time are equal,
When the sun is at greatest and least,
The four Lesser Sabbats are summoned,
Again witches gather in feast.

Thirteen silver moons in a year are,
Thirteen is the coven's array.
Thirteen times at Esbat make merry,
For each golden year and a day.

The power was passed down the ages,
Each time between woman and man,
Each century unto the other,
Ere time and the ages began.

When drawn is the magical circle,
By sword or athame or power,
Its compass between the two worlds lies,
In Land of the Shades for that hour.

This world has no right then to know it,
And world of beyond will tell naught,
The oldest of Gods are invoked there,
The Great Work of magic is wrought.

For two are the mystical pillars,
That stand at the gate of the shrine,
And two are the powers of nature,
The forms and the forces divine.

The dark and the light in succession,
The opposites each unto each,
Shown forth as a God and a Goddess:
Of this did our ancestors teach.

By night he's the wild wind's rider,
The Horn'd One, the Lord of the Shades.
By day he's the King of the Woodland,
The dweller in green forest glades.

She is youthful or old as she pleases,
She sails the torn clouds in her barque,
The bright silver lady of midnight,
The crone who weaves spells in the dark.

The master and mistress of magic,
They dwell in the deeps of the mind,
Immortal and ever-renewing,
With power to free or to bind.

So drink the good wine to the Old Gods,
And dance and make love in their praise,
Till Elphame's fair land shall receive us
In peace at the end of our days.

And Do What You Will be the challenge,
So be it in Love that harms none,
For this is the only commandment,
By Magic of old, be it done!

Eight words the Witches' Creed fulfill:
If it harms none, do what you will!
                              —Doreen Valiente, *Witchcraft for Tomorrow*

COMMENTARY

This text basically outlines Wiccan practices and philosophies connected with the rituals of the seasons and the worship of the God and Goddess. In the opening we find a reference to the time of the Inquisition when witches met at night in secret places. The Burning Time, as it is called, lies deep in the spirit of witches today, a remembrance of the violent persecution and a recollection of the bravery and suffering of so many who died by order of the church.

The magickal power of witches is referenced in the second stanza, the ability to evoke the very substance of Creation itself: earth, air, fire, and water. Here we also find the words of the Magus or Master of Magick: to know (one's will), to dare, and to be silent. Power shared is power lost.

The third through sixth stanzas address the seasonal and lunar rites. The periods of the eight Sabbats mark the time of powerful tides of energy that flow across the earth. To participate in ritual at these times is to become saturated with the energies associated with the season. Thus one becomes aligned with the vibration within Nature and the chakras resonate in harmony to the frequency. Aradia (an Italian witch of the fourteenth century) taught that the powers of a witch could only be maintained by an unbroken participation in the rites of the wheel of the year.

The seventh stanza contains the ancient teaching that initiation was to pass between people of the opposite sex. This is an issue dealing with sexual polarity and the psychic/magnetic energies associated when opposites come into contact with each other. The resulting energy opens up channels within the psyche and stimulates the chakras. This in turn makes the initiate more receptive and the initiator more energized. I will not debate here the subject of heterosexuals vs. homosexuals, but wish only to pass on the teaching of polarities.

The eighth and ninth stanzas remind us that a circle properly cast exists between the physical world and the astral world. It is, in effect, a corridor linking these dimensions. Wiccans refer to it as the world between the worlds. Here magick can be performed and the gods may be evoked. This dimension is neither substance nor dream. It is the shadow's edge between both realms of existence. Therefore magick is the law of metaphysics here, creating a micro-cosm according to the design of those who gather within the sacred circle.

The tenth and eleventh stanzas reveal the polarities of Divine Consciousness. These are the God and Goddess, the mystical pil-lars of light and darkness. Within Wicca, the Source of All Things (the Great Spirit) is perceived of as a great Consciousness com-prised of masculine and feminine qualities. The God and Goddess are equal but different aspects of Divine Consciousness.

Stanza twelve describes the God-Force as the Horned God of the Woodlands. This is a symbol of the antiquity of his aspect dat-ing back to the days of the hunter-gatherer. He is also seen as the Lord of the Underworld who draws the departed souls from the physical world into the realm of the spirit world. In the ancient mythos, he was the Sun God who rose each day from the Under-world and moved across the sky, gathering the souls of those who had died during the night. As the Sun set, the God descended into the Underworld carrying with him all of the newly departed souls.

Stanza thirteen describes the Goddess as she is associated with the moon. She is ever changing and ever renewing, just as the moon is. She appears waxing with youth or waning with age as she pleases. She is the Maiden, the Mother, and the Crone. The God-dess is the Queen of Heaven and the Mistress of Magick. In the ancient mythos she receives the souls from the God in the Under-world and carries them off to the moon. As the souls are collected, the light of the moon increases until it is full. As the souls are reborn again into the world, the light of the moon diminishes, eventually disappearing into the dark night.

Stanzas fourteen and fifteen tell us that the God and Goddess are also aspects of our own consciousness, dwelling deep within our subconscious mind. To love them and celebrate them is to gain liberation. To fear them and dread them is to become a prisoner to one's own mind. Therefore, Wiccans are encouraged to celebrate with wine, song, and love all in their praise.

Stanza sixteen contains the now-famous verses that comprise the Wiccan Rede. This addresses the issue of finding your true will and pursuing it, letting nothing stop you or turn you aside. This is to be done under love with harm to no one else. So the final stanza reads: If it harms none, do what you will!

The Great Rite Invocation

Assist me to erect the ancient altar,
at which in days past all worshipped;
The great altar of all things.
For in times of old, woman was the altar.
Thus was the altar made and placed,
and the sacred place was the point
within the center of the circle.
As we have of old been taught that the point within the
center is the origin of all things.
Therefore should we adore it;
Therefore whom we adore we also invoke.
O Circle of Stars,
Whereof our Father is but the younger brother,
Marvel beyond imagination, soul of infinite space,
Before whom time is ashamed,
the mind bewildered, and the understanding dark,
Not unto thee may we attain unless thine image be love.
Therefore, by seed and root, and stem and bud,
and leaf and flower and fruit do we invoke thee.
O Queen of Space, O Jewel of Light,
Continuous One of the heavens;
Let it be ever thus
that men speak not of thee as One, but as None;
and let them not speak of thee at all,
since thou art continuous.
For thou art the point within the Circle, which we adore;
the point of life, without which we would not be.
And in this way truly are erected the holy twin pillars,

*in beauty and in strength were they erected
to the wonder and glory of all men.*

**Altar of mysteries manifold,
the sacred circle's secret point
thus do I sign thee as of old
with kisses of my lips anoint.*

*Open for me the secret way,
the pathway of intelligence,
beyond the gates of night and day,
beyond the bounds of time and sense.
behold the mystery aright,
the five true points of fellowship,
here where the Lance and Grail unite
and feet, and knees, and breast, and lip.*

—Stewart and Janet Farrar, *The Witch's Way*

COMMENTARY

The opening verses refer to the fact that in ancient times a woman's body served as the altar in religious ceremonies. She lay on her back in the center of the ritual circle and served as the focal point for the rites. Today, because women's bodies have been used to sell products and magazines, many Wiccans no longer celebrate in the old way. Personal inhibitions along with the vestiges of former Judaic-Christian training also cause some Wiccans to avoid so intimate a setting.

As the text continues, there appear several references to the *point within the center of the circle.* This has several meanings depending on the context, but for our purposes it relates to the womb (both of the Universe and the woman). The invocations over the female altar draw on the universal aspects of God and Goddess which unite and are made manifest in the physical world through the womb gate. It is through the ancient star portals that avatars are born into the physical dimension (see chapter six).

The Holy Twin Pillars refer to two different elements. They are the polarities of Divinity itself as expressed in the personifications of Goddess and God. On a basic level they are aspects of masculine and feminine, positive and negative, active and receptive. In the second reference they allude to the legs of the woman upon the altar (although some modern covens focus on the breasts instead). With the knees bent, soles of the feet flat on the surface, the legs form two pillars flanking the opening to the womb, the Holy Temple containing the Great Cauldron of Rebirth.

The text continues with the anointing of the womb gate with kisses which are placed on a series of body points (see chapter fifteen). These are all connected with pulse sites and pressure points, which in turn can be used for blood flow restriction by binding cords to these areas. The ancient art can create certain states of consciousness when properly employed. Because of the dangers inherent in these workings, I will not discuss their application openly here.

The text concludes with a reference to sexual intercourse between the High Priest and the woman upon the altar. In many modern covens this has also been modified for much the same reason as the use of the female altar itself. Not all covens, however, compromise so thoroughly to the concerns of the Judaic-Christian Society in which they live, and still practice the old ways. There are also some covens in which the High Priest and High Priestess retire to a private setting in which the Great Rite may be concluded in whatever manner they personally elect.

Witches' Chant

Darksome night and shining Moon,
Hearken to the witches' rune.
East then south, west then north,
Hear! Come! I call Thee forth!

By all the powers of land and sea,
Be obedient unto me.
Wand and Pentacle and Sword,
Hearken ye unto my word.

Cords and Censer, Scourge and Knife,
Waken all ye into life.
Powers of the witch's Blade,
Come ye as the charge is made.

Queen of Heaven, Queen of Hell,
Send your aid unto the spell.
Horned Hunter of the night,
Work my will by magic rite.

By all the powers of land and sea,
As I do say, "so mote it be."
By all the might of moon and sun,
As I do will, it shall be done.

The Grimoire of Lady Sheba

COMMENTARY

The opening verses in this text relate to the ancient matrifocal beliefs and practices of the Great Goddess Cult in Old Europe. The Dark Night is the Mother of the Mysteries through which the moon was born. In this first passage we see that the cardinal points (portals) are evoked along with the moon. This tells us that the portals between the worlds must be opened under the influence of the lunar current when we celebrate or work magick.

The next two sets of verse are all commands to the tools set upon the altar to awaken beneath the enchantment which is being created through the evocations. This helps to focus the mind and direct the magickal concepts desired within the ritual circle. In other words, you are creating your own microcosm of the Universe and informing the objects within it with mental images of what is desired of them (thoughts become things in your magickal Universe). Thus all is in accordance with your will within the circle of magick.

The following verses call on the God and Goddess to send their power into the ritual/magickal working at hand. The images of the sun and moon are called on as reference points, defining the aspects of divinity being evoked. This serves to *fine-tune* the energy being evoked and directed by the power of personal will (see chapter nine). The statement—*as I do will, it shall be done*—is a magickal binding. It defines the power of the individual, referring to the person's training and abilities. It is the magickal equivalent of being known by one's word in one's own community.

Drawing Down the Moon

All ye assembled at mine shrine,
Mother Darksome and Divine.
Mine the Scourge and mine the Kiss,
Here I charge you in this sign
All ye assembled in my sight,
Bow before my spirit bright,
Aphrodite, Arianrod,
Lover of the Horned God,

Mighty Queen of Witchery and night,
Morgan, Etione, Nisene,
Diana, Bridgid, Melusine,
Am I named of old by men,
Artemis and Cerridwen,
Hell's dark mistress, Heaven's Queen.
Ye who ask of me a rune,
or would ask of me a boon,
meet me in some secret glade,
dance my round in greenwood shade,
by the light of the Full Moon.
In a place, wild and lone,
dance about mine altar stone;
work my holy mystery.
Ye who are feign to sorcery,
I bring ye secrets yet unknown.
No more shall ye know slavery,
who give true worship unto me.

Ye who tread my round on Sabbat night,
come ye naked to the rite,
in token that ye be really free.
I teach ye the mystery of rebirth,
work ye my mysteries in mirth.
Heart joined to heart and lip to lip,
five are the points of fellowship,
that bring ye ecstasy on earth,
for I am the circle of rebirth.
I ask no sacrifice, but do bow,
no other Law but love I know,
by naught but love may I be known.
All things living are mine own,
from me they come, to me they go.

I invoke Thee and call upon Thee
Mighty Mother of us all.
Bringer of Fruitfulness by seed and by root.
I invoke Thee by stem and bud.
I invoke Thee by life and love
and call upon Thee to descend into the body
of this Thy Priestess and Servant.
Hear with her ears, speak with her tongue,
touch with her hands, kiss with her lips,
that thy servants may be fulfilled.

The Grimoire of Lady Sheba

COMMENTARY

The ancient Roman Horace wrote in his *Epodes* (30 B.C.) that Italian witches had the power to call the moon down from the sky. This was also written concerning Greek witches in the days of antiquity. The Wiccan text presented here deals with this power as the invoking of the Great Goddess.

In the opening verses we find a reference to the dual nature of the Goddess as reflected in Neolithic times. She is both the Great

Mother and the Terrible Mother, the womb that gives life and takes life away. A list of various aspects of the Goddess follows, associating them with the Neolithic Horned God as consorts.

The verses then turn to a set of instructions for seeking favor with the Goddess. Her followers are directed to meet in a secret place away from the towns or villages. They are instructed to celebrate the Sabbats in a spirit of freedom, and as a sign of this they are to be naked during the rituals. In exchange, they are promised the revelation of secret mysteries.

The verses go on to say that live sacrifices during the rituals are inappropriate. The Goddess is the Mother of all living things, and it is she alone who will call to each when their life on earth has reached its end. The verses tell us that the Goddess may only be known through a heart that feels love. This is a love of self and others, a love that embraces Nature and Spirit alike.

The last set of verses is the actual invocation whereby the Goddess is asked to descend into the vehicle of the High Priestess. The alignments are addressed that define the mechanism of Nature through which the power is raised: *by seed and by root, by stem and by bud, by life and by love*. To one who has worshipped through the Cycle of the Year, and has been aligned with its mythos, the speaking of such words evokes the power of the experienced vibration of those currents. This is similar to when you smell a scent that reminds you of a certain summer day; for a moment you are back in that time feeling the way you once felt. This is the power of alignment and it serves to create the necessary states of consciousness for magickal workings.

The final verses direct the Goddess toward what is desired by the coven. This is the wish that she speak and act through the body of the High Priestess, using her physical senses to channel teachings or messages from the Divine realm to the physical realm. This can be a very powerful ritual, and should always be performed with great reverence.

Invocation of the Horned God

By the flame that burneth bright,
O' Horned One!
We call thy name into the night,
O'Ancient One!

Thee we invoke, by the moon-led sea,
By the standing stone and the twisted tree.
Thee we invoke where gather thine own,
By the nameless shrine forgotten and lone.

Come where the round of the dance is trod,
Horn and hoof of the goatfoot god!
By moonlit meadow, on dusky hill,
When the haunted wood is hushed and still,

Come to the charm of the chanted prayer,
As the moon bewitches the midnight air.
Evoke thy powers, that potent bide
In shining stream and the secret tide.

In fiery flame by starlight pale,
In shadowy host that rides the gale,
And by the fern-brakes fairy-haunted
Of forests wild and woods enchanted.

Come! Come!
To the heart-beats drum!
Come to us who gather below
When the broad white moon is climbing slow

Through the stars to the heaven's height
We hear thy hoofs on the wind of night!
As black tree-branches shake and sigh,
By joy and terror we know thee nigh.

We speak the spell thy power unlocks
At Solstice, Sabbat and equinox.

The Grimoire of Lady Sheba

COMMENTARY

This text really requires no explanation or special insights. Like the Horned God Himself, it is direct and powerful. I include it here because it is an important addition to sacred Wiccan text and should not be omitted. Thus we conclude this chapter and move on to explore the concepts of Wiccan deity in the following chapter.

CHAPTER
FOUR

WICCAN DEITIES

Just how the Celts conceived of their gods is very difficult to know, since, in every recorded story, people refuse to name their deity, always saying, "I swear by the gods that my people swear by..." This secrecy warded the gods from the scrutiny of outsiders, for only tribal members might partake in the mystery of their god, which included the knowing of his or her names and titles. And so, our knowledge of Celtic mythology is a tentative mixture of speculative archaeology and texts transcribed during the early Middle Ages.

—Caitlin Matthews, *The Celtic Tradition*

The traditional image of deity is represented in Wicca by a crescent-crowned goddess and a horned god. This divine couple imagery is commonly found in southern Europe, some examples being Diana and Pan or Artemis and Dionysus. Although in ancient Celtic iconography we do find a moon goddess and a horned god, we find no divine couple icons of the two figures together. For example, the Celtic moon goddess Cerridwen was the wife of Tegid, and not Cernunnos, the Celtic horned god. There are several possible reasons for this, which we will examine further in this chapter.

The majority of our knowledge concerning Celtic religion derives from the discovery of icons and inscriptions from the Roman period. The Celts of the Iron Age did not depict physical representations of deity with enough regularity to constitute an artistic or cultural tradition of such expression. However, after the influence of the Romans there is a sudden surge of Celtic deity representations reflective of the Roman tradition of iconography.

In her book *Symbol & Image in Celtic Religious Art* (Routledge, 1989), Miranda Green states that some scholars believe that the Celtic gods depicted in art may have come into existence only after Celtic submission to Rome and the formation of Romano-Celtic provinces. (Green is a tutor in Celtic studies at the University of Wales College of Cardiff, and an Honorary Research Fellow at the center for advanced Welsh and Celtic studies at Aberystwyth.) She believes it is more likely, however, that most Celtic gods appearing in iconography did exist in the pre-Roman era, but that their natures were no doubt modified by Roman influences. Concerning this influence, Green writes:

> *The Romans brought to Celtic lands the recurrent tradition of representing deities by images which were more or less mimetic, where artists used naturalistic human and animal models as the basis for image-projection...lastly the Romans introduced divine concepts which were on occasions absorbed and adapted by indigenous belief-systems.*

According to Green, it is apparent that the iconography which preserves the Celtic god forms is owed in a large part to the Mediterranean artist tradition. She states that some images of Celtic divinities occur for the first time only under Roman rule. These she lists as the Mother-goddesses, divine couples, and Nehalennia. She goes on to say that these aspects cannot be traced back prior to Roman times. According to author Caitlin Matthews, (*Ladies of the Lake*, Aquarian Press, 1992), the Celts had no creation myths as such; perhaps this is why the Mother goddess does not appear in Celtic religion prior to Etruscan and Roman influence. It is possible that evidence of their pre-Roman existence may once have been depicted on wood (now long since disintegrated) if such was ever the case, for we are reminded by Green that the Celtic king Brennus, in the third century B.C., laughed at the Greeks for creating human-like images of their gods.

The Kurgan/Indo-European invasion of central Europe resulted in the abrupt decline of the indigenous Neolithic Goddess Cult. The Celts originated in central Europe centuries after the patriarchal transformation of the Old European Goddess religion in that region. This may also shed some light on the issue of the Mother Goddess in pre-Roman Celtic religion. Chapter eleven addresses this in greater depth, and also examines the Tuatha de Danaan who worshipped a Mother Goddess—therefore we will not pause here to consider it further. As this chapter continues we shall examine the basic concept of *Deity* within Wiccan Religion, and seek out historically traceable lines leading to the roots of Wiccan theology. Generally speaking, we can say that most Wiccans conceive of deity as the Creative Source which is both masculine and feminine. These polarities are personified as the Goddess and the God, each known by many names within the various traditions comprising Wicca. However, some traditions (particularly the Dianic) conceive of Deity as a Goddess with both masculine and feminine aspects.

In mainstream Wicca, Nature establishes the pattern and therefore the God and Goddess exist in Wiccan theology as symbols of this polarity. We know that in Nature the physical manifestations of distinct male and female entities exist in order to procreate. There are some creatures, such as the snail, that possess both male and female sexual organs and can self-reproduce, but for the most part the natural pattern appears to require both separate male and female entities in order to maintain a species. We can discern from this that the Creator/Creators set forth a pattern reflected within Creation of both male and female agents. In this pattern there exists something of the nature of the Creators as well.

The ancient axiom of "as above, so below" addresses the issue of the Physical Dimension reflecting the Spiritual Dimension (see chapter two). Essentially this means that whatever results from the action of a catalyst is itself a reflection of the nature of that catalyst. From this perspective we can conclude that the Great Spirit is both male and female, God and Goddess. This is not meant to discredit or deny Judaic-Christian perceptions or those of the Dianic Tradition, but simply to explain mainstream Wiccan concepts of Deity and the reasoning behind them.

In this chapter we will examine the nature and origin of both of the Wiccan concepts of Goddess and God. The origins of these deity forms are quite ancient. Cave drawings from the Ice Age depict them associated with such human concerns as hunting, reproduction, and basic survival. Ancient burial sites reveal that early humans believed in an afterlife and provided tools and other items for the deceased to use in the Other World. It is possible that dreaming (no doubt mysterious to primitive minds) led humans to believe in other types of existence outside of everyday life.

In dreams, humans performed acts that they could not accomplish in everyday life. They also experienced fear, happiness, pain, and pleasure. Early humans knew that this world of dreams was somehow different from the waking world. This mentality led to a concept of other realms and other lives. The forces of Nature also played a role in forming religious thought. Thunder and lightning, volcanic eruptions, and earthquakes all presented humans with a need to understand what caused them and how to appease their source. Thus were born the old gods.

This leads us to what some occultists call egregores or "divine thought-forms" and how they function. I am speaking here of metaphysical principles and occult concepts, neither of which can be fully expressed in a few paragraphs. An egregore is essentially a composite entity, comprised partly of human energy and divine energy. When a tribe carves an image of their deity and offers it rituals of worship, then this image forms within the etheric material of the astral dimension. At this stage the deity is what we call a thought-form (energy formed into a mental image). The more ritual energy provided by the worshippers, the more cohesive the thought-form becomes.

Pre-existing Divinity, dwelling within a higher dimension, becomes aware of this formation due to the *ripple effect* or *domino effect* natural to the function of the seven planes of existence (see chapter seven). Because it is the nature of Divinity to respond to contact or communication, it then issues forth a *life spark* of its own essence and passes it into the thought-form. The form is thus given life by this emanation and is animated by it. It has now become a conscious god or goddess with the attributes perceived by the worshippers.

This is essentially the reason the old Wiccan teachings tell us that the gods need us as much as we need them. They are maintained by our rituals, which provide them energy and by our consciousness, which sustains their connection to us and to their source. The older the egregore, the more powerful it becomes. When a cult disappears then the egregore sleeps in the mist of the astral dimension, but it can be awakened again when worshippers recall its name and perform its rites, as is evidenced in the case of reconstructed traditions seen in Wicca today.

It is important to understand that not all gods and goddesses are egregores. The Great God and Goddess have always existed prior to the appearance of humankind. These are the archetypes, and the egregores are their children. Here we shall consider their origins and importance in Wiccan religion, so let us now turn to the Great God and the Great Goddess of Wiccan theology.

THE GOD

In the initiate level teachings of Wicca, the god has three aspects. He is the Horned One; the god of the forest, representing the untamed nature of all that is free. In this aspect he marks the stage of the hunter-gatherer. Secondly he is the Hooded One (hooded-in-the-green); the Lord of the Harvest, the Green Man image. Here he reflects the cultivated nature of all that is patterned. In this aspect he marks the stage of agricultural development. Lastly he is the Old One, and symbolizes the cumulative wisdom of human experience. In this aspect he marks the stage of civilization (defined as the building of cities and their supporting systems).

In Celtic mythology we find a god trinity under the names: Teutates, Esus, and Taranis (though they have little in common with Wiccan concepts today). Teutates was considered to be the most powerful aspect of the triple godhead. He was also the oldest and most sinister form, appeased with blood sacrifices on his ancient altars. Esus was associated with the bull and later with the god Cernunnos. Esus was appeased with sacrifices involving hanging humans from trees; eventually he developed into an Underworld god. Taranis was a sky god connected to the powers of thunder and lightning who demanded human sacrifice in ritual fires. Lug later replaces the god Taranis as the mythos evolves.

Examining the concepts of ancient god images from the past will help us to understand his Wiccan Mysteries.

THE HORNED GOD

The earliest carved icons of Neolithic god figures have been found in the area that was once Old Europe (c. 4300 B.C.). There are much older Paleolithic paintings and carvings in southern and western Europe, but we are concerned here with practical ritual items because they address the issue of a formalized cult. The meaning and purpose of cave wall images are open to debate, but statues indicate a "hands-on" approach to religion. According to Professor Gimbutas (*Goddesses and Gods*), only two to three percent of the figurines found in Old Europe are male images. These are mostly horned figures, human-like in appearance, and are said to represent metaphors of rising and dying vegetation.

The oldest image of the Horned God in Wicca is that of a god with the horns of a stag. In this form he represented the Lord of the Forest, providing for the needs of both human and animal life. In chapter fourteen (Men's Mysteries) we will explore the reason the stag was specifically chosen as a symbol. We begin our search for the early god of Wicca where his icons first appear, south of the Alps in Old Europe. This god-form continued to be worshiped up until the shift to agricultural dependence, and we will follow his evolution throughout this chapter.

As humans settled in one place to grow crops they also further developed the practice of domesticating animals. The importance of goats grew and eventually replaced the symbol of the stag in human culture. Thus the stag-horned god of the hunter-gatherer society was transformed into the goat-horned god of the agricultural community. At this stage of development he took on other aspects reflecting the development of human understanding, for these humans were no longer primitive forest dwellers, they were now the builders of civilizations. It is interesting to note, however, that the goat-horned god still retained the wild nature of the stag within himself, as seen in the nature of the god Pan.

The Wiccan God was known by many names in ancient times. He was originally known as the Horned One. In Latin this would have been Cornuno; *cornu* meaning horn and *uno* meaning one. This is the basis for the name of the Celtic stag god Cernunnos, whom the Romans recognized and named in their contacts with the Celtic people. He was also known by the name Dianus (from the Latin *divianus*, meaning the divine one) and as Dionysus (meaning the divine one of Nysea). In the Celtic regions he is called Myrddin, Suibhe Geilt, Cernowen, or Hu Gadarn, and many other names in addition to Cernunnos.

Stag-Horned God

Bull-Horned God

Goat-Horned God

Evolution of the Horned God

The images of drunken orgies and outrageous acts of frenzy associated with the cult of Dionysus are as much a distortion and corruption of the original cult practices as are the alleged practices of the Witch Cult during the time of the Inquisition. The esoteric practices of the mystery cult of Dionysus were not the drunken revelry of Pagans and the rampaging of crazed maenads across the countryside as reported of the exoteric cult. Divine intoxication rather than alcoholic intoxication was the basis of Dionysian practices, although wine was certainly in abundance during his rites. To fully understand Dionysus as a mystery god-form within Wicca, we must look to his agricultural nature wherein we find the intoxicating essence of his divine nature. For the moment we will regard him in his aspect as a horned god.

Dionysus was commonly portrayed in classical mythology as both a goat-horned god and a bull-horned god, whose cult is said to have originated in Thrace. Professor Gimbutas includes Thrace in her description of the region comprising Old Europe (*Goddesses and Gods*), and she states that Dionysus was a pre-Indo-European god of great antiquity, symbolizing renewal and brimming with virility. The employment of bull horns and the appearance of serpents associated with Dionysus are said to have originated as symbols of his connection with the lunar rites of Old Europe, and with his role as the divine son and incestuous lover of the Great Mother. Ancient pottery from Old Europe depicts bull horns as symbols of crescent moons, and therefore may be among the earliest representations of the concept of balanced polarities, male and female.

Crescent moons in Neolithic matrifocal culture appear to be exclusively female symbols. Stag horns of this period, forming crescent moons, appear earlier than do bull horns and are employed to express the union of male and female symbols in composite imagery. Therefore, since Dionysus had bull horns in Old Europe, he would have possessed stag horns at an earlier time. For example, in the ancient Homeric tales (a bardic tradition predating classical mythology) we know that Dionysus was consort to Artemis, thus confirming his forest nature (later in classical mythology he married Ariadne). Artemis was a woodland goddess associated with forest animals. Therefore her horned consort would logically have borne the horns of a forest dweller, not the horns of a bull. The bull is pastoral and its connection with Dionysus would have evolved after the hunter-gatherer period of human development. It is in the relationship with Artemis that his oldest god form is uncovered, that of the stag-horned god of the forest. This powerful early divine couple image, the crescent-crowned goddess and her horned consort, is the basis for Wiccan concepts of divinity from ancient to modern times.

When the Greek cult of Dionysus spread to Italy it became the cult of Bacchus, merging with the peaceful local forms of worship. The Romans recognized him as the Etruscan god Fufluns, who they had earlier absorbed into their agrarian religious mythos as Dianus. Although this Italic cult was an agricultural society focusing on the vineyards, the memory of the horned one is quite evident in the fact that the Romans portrayed the followers of Bacchus as satyrs. The fact that these minor horned deities of the woodlands were followers of Bacchus further attests to his aspect as a horned forest god. The Senate of Rome outlawed the cult of Bacchus in 186 B.C., but it survived as a secret society and publicly returned in the first century A.D. as a popular Mystery Religion.

The priests of Bacchus retained the horn imagery by associating Bacchus with Dianus, and thus Bacchus became the naturalized horned god of the Italic people. In art he was portrayed with a crown of leaves and vines, behind which lay his sprouted horns. They are often depicted in art as the budding horns of a goat. As mentioned earlier, the goat-horned god is simply the stag-horned god transformed in the passage from a hunter-gatherer society to an agrarian community. The practice of merging deities of the same nature in Italy is best characterized in the book *Roman and European Mythologies* (University of Chicago Press, 1992), compiled by Yves Bonnefoy:

> *A student of the ancient Italian gods must never lose sight of the religious unity of classical civilization, that is, the fundamental unity of the Greek and Roman religions. Beyond the traits that, on the level of imagination, mentality, and behavior, differenti-*

ate the relations that Greece, Etruria, the Italic populations, and Rome maintained with the sacred, it is evident that their ideas of the personalities, functions, looks and attributes of the main divinities are essentially the same.

The ancient Greek historian Strabo (63 B.C.–A.D. 19) wrote that the Druidesses were "the devotees of Bacchus" and mentions that Celtic women paid him homage on an island in Okeanos (the specific location is unknown but generally believed to be somewhere in the British Isles). Here they formed an exclusive female society maintaining his mystery tradition and performing ancient rites of initiation. Author Gerhard Herm, in his book *The Celts— The People Who Came Out of the Darkness* (Barnes & Noble Books, 1976), writes:

We are left with the question whether the Celts really did have cults similar to the bacchanalia. To suppose that Strabo merely picked up wild rumors would be too hasty. As we have seen, he generally described the Gallic people quite accurately and without prejudice....

The Druids were also associated with the Celtic horned god Cernunnos (though more commonly as Hu Gadarn), who arose out of the indigenous beliefs of the Celts and later absorbed the Mystery Teachings imported by the Romans. In the Celtic Cauldron Mysteries we find a connection between the nine Maidens who tend the fire beneath Cerridwen's cauldron and the nine Muses of Greek mythology. The Maidens of Cerridwen are clearly based on the earlier mythos of the Greek Muses, as is evident by simple comparison (see chapter twelve). It is no coincidence that the Greek Muses are also associated with Dionysus. In chapter twelve we will explore this in greater detail.

Images of horned beings appear to be the earliest portrayals of masculine divinity. They first appear as paintings and etchings on cave walls in the Paleolithic period, and then later as statues and icons of the Neolithic era in Old Europe. The most famous painting of a horned male figure is what archaeologists have titled the "Sorcerer" of Les Trois Freres (in southern France). This image is said to portray a man dressed in animal skins and horns, perhaps a shaman, apparently connected with hunting magick or an associated ceremony involving the prey.

The most ancient wall carving of a stag-horned god (as opposed to a stag-horned man) is found in a cave at Camonica in northern Italy, dated around 400 B.C. This carving portrays an entity with a human body and a stag's head. Beside him appears a worshipper, and the god lifts up a serpent. The serpent was associated with the rites of Dionysus and was in use as a connective symbol over a thousand years before the time of this carving. Upon the figure's arm hangs a crescent-like object, further linking him with lunar rites. It is interesting to note that the Celtic horned god Cernunnos was also associated with the serpent, and held a crescent-like symbol known as a torc.

Many people believe that the Camonica figure is actually the Celtic god Cernunnos and that the symbol he holds is a Celtic torc. However, the Mediterranean people also possessed a similar torc reflected in the well-known Caduceus symbol. The Italic torc was one of the military symbols of authority carried by Roman officers (see illustration below). It is also possible that the torc and serpent were later engraved upon the original Italic stag image by the Celts during their occupation of northern Italy. It should be remembered that the Celtic king Brennus, in 300 B.C., laughed at

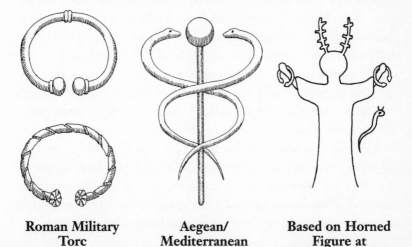

**Roman Military
Torc**

**Aegean/
Mediterranean
Caduceus**

**Based on Horned
Figure at
Val Camonica, Italy**

the Greeks for creating images of their deities; therefore it is unlikely that 100 years earlier they had carved an image of one of their own deities on a cave wall in northern Italy. In any case, since the religion of Old Europe began south of the Celtic lands and originally encompassed Italy, this deity is more likely an early depiction of the indigenous Italic horned god.

When the Romans occupied the Celtic lands to the north and west, they encountered a stag-horned deity not unlike the ancient Italic god in appearance. The Romans recognized the similarities and gave him the Latinized name Cernunnos, the horned one. Although the basic religious beliefs of the Celtic people probably remained relatively intact, there is no doubt that the influence of Roman occupation modified them in many ways. This is evident in the proliferation of Romano-Celtic altars, inscriptions, and icons. The Celts readily absorbed the Mystery Teachings of the horned Roman god, particularly because of his mystery association with the bull (from the cult of Dionysus). The importance of the bull to the Celts in the pre-Roman period of their pastoral economy was quite significant, and his symbol held much meaning.

The significance of the horned god was his power over the animal kingdom and all forest life in general. Gimbutas calls him the "Master of Animals" (*Goddesses and Gods*) and he played an essential role in early magickal and religious thought. His time-honored symbols were the syrinx (Pan pipes), the shepherd's crook, and the pine twig. He was himself the symbol of the covenant between human hunters and animal prey. The horned god provided meat for humans and renewed life for animals. The humans, for their part, performed certain magickal ceremonies, returning life energy back into the forest. This was the *secret mystery* of the hunter's cult, the *same* individual animals who were slain arose again to life through the stag-horned god ceremony.

Joseph Campbell, in his book *The Masks of God: Primitive Mythology* (Penquin Books, 1968), states that this basic theme of the covenant between hunter and prey was essential to all hunter societies. One important aspect of the hunter society was to retain an imperishable object from the animal itself. Through this it was believed that the life energy of the animal survived and only his physical body was slain. Joseph Campbell says of this concept:

> *The bone does not disintegrate and germinate into something else, but is the undestroyed base from which the same individual that was there before becomes magically reconstructed, to pick up life where he left it. The same man comes back; that is the point.*

In Wicca, this concept led to the practice of wearing a set of stag horns as a symbol of the priesthood. Prior to the religious symbolism of this crown, it was worn by the leader of the hunter society as a sign of his personal power and authority. Many Wiccan priests also wear a piece of horn on a necklace which symbolizes the sacred bone of the hunter's covenant with the animal kingdom. The gold charm called the "Italian horn" (known as the corno) commonly seen today originated in the hunter/warrior cult as a symbol of courage and virility. As a fertility symbol it also represented the phallus of a goat, an animal always associated in ancient times with sexual prowess.

As humans enjoyed the benefits of growing their own food and raising their own animals, they still felt the connection to the forest where life ran free. Thus the importance of the stag image and mythos remained for a time within the practices of Wicca. Eventually the impact of the seasons on the crops replaced the former importance of seasonal associations with the hunt (animal migrations and so forth). Wiccan religion moved into a deeper connection with divinity through the times of planting and harvesting. So we turn now to the Lord of the Harvest and the symbolism of the Green Man.

THE HARVEST LORD/GREEN MAN

Agriculture developed first in the Middle East, approximately 11,000 years ago. The most notable early developments were around the Tigris and Euphrates Rivers and the Nile River Valley of Egypt. Around 3000 B.C. the inhabitants developed methods of irrigation and the ox-drawn plow. Not long after this period the Greeks also began to develop as an agricultural society.

Because European farming began in the southern region of Old Europe, the development of agricultural deities and their mystery cults also began there. Logically, we look here for the origins of the Agricultural Mysteries. According to Professor Marija Gimbutas (*Goddess and Gods*), the most ancient non-Indo-European god of Old Europe (also associated with the plant kingdom) is Dionysus. Therefore it seems wise to study him in our quest for the mystery origins. In the course of this chapter we will see how his cult mysteries laid the foundation for many of the Mystery Traditions within Wicca.

The Romans began farming prior to 500 B.C. and introduced advanced methods of farming into northern and western Europe: the ox-drawn plow, irrigation, crop rotation, and the practice of leaving a field fallow. They also naturally passed along the Mystery Teachings associated with agriculture, which was by then a blend of Italic Paganism mixed with teachings inherited from the Etruscans, Greeks, and Syrians. We know historically that the Etruscans were famous for their occult knowledge of divination, magick, and the inner Mystery Teachings. The Romans who eventually conquered them absorbed much of their culture and based many of their religious practices on Etruscan tenets.

The Celts were mostly herders and dairy farmers when the Romans encountered them, although there is some evidence of simple farming among the Celts in pre-Roman times (although largely connected with cattle feed, as evidenced in archaeological finds among Celtic settlements). Historically, the people of western and northern Europe were a more pastoral nomadic culture while advanced agricultural societies were flourishing in the south. The rich fertile farm lands of Italy obviously attracted the Celts, one of several factors that drew them into contact with the Etruscans and Romans.

In the early days of humankind, prior to the knowledge of farming, women would gather roots, tubers, nuts, and various types of plants and mushrooms for food. They would bury some in order to control the distribution of this precious source of food for the tribe. Naturally some of the buried items rooted or seeded and sprang up from the ground as a new plant. The awareness of this connection gave birth to the concept of farming, and was also the origin of one of the Female Mysteries (see chapter thirteen).

The association of the god with plant life appears in abundant images throughout all of Europe. In the imagery of Old Europe it is best captured in various depictions of Dionysus. He sometimes appears as a bearded man with a crown of ivy. Other times he appears as an effeminate youth, wearing a fawn skin and crowned with a wreath of laurel and ivy (he is also depicted with a panther skin or a black robe). In later times, Dionysus is portrayed with long curly hair, crowned with vine leaves and grapes. He holds a thyrsus in one hand and a chalice cup in the other.

The thyrsus is a wand comprised of a fennel stalk capped with a pine cone. This composite symbol of plant and seed represents the union of Dionysus' forest nature (pine cone) merged with his agricultural nature (fennel). The chalice he holds represents first the womb of the Great Mother from which he issued forth (for he is the Divine Child of European mythology, the Child of Promise). Second, the chalice represents the offering up of his divine nature, for it contains his liquid essence. Thus he stands before us as the ancient Lord of the Harvest, the slain god to be (chapters twelve and fourteen).

The ritual items he carries are the wand and the chalice, and in this image we find the first ancient depiction of Wiccan ritual tools together with their traditional symbolism. It is interesting to note that along with these symbols in relief art, circa 30 B.C., the rituals of Dionysus also depict women presiding over blindfolded initiates. A picture of this is found in the book *Mystery Religions in the Ancient World* by Joscelyn Godwin (Harper & Row, 1981). In Wicca, the wand represents the phallus of the god and the chalice represents the womb of the goddess. Thus the thyrsus is the stalk and the seed, meaning that it is the shaft of the phallus and the semen issuing forth. The chalice is the opening to the womb and the lining of the uterus. Dionysus holds them both, displaying the male and female polarities which when united bring forth the Child of Promise (himself).

The Green Man

What, then, is the Child of Promise? This is a complex theme and marks the further evolution of human understanding concerning the secrets of Nature. The Child is essentially two different principles, the son (and lover-to-be) of the Goddess and also the product of magick (meaning that it is what results from a work of magick). He appears in both the religion of Old Europe and also in the Mystery Teachings of Witchcraft and Celtic Wicca. The Child of Promise is further explored in the following Goddess section. So for now, let us return to the Lord of the Harvest, also known as the Green Man.

It is interesting to note that the earliest known Celtic image of the Green Man comes from the fifth century B.C. It is reproduced in the book *The Green Man—The Archetype of our Oneness with the Earth* by William Anderson (HarperCollins, 1990). As the author notes, this image (now called the St. Goar pillar) is a blend of the earlier Etruscan art style with that of the Celtic La Tene culture. This again points to the region of Old Europe as the origin of deity forms now associated with the Wiccan Mysteries. Anderson attempts to link Cernunnos to the Green Man image and seems to believe that Dionysus and Cernunnos are "cousins" derived from an earlier deity who was the son/lover of the Goddess. However, as we are seeing in the progression of this chapter, Dionysus is actually the origin of all of these aspects himself.

The Green man image as seen within the Agricultural Mysteries is always associated with the essence of intoxication (whether spiritual or physical). Sometimes it is in the use of hallucinogenic plants such as mushrooms, known to have been employed by early shamans and also by the European Witch Cult. More commonly it is in the use of grapes and grains for the production of beer and wine. Such types of intoxication are meant to reflect the transforming nature of the essence that resides in the spirit or god-nature of the plant. To consume the nature of the Harvest Lord is to become one with his spirit. This is the basis of the Rite of Communion found in many religions.

One of the problems inherent with trying to associate Celtic deities with the Agricultural Mysteries in pre-Roman times is that the ancient Celts drank mead and not beer. Mead is made from fermented honey and not from grain. Therefore, in this respect, the grain and grape aspects of the Harvest Lord did not exist in Celtic religion prior to the arrival of the Romans from Italy. The historian Tacitus tells us that the Celts (and some Germanic tribes) first brewed beer sometime around A.D. 100. Pliny the Elder mentions earlier that beer was already being brewed in the Mediterranean. Prior to the Roman era, the inhabitants of northern and western Europe were pastoral nomads, and were not a true agricultural society (although they were certainly farming, but on a relatively smaller scale). Agrarian societies of this time period were found south of the Alps. We know, for example, that the Celts were trading with the Etruscans for wine around 400 B.C. and that the Romans introduced viniculture into Gaul after their conquest of this region (circa 50 B.C.). This does not mean that the Celts were without any indigenous Green Man mysteries. I am simply trying to maintain the proper chronological flow of the agricultural Mystery Teachings from Old Europe to Celtic Europe.

In addition to the Agricultural Mystery Teaching of the indwelling essence is the teaching of transformation. As previously mentioned, the earliest god forms are associated with the rising and dying of vegetation. All of the tenets of belief connected with reincarnation and transmigration are to be found in the cycles of the plant kingdom. The seasons of the earth, ever returning in the wheel of the year, are but amplifiers and signalers of the mystical powers of Nature at work in the fields and forests.

To link oneself to the mythos of the dying and returning god is to assure oneself of "salvation" from the forces of death and annihilation. This was the essential premise of the Dionysian cult, the Eleusinian Mysteries, and even Christianity. Plutarch consoled his wife in a letter written in response to the death of their daughter, assuring her of the immortality to be found in the Dionysian mysteries. This linking to the cycles of Nature (physical and metaphysical) is also reflected in the ritual observances of the Wiccan Wheel of the Year, the eight Sabbats.

We also find evidence of the transformation mysteries of agriculture in the Celtic tale of Taliesin (circa A.D. 500), influenced by the Roman tradition which was absorbed in Gaul and Britain over centuries of Roman occupation. In this tale, the character Gwion accidentally receives enlightenment from three drops of magickal elixir (concocted by the goddess Cerridwen). He flees and is pursued by the goddess. During the chase he is magickally transformed into various creatures, and Cerridwen changes herself into a form that preys upon each form that Gwion takes on. Finally he becomes a grain and is swallowed by Cerridwen in the form of a bird. This grain impregnates her and she later gives birth to the bard Taliesin.

The mystical theme of transformation associated with agriculture is found in many European folk tales. Gimbutas tells us that the mythos of the Harvest Lord is preserved in texts dating from Homer and Hesiod, up into modern folklore. It is perhaps best preserved in the story of the passion of the flax and the dying god. In ancient Greece he was Linos, in Lithuania he was Vaizgantas and in Scotland he was known as Barleycorn. It is interesting to note that the common word for flax in European language unites Old Europe with Celtic Europe. In Greek it is *linon*, in Latin *linum*, and in both Old Irish and Old German it is *lin*.

As Gimbutas points out in *The Language of the Goddess*, this mythos is also reflected in Hans Christian Anderson's story of the flax and in the Danish tale of Rye's Pain (Rugen's Pine). Essentially these stories address the planting of the seed and its struggle to sprout from the earth. This is followed by the plant having to endure the elements. Then, in its prime, it is pulled out of the ground and subjected to thrashing, soaking, and roasting. Eventually it is combed with hackle-combs and thorns, spun into thread and woven into linen. Finally it is cut and pierced with needles, and sown into a shirt. Here indeed we find the sacrifice of the Harvest Lord for the welfare of his people.

In the classical Greek myth of Dionysus, he is first slain and then dismembered. Next he is boiled, roasted, and then devoured. The Orphic myth of Dionysus includes the same sequence but adds the recomposition and resurrection of the bones. Heraclitus says that Dionysus and Hades are one and the same, thus associating Dionysus with the Underworld (a classic Wiccan Mythos, the

Lord of the Shadows). Further evidence of this connection comes from a tale about the labyrinth of the Minotaur and Dionysus and Ariadne, retold in *Ecstasies: Deciphering the Witches' Sabbath* (Pantheon, 1991), by Carlo Ginzburg:

> *...That the Labyrinth symbolized the realm of the dead and that Ariadne, mistress of the Labyrinth, was a funerary goddess, are more than probable conjectures. In Athens the marriage of Dionysus and Ariadne was celebrated every year on the second day of the Anthesteria: an ancient springtime festival that coincided with the periodic return to the earth of the souls of the dead, ambiguous harbingers of well-being and harmful influences, who were placated with offerings of water and boiled cereals.*

This passage is of particular importance because it connects Dionysus with the souls of the dead and the Underworld. This aspect of Dionysus is also confirmed by the ancient historian Herodotus in his work *The Histories*. In this one god we now see all of the aspects of the Wiccan God: Horned God of the forest, Lord of the Harvest, God of the Underworld, Son/Lover of the Goddess, the Child of Promise, and the Green Man (bearded man crowned with ivy, the Old One). It is interesting to note that no other single European deity outside of the Mediterranean contains each and every aspect of the God-form found in Wicca. This confirms that our Quest was not in vain, for in Dionysus we have found the origins of the Wiccan God's Mysteries.

THE GODDESS

The most ancient concept of deity within early human culture was that of the Great Mother Goddess. The vast amount of statues and carvings of this deity first appear from 6500 to 3500 B.C. in southern and southeastern Europe (Old Europe). In western Europe they appear from 4500 B.C. to 2500 B.C. and are not as abundant. In Wicca today the Goddess is perceived as a three-fold goddess: Mother, Maiden, and Crone. However, the Old Religion was a lunar cult; in the initiate levels it was taught that each phase of the moon pertained to an aspect of the Goddess: Maiden, Mother, Crone, and Enchantress. When the waxing crescent appeared it was seen as the chaste Maiden, when the moon was full it represented the Mother, and the waning crescent represented the Crone. When the moon was dark and unseen it represented the Enchantress (who was also called the Temptress).

In this section we will independently examine the natures of the Goddess as they imprint their influences upon the mysteries. Therefore, we will look to the Mother Goddess, Moon Goddess, and the Triple Goddess of Fate.

THE MOTHER GODDESS

The Mother image is perhaps the most powerful and certainly the most enduring of all goddess types. She is the totality of all that is feminine. The Mother is the vessel through which all things enter into the world. Her most obvious attribute is fertility; in the Old Religion she governed the fecundity of animals as well as humans, and all life existing in the wild. One of her oldest titles is the Lady of the Beasts.

She was also known in ancient times as the frightening Terrible Mother, for she who generated life was also she who took it back into herself. Where the Great Mother held power over life and birth, the Terrible Mother held power over death and destruction. Life and birth are intimately connected with death and destruction; the life-generating womb of the earth eventually transforms into the devouring mouth of the Underworld. It is from this connection that the Mother Goddess took on the aspects of the power of light and darkness.

Caves were early symbols of the Mother Goddess and represented both the womb and the grave. In time she came to be worshipped in a grotto, a practice still seen in modern times in the veneration of Mary by the Catholic Church (the Mother of God). In early Pagan symbolism the Mother possessed large breasts and buttocks, symbols of abundance. A fat body indicated that food was abundant, the world was fertile, and well-fed women produced healthier babies. In the Christian image of Mary as Mother of God, she appears without any noticeable breasts and her hips are hardly even suggested.

In Neolithic times the Goddess appears as the Great Goddess of Life, Death, and Regeneration. In the iconography of this period her powers are reflected in images of certain insects and animals. The bee and butterfly are ancient feminine symbols of regeneration, and in the Minoan culture the butterfly is transformed into the double axe symbol. In the animal kingdom her powers are depicted by the deer, bear, hare, hedgehog, dog, toad, and turtle. All of these creatures are found flanking the goddess in Neolithic art. In every case these companions are male creatures, signifiers of the impregnating forces of Nature empowering the Great Goddess.

Images of the Triple Mother first appeared among the Celts in the Roman period. Miranda Green (*Symbol and Image*) tells us that the imagery of this concept owes itself to the original Roman form of the *Iunones* (a female spirit flanked by the feminine Genius and the Nursing Goddess). Green states that the Celtic triplicity is an intensification of the original Mediterranean *Iuno* concept. Its use among the Celts was designed to retain the indigenous elements of Celtic religion by means of triplication.

There are essentially two early male forms associated with the Mother Goddess: the Divine Child (or Child of Promise) and the Year God (lover of the Goddess, her consort). The Year God cycle begins with the birth of the Divine Child. In ancient art the Goddess nurses him and is depicted wearing the mask of a creature such as a bear or snake. The infant correspondently appears as a cub or newborn snake. The Divine Child is symbolic of the newly emerging vegetation and as such is the indwelling spirit providing renewed vitality. A curious element always associated with this personage is that shortly following his birth, he is always hidden away and reared by someone other than his biological mother. This same theme is present in the myth of Dionysus who, shortly after his birth, is hidden from Hera and raised by nymphs in the woods.

The Year God is known as both the lover of the Goddess and as the Sorrowful God. He is both the son and the sexual lover of the Goddess. His ancient Neolithic symbols are the phallus and the mushroom (see chapter thirteen). In iconography he is usually depicted as a horned god, usually a goat or a bull (but in Paleolithic times as a stag). As such he was associated with fertility and virility. This correspondence led to what Gimbutas (*The Language of the Goddess*) calls the "Sacred Marriage":

> *Since many elements of the year-god's festivals are represented in the sculptural art of Old Europe, it seems not unreasonable to assume that festivals took place in Neolithic and Chalcolithic Europe. Possibly the central idea of ritual drama, the "Sacred Marriage," the ritual coition of the male god and a female goddess, is reflected in the little sculpture from Casciorele.* [this late 5th millennium B.C. artifact is pictured in *The Goddesses and Gods of Old Europe*, Gimbutas].

Ancient Year God icons usually depict him seated with one of two characteristics. He is shown either as a young male figure with a large erect phallus, or as an older male with flaccid genitalia (or nothing displayed). Clearly the youth represents the waxing power of Nature and the aged figure the waning power. Gimbutas writes that some of these icons have been found buried in tombs together with images of the Great Goddess. This is an important find because many ancient divine couple images and Great Goddess images were destroyed throughout Europe due to the patriarchal Kurgan invasion.

In southern Europe the Great Goddess survived the Indo-European cultural transformation that spread almost everywhere in Europe. Gimbutas tells us that She survived the Bronze Age, and then the Classical Age of Greece, and continued into later times where She was absorbed by the Etruscans. The Celts embraced the Great Goddess through contacts with the Greeks, Etruscans, and Romans. Her cult had already been displaced by the patriarchal concepts of the Kurgan/Indo-European invaders in central Europe long before the Celts arose there as a distinct people (see chapter eleven).

There is an interesting connection between the Celtic goddess Artio and the Mediterranean goddess Artemis. This appears in the form of a bear, an ancient symbol of the Mother. Artio was a bear goddess venerated by the Celts, and in some legends she was associated with the horned god Cernunnos. Artemis was associated with the horned god Dionysus. Athenian girls danced as bears in honor of the goddess Artemis, and she also bore the title Artemis-Kalliste, associating her with the bear. This connection is rooted in the Greek myth where a woman named Kallisto is transformed into a bear. In Greek *artos* means bear, in Latin it is *arctus*. The Roman writer Porphyry (A.D. 233 to 304) associates Artemis with the bee and with honey, under the name Melissa. The association with bears and honey is obvious here. Porphyry says it was Artemis' province, as moon goddess, to bring about birth. He also makes a curious statement that the moon is a bull and bees are begotten of bulls. This would bring us back to Dionysus again as a consort figure, and we seem to have come full circle.

Gimbutas identifies the surviving Great Goddess of Old Europe as Artemis, and describes her as a non-Greek and non-Indo-European goddess (in name and character). Under the name Atimite (a-ti-mi-te) she appears on Linear B tablets from Pylos, but she was also known by many other names: Enodia, Hekate, Diana, Diktynna, and Kallisto. In both ancient Greek and Roman art she was still depicted with her Neolithic consorts, the deer and the dog. She was believed to be present at births and was called "Opener of the Womb" by the Romans who knew her as Diana. Through this association with Diana/Artemis, the Great Mother Goddess became linked to the Moon. Porphory wrote that Hekate was Artemis on the earth and Hesiod tells us in the *Theogony* that Hekate rules over the three great mysteries: Birth, Life, and Death. There were, of course, other reasons for this association of the Mother with the Moon as we shall see in the following section.

THE MOON GODDESS

The Great Goddess came to be associated with the moon for a variety of reasons. The most obvious relationship is found in the swelling of the moon and its subsequent decline, reflecting the changes in a woman's body due to pregnancy. On a deeper level the

Goddess governs growth and therefore time itself. The earliest cal-
endars measured time by the moon and not by the sun. The
ancients believed that the moon influenced a woman's menstrual
cycle, thus linking the moon to fertility. It was from this belief in
Her power over time and fertility that the Great Goddess was also
associated with Fate. This aspect will be explored in the section
following this one.

As we noted earlier, in the Mystery Tradition the Moon Goddess is known by traits linked to the four phases of the moon: new,
waxing, full, and waning. In the public tradition of ancient times,
the Moon Goddess possessed three aspects: Maiden, Mother, and
Crone. In the Initiate level her fourth aspect was revealed as the
Enchantress. Thus each phase of the moon is identified with an
aspect of the goddess:

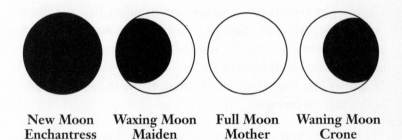

New Moon   **Waxing Moon**   **Full Moon**   **Waning Moon**
Enchantress   **Maiden**   **Mother**   **Crone**

The new moon (when the moon is unseen for three nights) is
the time of the Enchantress. Actually, whenever the moon cannot be
seen or is obscured by clouds is also her time of power. The waning
moon is the time of the Maiden. The full moon is the time of the
Mother, and the waning moon is the time of the Crone. The
Enchantress does not follow an order of appearance as does the
Maiden, Mother, and Crone. Her nature can appear in any of the
other three aspects of the Goddess, and can also be reflected in the
human counterparts. She weaves her way in and out of the other
three natures as she pleases, just as one would expect of a goddess so
named. The Lunar Mysteries were not of a linear orientation, like
the Solar Mysteries, and so the progression of the personified phases did not necessarily follow a set pattern. The need to establish a

chronological order is something we as modern people have inherited from our patriarchal ancestors.

The nature of the Enchantress can appear within women in any of the phases of Maiden, Mother, and Crone, for the Maiden can be alluring and enchanting/tempting just as the Mother can; the natures are different aspects of sexuality. The crone can be enchanting/tempting as well, attracting through her grace, knowledge, and experience. This is why the Enchantress was also known as the Temptress. Temptation, to a Pagan mind, does not carry a negative connotation and simply means being drawn away from one's originally intended course. A woman (or a goddess) as a temptress figure need not be associated with sexuality or negativity.

The Great Moon Goddess is known by three mystical natures within the Mystery Tradition. She is connected to *virgin births*, associated with *life and death*, and is the *giver of visions or lunacy*. Virginity, in ancient times, simply meant unmarried and did not carry the meaning we think of today. To refer to a virgin giving birth merely meant that the woman was unmarried, not that she had never had sexual intercourse. In the book *Women's Mysteries*, by M. Esther Harding (Harper Colophon, 1976), the author addresses this ancient concept:

> *The term virgin, then, when used of the ancient goddesses, clearly has a meaning not of today. It may be used of a woman who has had much sexual experience; it may be even applied to a prostitute. Its real significance is to be found in its use as contrasted with "married."*

The ancient Moon Goddess was a goddess of sexual love not associated with marriage. This is the true chaste nature of the goddess Diana or Artemis. No male can influence the conduct of a virgin moon goddess; she rules over her own nature and does not compromise as one would in a love relationship such as marriage. In mythology, the Moon Goddess typically controls a son who grows up to be her lover. He then dies only to be reborn once again as her son. This reflects the Lunar Mysteries in which chronological events are meaningless, for the Moon Goddess controls time itself. Thus She can be impregnated by her son, who is her lover (and sometimes her brother) before he is her child. Her power over time is why the Moon Goddess is also the Queen of the Fairies, for mortal time and fairy time are not the same thing in European folklore (see chapter eleven for further information).

The Moon Goddess is also known as the bringer of life and death. She sends rains, storms, floods, and moves the tides of the ocean. The water she provides in order for life to exist (water) is also the water (storms) with which she removes life. This is also reflected in the menstrual period of women—the providing for life and then its abrupt denial. Thus the Moon Goddess is strongly linked to fluids of all kinds. In ancient times she was also known as The Dewy One, for in the dry, warm climates of southern Europe the dew was essential for plant life. The life-giving and fertile quality of liquids under the power of the Goddess is apparent in an ancient fertility rite from southern Europe. A woman who wished to become pregnant would lie nude upon her back beneath the full moon until sunrise. Thus she was covered with a bath of dew, considered to be a powerful potion for fertility. Plutarch, in his work *Isis and Osiris*, writes:

> *The moon, having the light which makes moist and pregnant, is promotive of the generating of living beings and of the fructification of plants.*

Just as the moon was viewed as having power over the forces of the outside world, it was also believed to have power over the forces of the inner world of Humankind, the mind and the spirit. Therefore the Moon Goddess could bestow psychic visions to an individual or insanity, as she pleased. This is reflective of her dual nature of Light and Dark, Waxing and Waning. In the Mystery Teachings, darkness is the Mother of the Moon. It is the first power and therefore it was approached with both fear and reverence under the title of Anthea, the Underworld Queen. Her name meant "The Sender of Nocturnal Visions." Later she was known as Hecate Triformis, a Greek moon goddess associated with the powers of darkness and the moon.

In ancient times, the light of the moon itself was the power of the moon. There was nothing symbolic about it—it was the actual substance of magick. This is why, in iconography, we find torches in the hands of Hecate and Diana Lucifera; they are displaying the power they wield in their hands. From this concept arose the ritual practice of employing candles, torches, and bonfires in lunar ceremonies. This was designed to encourage the light of the moon, as seen in the ancient rite of carrying torches around a newly planted field at night.

In ancient Greece, the torches of Hecate were placed in a circle around freshly sown fields to aid in the germination of the grain. Italian witches employ an invocation during the time of the full moon, requesting that the light of the moon impart occult knowledge to them in their dreams. In ancient Italy, on the festival day of Diana (August 13), a multitude of torches were lighted to honor the moon goddess, and to secure her favor not to send storms that might harm the coming harvest. The practice of employing candles in moon worship is also the basis for the Wiccan Sabbat known in some traditions as Candlemas, celebrated on February 2. In ancient Celtic times, torches were lighted for the moon goddess Bridget or Brigentis just as they had been earlier in Greece.

THE TRIPLE GODDESS OF FATE

In ancient times the power of the Great Goddess over time itself evolved into the concept of Her as a goddess of Fate. The most ancient Western Civilization personifying this concept was Greece, and we find later in history an almost identical mythos among the ancient Germanic tribes. To the Greeks, fate was administered by three sisters known as the Moerae (the Fates). Among the Germanic people there were also three sisters dispensing fate; they were known as the Norns (the Wyrrd Sisters). These basic myths are too close to be coincidence, as we shall see, and only their names constitute any real differences. The Greeks called them Klotho, Lachesis, and Atropos. The Germanics gave them the names Urd, Verdandi, and Skuld (also known as Wyrd, Werthende, and Skould).

The Moerae were associated with streams and fountains. The Norns came from the fountain of Urd, the source of life from which the great ash-tree Yggdrasill drew its strength. In both cultures the three sisters spun the thread of life and then cut it, bringing a person's time upon the earth to an end. In Greek mythology, Klotho (the youngest) put the wool around the spindle, Lachesis (the middle sister) spun it, and Atropos (the Eldest) cut if off. In Germanic lore it was Skuld (the youngest) who cut the thread, while Urd (the Eldest) wrapped the wool and Verdandi (the middle sister) spun it. In the Mystery Tradition activities such as weaving, plaiting, and knotting are governed by women under the auspices of the Fates. The Moerae govern the Triple Mysteries: *birth, life, and death, past, present, and future, beginning, middle, and end.* The sisters are also aspects of the Lunar Mysteries and reflect the phase of the moon: *waxing, full, and waning.*

In the Mystery Teachings the Great Goddess bears the title of the *Triple Goddess of Fate.* Marija Gimbutas (*The Language of the Goddess*) notes that She is the Fate or three Fates: the Greek *Morae,* Roman *Fata* or *Parcae,* Germanic *Norns,* Baltic *Laima* and the Celtic triadic *Brighid.* In ancient times the Triple Goddess of Fate held power, over even the highest gods. Gimbutas also notes that the image of a triple goddess is well evidenced in the sculptures and frescoes of ancient Greece (and Rome) from as early as the seventh century B.C. Since we know that the Celts first emerge as an identifiable people around 700 B.C., it appears that the triformis aspect of the Goddess was also not of Celtic origin, but has its origins in the earlier religion of Old Europe.

This is evident as we research certain goddesses back to their Neolithic origins as Mediterranean bird deities; the bird goddess symbol was always accompanied by triple lines above or below. The most graphic visual example of this is found in the ancient deity forms of the Egyptians, where gods and goddesses have various animal and bird heads. The vulture is a common bird goddess associated with certain Egyptian deities and with the Greek goddess Athena (who could also transform herself into a dove). One of the common names of the Celtic Triple Goddess in Ireland is *Badh*, which means "crow." Throughout Europe the ancient gods and goddesses either bear names derived from certain animals, or are in the company of animals symbolic of their more ancient natures.

The Sirens and Harpies of Greek mythology are birds of prey in female form. They have a human head, the feet of a vulture, and appear in groups of three. A Siren possesses the power to lure a person through her song, the end of which brings death. They are called the Keres (Fates) of Death, and Gimbutas states that they must have descended from the Old European Vulture Goddess or Bird of Prey Goddess (*Goddesses and Gods*). In the Mystery Tradition it is taught that the animals associated with a god or goddess are actually their ancient totem forms. Neolithic goddesses often appear now in European folktales as birds. Gimbutas says of this:

> *The Bird Goddess and anthropomorphic Life-giving Goddess continue as a Fate or Fairy and also as a luck-and-wealth-bringing duck, swan, and ram. As a prophesier she is a cuckoo. As a Primeval Mother she is known as a supernatural deer or bear.*

The ancient tales of Homer relate that the gods were able to shapeshift at will. Zeus is probably the most common example of this, changing into various animals whereby he seduces goddesses and mortal women. Hera was known to take on the shape of a dove, and the Baltic goddess of Fate (Laima) assumed the form of a cuckoo or a dove. The migration of birds and their joyful return in the spring linked them with the Goddess who oversaw the cycles of time, of life and death, and the seasons of Nature. It was due to their association with the mystical powers of fate that the appearance of certain birds later became omens and signs.

CHAPTER
FIVE

THE WATCHERS

"...Then Diana went to the fathers of the Beginning, to the mothers, the spirits who were before
the first spirit..."

—Charles Leland,
Aradia—Gospel of the Witches

This chapter is an enhanced and expanded version of one from my earlier book *Ways of the Strega* (relating the Witchcraft Tradition of Old Europe in Italy). In this book I have focussed on the views of Wicca concerning those beings known as the Watchers. Aspects of Wiccan belief not shared by the Strega (Italian witches) are included here, along with certain tenets not covered in *Ways of the Strega*. The key fact is that the Watchers, by whatever cultural name employed, were known in ancient Mesopotamia long before the Italians or Celts came to learn of their existence.

The Watchers is a concept common to most Wiccan Traditions, although they are viewed differently by the various systems within Wicca. In this chapter we will look at the oldest form of the Watchers, dating back to the early Stellar Cults, as well as the modern concept of Watchers as Elemental Rulers, as employed in many Wiccan Systems today. Among the Witches of southern Europe, the Watchers are called the *Grigori*, particularly by the Tanarric witches of Italy who are known as the *Star Witches*. The Tanarra have preserved the ancient Stellar Mysteries and it is through their teachings that we can understand who the Watchers really are in a higher sense. The fact that ancient stellar secrets were preserved in Italy is apparent in the writings of Amerigo Vespucci. He accurately described the constellation of the Southern Cross and mentioned that it was visible from ancient Mesopotamia. His description was written long before any Western navigator had sailed far enough south to see this constellation as a whole. It was also written before any Westerner would have known that the constellation was entirely visible from Mesopotamia in ancient times.

In the witchlore of Italy the Watchers are referred to in an old Strega myth (recounted in Leland's *Aradia—Gospel of the Witches*, published in 1890). In this tale we find the words: "Then Diana went to the fathers of the Beginning, to the mothers, the spirits who were before the first spirit...." These spirits are the Grigori, also known in some traditions as *The Old Ones*. The Watchers are an ancient race who have evolved beyond the need for physical form. In the Mystery Teachings they once lived on the earth and may well be the origin of the legend of ancient Atlantis or Lemuria. In some legends the Watchers were said to have originally come from the stars. It may even be possible that the Watchers have a connection with ancient Egypt. In the Mystery Teachings of Egypt, one of the password phrases to gain access to the temple was: "Though I am a child of the earth, my Race is of the stars."

In the early Stellar Cults of Mesopotamia there were four "royal" Stars (known as Lords) which were called the Watchers. Each one of these Stars "ruled" over one of the four cardinal points common to astrology. This particular system would date from approximately 3000 B.C. The Star Aldebaran, when it marked the Vernal Equinox, held the position of Watcher of the East. Regulus, marking the Summer Solstice, was Watcher of the South. Antares, marking the Autumn Equinox, was Watcher of the West. Fomalhaut, marking the Winter Solstice, was Watcher of the North.

Towers as a form of worship were constructed bearing the symbols of the Watchers, and their symbols were set upon the towers for the purpose of evocation. These towers were called Ziggurats (cosmic mountains) and were said to have been 270 feet high. In part they served as primitive astronomical observatories, and were built with seven terraces representing the seven known planets of their era. During the "Rites of Calling" the Watchers' symbols were traced in the air using torches or ritual wands, and the secret names of the Watchers were called out.

In the Stellar Mythos the Watchers themselves were gods who guarded the Heavens and the Earth. Their nature, as well as their "rank," were altered by the successive Lunar and Solar Cults which replaced the Stellar Cults. Eventually the Greeks reduced them to the Gods of the four winds, and the Christians to principalities of the air. Their connection with the Stars is vaguely recalled in the Christian concept of heavenly angels.

Cabalists organized them into Archangels, which I assume they derived from the early Hebrew concept of an order of Angels known as the Watchers. According to this belief the Watchers were ruled over by four great Watchers known as Michael, Gabriel, Raphael, and Auriel. The Hebrews no doubt borrowed this whole concept from surrounding cultures which were Stellar and lunar in nature. The Hebrew religion was highly eclectic in ancient times.

In many traditions of Wicca these Ancient Beings are the Guardians of the Dimensional Planes, protectors of the ritual circle, and witnesses to the rites which have been kept down through the ages. Each of the ruling Watchers oversees a "Watchtower," which is now a portal marking one of the four quarters of the ritual circle. In ancient times a "Tower" was a military fighting unit, and a "Watchtower" was a defending home unit, similar to a National Guard.

Originally the Watchers were "lesser gods" who watched over the earth and the heavens. Among Italian Witches the Watchers were the Guardians of the four entrances to the Realm of Asteris, which is the home of the gods in Strega mythology. In modern Wicca they are often conceived of as rulers of the Elemental Kingdoms, known as the Lords of the Watchtowers. The Elder traditions of Wicca believed them to be ancient gods known as the Old Ones who guarded the portals to the Other World.

Outside of the Wiccan structure, the Watchers are most easily linked to the Judaic/Christian concept of "guardian angels." In the Old Testament (Daniel 4:13–17) reference is made to the *Irin*, or Watchers, who appear to be an order of angels (in early Hebrew lore the Irin were a high order of angels who sat on the supreme Judgment Council of the Heavenly Court). In the *Apocryphal Books of Enoch and Jubilees*, the Watchers are mentioned as Fallen Angels who originally were sent to Earth to teach men law and justice. In the *Secret Book of Enoch*, the Watchers (called therein Watchers) are listed as rebellious angels who followed Sataniel in a heavenly war.

Gustav Davidson, in his *Dictionary of Angels*, portrays the Watchers as a high order of angels known also as the Watchers. In Rabbinic and Cabalistic lore, the "good" Watchers dwell in the Fifth Heaven, and "evil" Watchers dwell in the Third Heaven. The Watchers of the Fifth Heaven are ruled over by the archangels Uriel, Raphael, Michael, and Gabriel. In the *Apocryphon of Genesis*, it is said that Noah is the offspring of a Watcher who slept with Bat-Enosh, his Mother.

In the *Dictionary of Angels*, the Watchers are listed as the Fallen Angels who instructed humankind in the ancient arts. The most common associations found in various texts on Medieval magick regarding the Watchers are as follows:

Araqiel: taught the signs of the earth.

Armaros: taught the resolving of enchantments.

Azazel: taught the art of cosmetics.

Barqel: taught astrology.

Ezequeel: taught the knowledge of the clouds.

Gadreel: taught the making of weapons of war.

Kokabeel: taught the mystery of the Stars.

Penemue: taught writing.

Sariel: taught the knowledge of the Moon.

Semjaza: taught Herbal enchantments.

Shamshiel: taught the signs of the Sun.

It is these same Angels who are referred to as the Sons of God in the *Book of Genesis*. According to Christian mythology their "sins" filled the Earth with violence and the world was destroyed as a result of their intervention. This, of course, is the Biblical account and has little to do with Wiccan beliefs. Richard Cavendish, in his book *The Powers of Evil*, makes references to the possibilities of the giants mentioned in Genesis 6:4, being the

Giants or Titans of Greek Mythology. He also lists the Watchers as the Fallen Angels that magicians call forth in ceremonial magick. Read *Genesis* 6:1–7 for the background in Biblical reference. Despite the debatable accuracy of information in most books by Cavendish, he does draw some interesting parallels and even mentions that the Watchers were so named because they were stars, the "eyes of night."

St. Paul, in the *New Testament*, calls the Fallen Angels "principalities": "For we are not contending against flesh and blood, but against the principalities, against the powers...against the spiritual hosts of wickedness in High Places." It was also St. Paul who called Satan "The prince of power of the air," and thus made the connection of Satan (himself connected to "a star," *Isiah* 14:12–14) and etheric Beings, for they were later known as Demons and as principalities of the Air.

This theme was later developed by a French theologian of the sixteenth century named Sinistrari, who spoke of Beings existing between humans and angels. He called them Demons, and associated them with the Elemental natures of Earth, Air, Fire, and Water. This, however, was not a new concept but was taught by certain Gnostic sects in the early days of Christianity. Clement of Alexandria, influenced by Hellenistic cosmology, attributed the movement of the Stars and the control of the four Elements to Angelic Beings. Sinistrari attributed bodies of fire, air, earth, and water to these Beings, and concluded that the Watchers were made of fire and air. Cardinal Newman, writing in the mid-1800s, proposed that certain angels existed who were neither totally good nor evil, and had only "partially fallen" from the Heavens. This would seem to support Davidson's text which places the Watchers in two different "Heavens."

Many modern Wiccan Traditions view the Watchers as Elemental Rulers, "Lords" of the four Elements of Creation: Earth, Air, Fire, and Water. These Elements are believed to be empowered by spiritual creatures known as *Elementals*. Within the Element of Earth dwell the *Gnomes*, within Air the *Sylphs*, within Fire the *Salamanders*, and within Water the *Undines*. These Elemental Races each have their own Ruler. For Earth the ruler is *Gob*, for Air

Paralda, for Fire *Djin* and for Water *Necksa*. In some Wiccan Traditions, such as the Alexandrian, old Roman deity names for the gods of the four winds are used instead: Boreas, Eurus, Notus, and Zephyrus.

In part, the modern use of elementals associated with the Watchtowers originates from the works of Dr. John Dee and his research into Enochian Magick. In Enochian Magick there is a great emphasis on the Elemental Quarters and the Watchtowers. Some people feel that Gerald Gardner incorporated these things into Wicca through his contact with Aleister Crowley. Crowley was very much involved in Systems of Ritual and Magick that incorporated Enochian and Egyptian Teachings. However, the presence of these aspects in The Old Religion actually stems from a much older magickal theology.

In the Mystery Teachings of Wicca there appear two sets of portals within a ritual circle: the Elemental Portals and the Watcher Portals. In the diagram pictured here you will note a circle within a circle (see illustration). The corridor section that lies between the circles is called *The World between the Worlds*. From a metaphysical perspective this dimension must exist in order for magickal/ritual energies to flow between the Worlds. It is here that the Elemental Portals come into use, as they represent the access points to the Plane of Forces (Elemental Plane), which exists between the Physical and Non-Physical (Astral) Dimensions. See chapter seven for a much more detailed examination of the interplay of the dimensions.

Just beyond the Elemental Portals, lying directly on the *other side* of the corridor, are the Watcher Portals. While the Elemental Rulers *guard* the immediate portals between this World and the Plane of Forces, the Watchers *guard* the direct access points to the Astral Plane. This is where the aspects of Low Magick (Elemental) and High Magick (Astral) come into play. Low magick is more simplistic and High Magick is more ritualized. Essentially it is the difference between Shamanism and Ceremonial Magick.

My purpose in presenting these associations is to show some examples of how a central theme can be divided and transformed. Today, even among Craft Traditions, there exists a great deal of

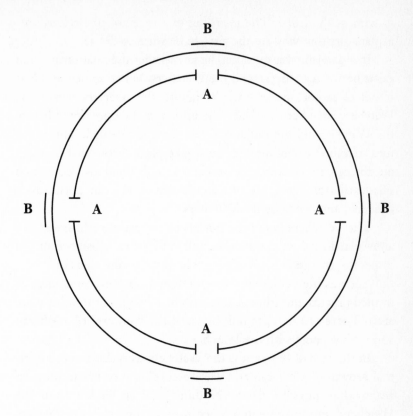

Circle Portals

Elemental doorways (A) open into the magickal corridor between the worlds. Astral portals (B) border on other side of corridor (the Watch-towers).

confusion concerning the Watchers. Some systems view them as Elemental Rulers, Demi-Gods, Guardians, Spiritual Teachers, or Planetary Intelligences. All of these concepts are indeed aspects of the Watchers. The Watchers also are associated with the Judaic/Christian angels, but those associations are so distorted and biased that they serve only to cloud the issue.

To really understand the Watchers we need only look to their role in Wicca as a religion. Our first encounter with these entities usually occurs when casting a ritual circle in which to practice the rites. The Watchers are called, or evoked, to guard the circle and to witness the ritual. The guarding of a ceremonial circle is self-explanatory, but why are the rites to be witnessed?

In answering this question, let us consider the relationship that exists between a Wiccan and the Watchers. When someone is first initiated, he or she is brought before the quarters where the Watchers have been evoked. The initiate is then presented before the Watcher and the initiate's Craft name is revealed. This is the first step in the bonding that must take place. From that moment on, the initiate is "watched" and aided. This bond also serves as a safeguard, for every act of magick that a Wiccan performs is observed and noted by the Watchers.

The Watchers guard the portals to the astral realms, and can allow a magickal act to establish itself in the astral substance, or can dispel the charge. This is why certain gestures and signs of evocation such as the pentagram were designed, so as to "announce" a trained practitioner (that is, one who had sworn not to misuse the arts). There is a definite link between the "powers" of a Wiccan and their rapport with the Watchers.

In the lore of Wicca it is the Watchers who assist in the spiritual growth of a Wiccan and who "escort" him or her to the next realm after physical death. Nothing is ever hidden from the Watchers, and in the end a Wiccan may come to know them as either the "Dread Lords of the outer spaces," or as the "Mighty Ones, the Guardians." This is not to be viewed as a situation in which these entities will "get you" if you're not "good," but rather as an assurance that Karma will be delivered promptly.

Among many Neo-Wiccans there is a tendency to dismiss the concepts of *good* and *evil*, and to view things as simply *cause and effect*. This new philosophy grew from a rejection of the Judaic-Christian teachings concerning Satan and Hell. However, the vast majority of ancient religions typically personified evil in their myths; it really is an ancient concept pre-dating Christianity. Many Neo-Wiccans view Karma as simply an energy of action and reaction, and have dismissed the ancient concept of Divine Intervention, as well as the role of the Watchers as "Lords of Karma."

Stewart and Janet Farrar, in their book *The Witches' Way*, perhaps best relate the role of the Watchers in their discussion concerning the Lords of Karma:

We have spoken of Karma as an almost impersonal process, set in train by the inexorable laws of cause and effect. And it is its basic principle of action. But that does not mean there is no intervention or that what are sometimes called 'the Lords of Karma' are mere observers. Higher entities of many kinds do exist and function on the non-material planes, intermediate between humankind and the ultimate creative force, as every religion has recognized.

—Janet and Stewart Farrar, *The Witches' Way*

As we saw in the first part of this chapter, the Watchers were linked to certain stars that marked the Solstices and Equinoxes, being the cornerstones of the year if you will. On a greater scale the Watchers oversaw the "seasons" of the Heavens as well. It is important to remember that the Watchers are Stellar Beings, not lunar. Their association with a Lunar Cult, rather than a Solar, is obvious on a mundane scale. Stars are associated with the night (as is the moon) for they share the heavens together. The sun is seemingly alone in the sky (at least most of the time). The Stellar and Lunar Cults are older than the Solar Cults, which later adopted (and adapted) the Inner Teachings of the previous ones.

Ancient lore reveals that the Watchers once had bodies of physical matter, but they evolved beyond the need for physical expression long before the rise of humankind. They became Beings of Light, and this was most likely one of the first parallels between Watchers and Angels. Yet, these Beings of Light were linked to the stars even before their evolution, for the old legends say that the Watchers came from the stars. In the early Stellar Cults this association was so strong that the Watchers were considered to be stars who had descended to earth.

From their original worship as demi-gods, the Watchers have come to be honored as a spiritual race that oversees the worlds. In

between we have seen what became of them. Today we acknowledge them as guardians of the entrances and exits to and from the
worlds that connect to the physical plane. We also know them as
the Keepers of the Ancient Wisdom and Guardians of the Art.

————————————

CHAPTER
SIX

THE CYCLE OF
REBIRTH

All things are changing, nothing dies. The spir-
it wanders, comes now here, now there, and occu-
pies whatever frame it pleases. From beasts it
passes into human bodies, and from our bodies
into beasts, but never perishes.
— Pythagoras, *Metamorphoses XV*

One of the basic tenets of Wiccan belief is that the soul passes through many lives before it achieves release from the wheel of rebirth and can remain in a spiritual dimension. In the theology of Wicca there exists a realm known as the Summerland in which souls rest and are renewed for their next experience. Reincarnation (sometimes called *transmigration of the soul*) was one of the Mystery Teachings in ancient Greece (the Orphic Mystery), and was a tenet of Roman Mystery Cults as well. In Rome it was not accepted as a public viewpoint, but in Greece it was openly debated by the great philosophers.

In ancient Greece, reincarnation was known as *Palingenesis,* which means "to have origin again." The Orphic teachings maintained that the soul was pre-existent and survived the physical death of the body it inhabited. It would return again in the body of a human or other mammal, eventually finding release whereby it could return to its former pure state. The Greek Philosophers Pythagoras (sixth century B.C.) and Plato (fifth century B.C.) believed in an immortal soul that passed through many incarnations. Such beliefs were well known in Greece generations before the arrival of the Celts.

The Druids also apparently believed in reincarnation, observed by Julius Caesar during his campaign against the Gauls and the invasion of ancient Briton. In Caesar's *Sixth Book of the Gallic War* he notes:

They wish to inculcate this as one of their leading tenets, that souls do not become extinct, but pass after death from one body to another, and they think that men by this tenet are in a great degree excited to valor, the fear of death being disregarded.

Pomponius Mela wrote that the Druids taught this doctrine because they believed it would make their warriors more fearless. He personally felt that the Druids themselves did not believe it, but were willing to dupe their warriors in order to produce fearless fighters. It seems clear that neither he nor Caesar believed in reincarnation themselves, although they would have been aware of the earlier Greek belief in this tenet, having been educated men of the Roman Empire (Greek Philosophy was introduced to the Romans in 155 B.C. by a Greek Philosopher named Critolaus). Pythagoras (born circa 580 B.C.) taught the doctrine of rebirth centuries before the Celts entered Greece circa 300 B.C. Some people believe that the Druids taught Pythagoras this doctrine, however the time frame does not support this. The earliest date mentioning the Druids comes from Diogenes Laertius (circa A.D. 200) who wrote that the Druids were known in the time of Aristotle (384–322 B.C.). Again, this is almost two centuries after the death of Pythagoras.

Ancient Greek historians such as Posidonius, Strabo, Diodorus, and Ammianus give us accounts of various Celtic beliefs concerning reincarnation. Diodorus, along with Ammianus and Valerius Maximus, equated the Druidic beliefs with the belief of Pythagoras concerning the survival of the soul and its journey from one body to another. Unlike the Greeks, the Druids taught that souls always returned to human bodies, while Pythagoras taught that they could reside anew in the body of any life-form. The ancient historian Hippolytus of Alexandria tells us that the legendary Thrachian Zalmoxis (said to have been both a slave and a student of Pythagoras) instructed the Druids in the Pythagorean *faith*. In Greek and Roman writings concerning Druidic beliefs in rebirth we are basically seeing an attempt to reconcile them with the Pythagorean and classical beliefs of southern Europe. Clearly the Celts seem to have embraced an earlier Aegean principle and later modified it from the Druidic teachings in accordance with aspects of their own indigenous beliefs. The earliest recorded Greek contact with the British Isles is noted by the Greek sea captain Pytheas of Massilia sometime around 320 B.C.

Reincarnation was also an early Christian teaching which the Church later labeled a heresy. The concept was preserved by the Gnostics after it was removed from traditional Christian theology. The Church, however, was not totally successful in deleting all of the references to reincarnation in the New Testament. We find an interesting passage in the gospel of John 9:1–3:

> *As he went along, he saw a man who had been blind from birth. His disciples asked him, "Rabbi, who sinned, this man or his parents, for him to have been born blind?" "Neither he nor his parents sinned," Jesus answered, "he was born blind so that the works of God might be displayed in him."*

Now if this man *had* been born blind because of his sins, how was he able to sin before his birth? It is interesting to note that Jesus does not denounce the question of this man's existence prior to this birth, but explains that it had nothing to do with his sins prior to his present life.

In the Old Testament it was prophesied that Elijah would appear again at the time of the Messiah. In the Gospel of Matthew 17:10–13, we read:

> *And the disciples put this question to him, "Why do the scribes say then that Elijah has to come first?" "True" he replied "Elijah is to come to see that everything is once more as it should be, however, I tell you that Elijah has come already and they did not recognize him but treated him as they pleased; and the Son of Man will suffer similarly at their hands." The disciples understood then that he had been speaking of John the Baptist.*

Here we see that the disciples understood Jesus to be saying that John the Baptist was Elijah from the Old Testament. Again we find no questioning in this passage of the New Testament concerning this former life concept.

Finally, there is one more such reference to John the Baptist as the reincarnation of Elijah. It is found in the Gospel of Matthew 11:14–15:

Because it was toward John that all the prophesies of the prophets and of the Law were leading, and he, if you will believe me, is Elijah who was to return. If anyone has ears to hear, let him listen.

In this passage Jesus makes it quite clear that he is saying that John the Baptist is indeed the Old Testament prophet Elijah. Therefore it seems clear that even the New Testament teachings do support the concept of reincarnation.

In Wiccan beliefs, it is taught on Initiate levels that the soul can find fulfillment in the rebirth process. In the Wiccan *Legend of the Descent of the Goddess* we find a passage that addresses the issue of rebirth:

...you must return again at the same time and at the same place as the loved ones; and you must meet, and know, and remember, and love them again. But to be reborn, you must die, and be made ready for a new body. And to die, you must be born; and without love, you may not be born.

This concept is similar to the Buddhist belief in the *Group Soul* and *Collective Karma*. It is also a teaching found among Hereditary Witches who take their bloodlines very seriously, due in part to this metaphysical principle concerning the soul's evolutionary process.

Another Wiccan text that contains the teaching of reincarnation is *The Charge*. This passage also contains the concept of rejoining with those who have passed from one existence to the next. Here we find mention of the Cauldron of Cerridwen, which is the Holy Grail of Immortality. In this text we read:

I am the Gracious Goddess who gives the gift of joy unto the heart of man. Upon earth, I give the knowledge of the spirit eternal; and beyond death I give peace, and freedom, and reunion with those who have gone before.

The concept of rejoining those known in past lives is a common theme in the Wiccan Mysteries. One of the teachings is concerned with what may be called the *Star Gates*, or the *Four Gates of Atavaric Descent*. These gates are associated with the four cardinal signs of the Zodiac. Their symbolic images are Man (Aquarius), Bull (Taurus), Lion (Leo), and Eagle (Scorpio). Through these Star Gates pass great energies that can be employed as paths of descent into the material plane by Spiritual Forces and Beings. The Avatar descends through one of these gates at the time of conception and is born after the term of pregnancy.

Aradia, an avatar to Italian witches, was born in August and so we assign her the portal of Scorpio which would have been her pathway at the time of conception. Generally speaking, Aquarius leads to a birth in November, Leo to April, and Taurus to a birth in February. Obviously there are many variables that would alter this occult assignment, and certainly not everyone conceived at the time of a Star Gate is going to be a highly evolved spiritual being.

According to the Mystery Teachings, when a couple is united in sexual union a composite energy field is formed. This field is a harmonic energy sphere resonating as a blend of the individual's own auras. As the sexual energy stimulates the nervous system and endocrine secretions, chemical changes take place in the body, heart rate and breathing increase and so forth. This creates a metaphysical response and a vortex of energy begins to swirl above the individuals. In some respects this is not unlike the cone of power raised in a magickal ritual setting. The vortex creates an opening in the etheric matter separating the physical world from the spiritual world. Souls awaiting rebirth, whose own vibrations are harmonious to the energy of vortex, are drawn into its current and thus into the auras of the sexual participants. This occult principle is reflected on a mundane scale in conception by the sperm which are drawn to the egg (as above, so below).

Different types of sexual union draw on different levels of the spiritual dimensions. Impregnation from sexual acts such as rape, prostitution, and molestation by a family member generally (but not always) draw earth-bound souls back into rebirth. Consensual sexual acts where mutual love is present typically draw upon the spiritual dimension just above the physical plane (where souls await rebirth). Magickal or ritual sex is often designed to draw upon the higher planes where souls dwell who have no need to return to the physical dimension. This type of sexual union (depending on the nature of the participants) can draw prophets and avatars back into rebirth. In the case of an avatar's birth however, the spiritual entity can cross through the planes in any vortex of its choosing. Ritual or magickal rites serve mainly as a beacon for the advanced soul.

In any event, if conception takes place, then the womb energy binds the soul to the physical plane and it is drawn into the physical substance of the egg, eventually dwelling within a fetus. In the case of twins and other multiple births, there is usually a very strong karmic link between the souls, drawing them into the same space and time. In Eastern philosophy it is usually believed that the soul dwells in the aura of the mother and is not drawn into the infant's body until the first breath is drawn. This image has no parallel in Nature and is therefore not a principle of the European mysteries (however, many Neo-Wiccans and New Age followers do embrace this foreign concept).

Once the infant is born, there begins a seven-day period during which the soul deeply merges with the physical life form (while in the womb the soul was not fully integrated into the physical dimensions). Day by day the new body draws the soul into itself, binding one physical function after another to the soul's consciousness. There is typically a great deal of discomfort associated with the process of a soul taking on physical form, and the infant often cries and shows other signs of distress. Generally this will pass within a week; any discomfort experienced by the infant from this point on will be due solely to mundane sensory responses.

Rebirth is for many reasons a fundamental aspect of the Mystery Teachings. The most important reason lies in the belief of what modern Wiccans call genetic memory. Primarily this is the belief that each of us carries the *essential distillation* of the memories of all of our ancestors within our DNA. In a physical sense this provides us with the survival skills that ensured the lineage to us in the first place. In a metaphysical sense this provides us with a channel to the past through which we can awaken the memories of past Pagan practices.

The Wiccan rites originating from the time of the persecution of witches contain references to being reborn among one's own people. This rejoining ensured that the ancient mysteries would not become lost and that powerful covens would always exist. This is the legacy of hereditary witches and is why so many still guard their secrets in an attempt to maintain a pure bloodline connected to the Old Ways.

The renowned author Manly Hall once likened the cycle of life, death, and rebirth to the work of a deep-sea diver (*Death to Rebirth*, Philosophical Research, 1979). He described the diver putting on the heavy rubber suit and diving helmet which allowed the diver to operate under water. This, he said, was like the soul putting on the mantle of flesh in order to operate in the physical dimension. The diver's work was to explore the ocean waters in search of discovery or reclamation, which Hall likened to the work of the soul in the physical world. Once the work of the diver is completed he or she returns to the world of earth and air. So, too, it is with the soul which returns to its natural environment once the physical body can no longer house it. The diver returns many times into the depths of the water in an attempt to complete the desired goal. The soul also returns many times into the realm of matter to complete its work.

In the Mystery Teachings it is propounded that the body is nothing more than a vehicle through which the spirit can operate in the physical world. The body and soul are linked together in a symbiotic relationship, each supplying the other with what is necessary for itself to function. As Hall pointed out, the vitality of the body was diffused throughout but did not originate from bodily functions. It was the soul that gave life to the flesh; the body simply maintained it. Feelings were transmitted by the nervous system but did not originate there. Thoughts were formed by the brain but did not originate as a biological reaction. It was the mind that employed the brain as a vehicle to manifest thought. Therefore, the body needs the soul in order to continue living, but the soul exists even without the physical body.

Religions differ in their teachings on what the soul experiences once it has passed out of the physical world. Some believe that the soul meets with corrective actions or rewards for the physical life it has lived. Others believe that the soul exists in a spiritual dimension where it continues to evolve with the experiences it gains there. The Wiccan Mysteries teach that the soul resides within the astral realm (whether called the Summerland, Tir nan og, or Luna) where it integrates the life experience from which it just passed. Then the soul is prepared to either be reborn into the world of matter for further learning experiences, or into a higher spiritual dimension as it moves ever closer to the Source from which it came.

In the book *The Fairy Faith in Celtic Countries*, by W. Y. Evans-Wentz (Citadel Press, 1990), the author tells us the Celts believed that the dead go to live beyond the ocean in the southwest, where the sun sets during the greater part of the year. Following the Winter Solstice the sun appears to be reborn in the southeast. In the book *Les Contes Populaires de l'Egypte* author M. Maspero tells us that the ancient Egyptians also held this belief. Evans-Wentz writes:

> *In this last Celtic-Egyptian belief, we maintain, may be found the reason why the chief megalithic monuments (dolmens, tumuli, and alignments), in Celtic countries and elsewhere, have their directions east and west, and why those like New Grange and Gravrinis open to the Sunrise.*
> —W. Y. Evans-Wentz, *The Fairy Faith in Celtic Countries*

The connection between fairies, souls of the dead, and entrances to the *Other World* all relate back to ancient concepts inherent in the Mediterranean Cult of the Dead (chapter twelve).

In this ancient cult we find the origins for beliefs concerning fairy mounds, secret entrances, and the distortion of time as experienced by mortals. For further information please refer to the Goddess section in chapter four and the Blood Mysteries section in chapter thirteen.

CHAPTER
SEVEN

THE PLANES OF
EXISTENCE

*First of all Chaos came into being, and then
Gaea, the broad Earth, the ever certain support
of all the deathless gods who dwell on the summit
of snowy Olympus, and also dark Tartarus in the
innermost part of the broad-pathed earth, and
also Eros...*

—Hesiod, *Theogony*

The existence of other worlds or dimensions is a part of most Mystery Traditions. Wicca has been influenced a great deal by Eastern philosophies in this regard, but has also retained the pre-Christian European concepts of the Old Religion. The Three Worlds from which all things issued forth, seen in such ancient Greek texts as the *Theogony* (700 B.C.) and later in Celtic lore, are still a part of many Wiccan traditions. Other Wiccan groups have fully embraced the Seven Planes of Existence common to Eastern concepts and do not operate within the Three World principle. There are also groups that have incorporated Western Occultism into Wicca. Since I have addressed the Greek and Celtic concepts in chapter eleven, this current chapter will mainly examine the modern Wiccan concepts of the Planes.

THE ASTRAL PLANE

An integral aspect of the Wiccan Mysteries is that of the Astral Plane. This is a dimension that is not so easily defined because it is actually comprised of several realities and relationships. The astral plane may be thought of as a parallel Space/Time continuum. It is also a state of consciousness, in some respects related to imagination but more in the realm of controlled mental imagery rather than the fragile fiber of daydreams. Where the physical plane is a plane of form, the astral plane is a plane of force. As J. H. Brennan said in his book *Astral Doorways* (Weiser, 1971): "Thoughts become pictures. Abstractions become symbols. Emotions become the driving forces behind them."

In many ways it is not unlike the dream world to which we journey each night. The main difference is that, in the dream world, when objects and situations change we simply go along with them. For example, when a bus pulls up and the doors open, we get on the bus without wondering where we are going. On the astral plane we react to objects and situations with the same rationale as we do in the physical world. In this make-believe scenario, the bus pulls up and we are aware of the setting and the situation; we can think to ourselves *what is this all about?*

The dream world is actually one of the gates to the astral plane. In the Mystery Tradition initiates are taught how to gain conscious control of their dreams. Once the setting and theme of a dream can be directed, then a portal or doorway can be created through which a person can enter the astral dimension at will. Some initiates prefer to establish a temple setting in the dream world through which they can transfer influences into the Astral material without having to personally enter the dimension itself.

The material of the astral dimension is known as *astral light*. It can be molded and shaped like clay through the energy of our thoughts and feelings. It is in this etheric substance that we create thought-forms that serve as channels for higher forces. This material is not only influenced by emanations from the physical dimension but also by those from the higher planes, including the Divine and spiritual realms. Thus situations and events that are generated from above take shape on the astral plane, eventually manifesting on the physical dimension (unless another energy alters the form in some manner). This is where the art of divination has its basis in metaphysical science. If a person can tap into the images forming on the astral plane then he or she can discern what is about to manifest on the physical plane.

It must be understood, however, that divination is simply the foreseeing of events that are moving toward manifestation. The astral images that are animating these events can be altered by the constant influx of currents passing through the astral dimension.

Therefore what we are really seeing in divination is what will occur if the patterns remain unaltered. In the Mystery Teachings nothing is fixed in time, nothing is absolutely going to happen in our lives despite our best attempts (except, of course, the death of our physical bodies). However, the major events of our lives are part of the pattern with which our spirits are *imprinted* when our souls are born into flesh. This is the metaphysical basis of astrology, the so-called Stellar imprint. Our natal chart can depict the major patterns laid out for us in each physical life, as well as the strengths and weaknesses of our spiritual state. We can work toward them or against them because we possess free will.

THE ELEMENTAL PLANE

The Mystery Teachings include the Elemental Plane, also known as the Plane of Forces. This plane represents the actions of the four creative elements comprising anything that is manifest on the material plane. Overseeing these elements, and the process through which manifestation takes place, is a fifth element known as spirit. This etheric element pervades the four elements. If the four elements are said to mark the quarters of the Cosmic circle, then the fifth element may be said to comprise the substance of the circle itself.

Earth is the element of solidity and reflects the metaphysical principle of Law. Air is the element of intellect and reflects the metaphysical principle of Life. Fire is the element of action and reflects the metaphysical Light. Water is the element of fertility and reflects the metaphysical principle of Love. The various aspects of the elemental plane are interwoven into everything a Wiccan does or experiences. Magickally they are involved in spell casting and the consecration of amulets, tools, and the ritual circle itself. In a metaphysical sense they reflect the psyche and the emotional stability of the Wiccan. The personality of an individual and any emotional disturbances are directly related to a balance (or imbalance) of the elemental natures residing within the person.

The consciousness of these elements can be thought of as mana, numen, or more commonly as *elementals*. To the element of earth we assign the beings known as gnomes. To air we assign beings known as sylphs. To fire belong beings known as salamanders and to water are creatures known as undines. Earth elementals are spirits whose vibrations are so close to those of the physical earth that they influence the mineral structures of the earth, and thus have power over rocks, flora, and fauna. Air elementals are spirits whose vibration is closely related to the energy emanated by the electrical nerve impulses of all living things. Thus they have power over the mind and the nervous system. Salamanders are spirits whose vibratory rate is very much like the emotional energy typically attributed to love, hate, fear, joy, and other powerful emanations. Thus they have influence over emotional states and the general metabolism of the body. Undines are spirits whose vibrations are quite similar to fluids. Thus they have power over moisture and fluid balances within Nature and all living things.

All of *Creation* is influenced and animated by the presence of these elements (or lack thereof). Every object that is subject to manifestation shares a tangible nature and a spiritual nature. The tangible nature gives it form and the spiritual nature gives it vitality. Thus everything physical has its spiritual counterpart or elemental nature. Metaphysical correspondences of the four elements exist within the Zodiac also, and contribute to the natal chart qualities of the individual born on any given day. Empedocles (a student of Pythagoras) was the first person in history to teach the Four Elements as a cohesive doctrine and to introduce the concept of the four elements into astrology. He taught in his native homeland of Sicily around 475 B.C., presenting the four elements as the *fourfold root of all things*. These are the traditional assignments in European Occultism derived from the teachings of Empedocles:

Earth:	Taurus, Virgo, Capricorn	Earth:	cold + dry
Air:	Gemini, Libra, Aquarius	Air:	hot + moist
Fire:	Aries, Leo, Sagittarius	Fire:	hot + dry
Water:	Cancer, Scorpio, Pisces	Water:	cold + moist

THE AKASHIC RECORDS

According to the Mystery Teachings, the Magnetic Sphere of the Earth (also known as bound ether) is an energy field containing the patterns of all deeds, thoughts, and actions from the past. This field is known in occult terminology as the *Odic Mantle* (see chapter nine). The material comprising this etheric material is called *Akasha*, and the patterns contained within it are known as the *Akashic Library*. It is said that this plane can be accessed through psychic abilities, astral travel, or trance states and is the source of what some people call channeled material. Occultists seek to mentally connect with this dimension and obtain the knowledge preserved and contained in the energy patterns.

An old Wiccan belief is that a witch can *understand the voice of the wind*. This tenet first publically appeared in Charles Leland's *Aradia—Gospel of the Witches*. Leland gives a list of the powers ascribed to Italian witches who follow the teachings of Aradia. To understand the *voice of the wind* is to be in harmony with the vibrations of the Akashic currents. Through this attunement one can gain knowledge *carried upon the wind* and remember things that were once lost in the past. Aradia taught that a person must participate in the *wheel of the year*, observing each Treguenda (Sabbat) in order to become one with the ways of Nature.

The Akashic records are best accessed as the sun rises. The Elemental portal of Akasha (see appendix) is often employed as a mental gateway into this dimension. The techniques employed in Western Occultism for accessing the planes were publically introduced by the Golden Dawn. You can use the Elemental Doorway techniques given in the appendix if you wish to experiment. When seeking to channel from the Akashic records, one should use the Akasha doorway and mentally seek out a temple library setting.

THE SUMMERLAND

The *Summerland* is a term generally used in Wicca to refer to the *Other World* into which the souls of the dead cross after physical life has ended. This can be thought of as a type of Pagan paradise not unlike the so-called *Happy Hunting Grounds* of some American Indian traditions. The Summerland of the Wiccans exists on the astral plane and is experienced differently by each individual, according to the spiritual vibration he or she brings to this realm of existence. How long one remains in the Summerland depends on one's ability to release and resolve that which the soul carries from life to life, causing it to be subject to rebirth within the physical dimension.

Existence in the Summerland allows an individual the opportunity to study and understand the lessons of the previous life and how they relate to other lives that the soul has experienced. In Wiccan theology this is called the time of rest and recuperation. Once this time period has passed the *Elemental Plane* begins to draw the individual toward rebirth into whatever dimension is harmonious to their spiritual nature at the time. The reincarnating soul is then subject to the Plane of Forces and can be drawn into the vortex of a sexual union occurring within the physical dimension. In the Mystery Teachings it is said that the soul is drawn to the aspects of the physical life which will best prepare it for the lessons required to ensure its evolution and eventual release from the Cycle of Rebirth.

In the Mystery Teachings a miscarriage or stillborn birth indicates a soul who no longer needed to return to the physical dimension but required a brief emersion in dense matter in order to balance the etheric elemental properties required for its spiritual body. The other reason for such occurrences is that the parents required the lesson of this loss for their own spiritual evolution, in which case this was provided by a soul who no longer required a physical existence. The service of such higher souls is often seen not only in this scenario, but also in the teaching concerning the reincarnation of Avatars such as Buddha or Jesus.

THE OCCULT DIMENSIONS

Occult philosophy maintains there are four realms that comprise Creation: Spiritual, Mental, Astral, and Physical. For the purposes of this chapter we will deal only with the inner dimensions since these function as part of the inner mechanism for the Mysteries. Just as there is a physical dimension, or plane of existence, there are also astral or spiritual dimensions. Each plane is believed to be a reflection of the one above it. An old occult saying, "as above, so below" originates from this concept, as we saw in chapter two. Essentially each descending plane manifests the "formed-thought" of the plane above it. In magick, one establishes his or her desire upon a higher plane so that it will return as the manifestation of that desire. The seven planes are as follows:

1. The Ultimate Plane.
2. The Divine Plane.
3. The Spiritual Plane.
4. The Mental Plane.
5. The Astral Plane.
6. The Elemental Plane (Plane of Forces).
7. The Physical Plane.

Directly above the physical plane is the elemental plane also known as the elemental plane of forces. Everything that occurs on the physical plane is directly linked to this plane. The dimensions react very much like a row of domino pieces; one triggers the other and a chain reaction takes place. This is the law of physics and also metaphysics (as above, so below), and this is how magick spells and religious prayers are transmitted.

This law is the inner mechanism working within the planes, each one vibrating in response to the next. Above the plane of forces is the astral plane, which is an etheric realm containing the formed thoughts of the Collective Consciousness. It is here that all the heavens and hells of religious belief exist, fed by the minds of worshippers on the physical plane. In this plane we can form images of what we desire (as well as what we fear).

Since we all bear the Divine spark of what created us, we also employ the same patterns. Our creative minds operate in the same manner as what gave us creative consciousness—the main difference being that we are limited since we are but the spark and not the Source. The creative process, however, is much the same and we use it to create magick.

For example, if I decided to create a stand that will hold papers during a speech, I would first need to formulate the thought. This would go through several stages represented by the seven planes. The Divine plane would receive the spark from the ultimate plane. The spiritual plane would conceive the plan, the mental plane would bring forth the visualizations, the astral plane would form the thought in etheric material, the Plane of Forces would carry the formed thought, and the physical plane would give it substance.

In simpler terms, the need arises (ultimate plane) and I begin to think of what I require to satisfy the need (Divine plane). Eventually I form an idea (spiritual plane) and then refine it into something I can visualize (mental plane). Once I can see the object in my mind's eye, I draw it out and give it form on paper (astral plane). Then I gather the materials required and begin to assemble the object (elemental plane). Once the labor is finished I have the physical object required to accomplish my task (physical plane).

The magickal art is one of creation. The material that we use is the astral substance. The power to create from our thoughts resides within us due to the divine spark. We create in accordance with the "divine formula" of the planes. The stronger the emotion, the more exact the thought, then so too is the corresponding astral response. In order to cause changes in the physical world (magickally) you must first cause them in the astral world.

The purpose of ritual magick is to raise and direct the energy (containing the thought-form) off into the astral plane. The symbols, gestures, colors, and other ritual trappings are all methods of astral communication. They also create the necessary mentality of all participants through which magickal images are communicated to the subconscious mind. Each one conveys its own vibration or energy and sets into motion subtle waves of stress and flow. Thought-forms can then begin to appear in the astral dimension and become channels for the higher forces of the other planes.

The ritual energizes these forms, channels then open, like responds to like, and the forces become potent. Then, according to the work and its nature, raised energy will ascend to the astral plane or divine energy will descend to the physical, in the case of rituals that invoke deity (see chapter ten).

CHAPTER
EIGHT

PSYCHIC CENTERS

*Whenever a place has had prayers and concen-
trated desires directed towards it, it forms an
electrical vortex that gathers to itself a force, and
it is for a time a coherent body that can be felt
and used by man. It is round these bodies of force
that shrines, temples, and in later days churches
are built; they are Cups that receive the Cosmic
down-pouring focused on each particular place.*
—Dion Fortune, *Aspects of Occultism*

Centers of power or magick are found both upon the earth and within the human body. In the Mystery Teachings the earth itself is a conscious living creature. In other words it is inhabited by a spiritual being, just as our own bodies are inhabited by a soul. The earth receives its nourishment from the radiation of other planetary bodies surrounding it. The physical nature of the earth is like the physical nature of those creatures who live upon her. It is subject to disease, aging, and decay. Today the rivers, streams, and oceans (its blood system) are filled with toxins created by human beings (very much like viruses and bacteria create toxins within our own bodies). The earth is very ill and is calling out to be healed.

According to the Mystery Teachings the earth possesses chakra centers just as does the human body. The following is a list of these centers as compiled by Western Occultists:

1. The sacred hill of Arunachala in southern India.

2. Trans-Himalayan region of the Gobi desert.

3. Cairo, Egypt.

4. A mountain approximately 100 miles inland from the coast of Peru, in the Andes region, directly opposite the globe from Aranachala.

5. Glastonbury, England.

6.   Ancient site of Sumer, on the lower Euphrates.

7.   Mount Shasta in California.

LEY LINES

Just like the human body, which possesses a system of nerve sensors and relays, so too does the earth. According to the Mystery Teachings, ancient civilizations erected sites of worship to mark the plexus of such points upon the earth's body. The energy that flowed from point to point (its nerve relay) is known in modern times as a Ley Line. There are many such ancient sites marked upon the face of the earth. They were erected to amplify the spiritual emanations of the earth. Later others were erected to modify and re-direct these emanations.

In Britain we find what ley researchers call *straight-tracks* or *cursuses*. These are often linked to Neolithic mounds and long barrows. In the Mystery Teachings these ley lines were designed to connect the dead with the energies of the Great Megaliths and other ancient structures. In this way the Collective Consciousness of the race was preserved in the standing stones that absorbed the energy flowing along the ley. In other words ley lines associated with mounds and monuments are designed to ensure the survival of ancestral memories. Ley lines are also known as *fairy tracks*, which further associates fairies with the *Cult of the Dead* (as seen in chapters seven, eleven, and thirteen). The geometric patterns found in the British Isles is reminiscent of similar patterns employed by the Etruscans in the layout of their cities, roads, tombs, farms, and other structures.

Geometric patterns are associated with shamanism, trance states, and the magickal use of psychotropic drugs (all of which have connections to spirits and the Cult of the Dead). In chapter six of the book *Shamanism and the Mystery Lines*, by Paul Devereux (Llewellyn Publications, 1993), we find some interesting results from a study in sensory deprivation. The so-called hallucinatory images discovered in the test fell into categories of shapes called:

lattice, *web*, *tunnel*, and *spiral*. These forms were constant and universal among the participants within the study and seemed to indicate a neuron reaction to sensory deprivation within the visual system of the brain. Even a casual glance at Neolithic designs in such works as *Goddesses and Gods of Old Europe* (Gimbutas) reveals the presence of the same images appearing in sensory studies. See chapter thirteen in this book for a look at Neolithic matrifocal designs.

THE CENTERS OF POWER
IN THE HUMAN BODY

Occult tradition states that within the human body there are located various centers of power. The first center is the Energy Center; this is also called the Fire Center or Serpent Center (operating within the genital region). This is the *seat of power* where concentrated life energies and psychic energies reside. It is essentially a transmitive center connected to the astral plane, in effect a type of portal or doorway. Like all psychic centers it is influenced by the lunar emanations associated with the four phases of the moon. The Serpent Center itself is linked to the new moon, whose energy is procreative, potential, and latent. The stellar enhancers of this center are found in the astrological signs of Pisces, Cancer, or Scorpio. Therefore the magickal uses of the Serpent Center are more profound when the moon *occupies* these particular Zodiac signs.

The second center is known as the Personal Center. This center is both receptive and transmitive. Its function deals with the condensation and manifestation of astral energies. It is one of several *gates* through which the astral body of the individual can exit from the physical flesh. Great amounts of energy can be drawn in and sent out from this area, which is used extensively in Shamanistic practices. The stellar influences that assist this center in the solidifying of astral material are the *earth signs:* Taurus, Virgo, and Capricorn.

The third center is the Power Center. This center is also transmitive and receptive, and deals with life energies. Through this center, both physical and astral bodies are nourished. This center

is linked to the full moon, at which time this center is most powerful. The astrological signs associated with this center are the *fire
signs:* Aries, Leo, and Sagittarius. This is the magickal fire of the
alchemists which transforms both matter and spirit. Among Italian
witches this magickal agent is present within the *spirit flame* (*Ways
of the Strega*).

The fourth center is called the Emotional Center. This center
is receptive in essence, but it is transmitive as well. The Emotional Center deals with human feelings and ethics. It is associated with
the creative element of water. This center enables us to sense
another person on an emotional level. It is most effectively
employed for magickal purposes when the moon is in one of the
water signs: Pisces, Cancer, or Scorpio.

The fifth center is the Vibrational Center. It is transmitive and
deals with causing actions and reactions. It is the most physical of
the nonphysical centers. This center is associated with the creative
element of air. Air is the medium that carries vibration and influences its effectiveness. This center is most effective for magickal
purposes when the moon occupies one of the *air signs:* Aquarius,
Gemini, or Libra.

The sixth center is the Psychic Center. It is basically receptive
but functions in a transmitive manner as well. This center is also
called the *Third Eye* and the Purity Center. It is a very active psychic center and another exit point for the astral body. Because this
center interprets etheric energy patterns and vibrations, it is associated with the Zodiac signs of the creative air element. Therefore
the most effective use of this center for magickal purposes is when
the moon is in one of the Zodiac signs associated with the creative
air element.

The seventh center is the Divine Center. It is receptive and
transmitive, and deals with "Deity-Consciousness." This is our
higher self and our place of union with what created us. It is viewed
as being outside of the body, and therefore it is not limited to the
associations attributed to the other power centers linked to the
body. Instead it serves to circulate energy from the other centers
and filter them. It also vitalizes the other centers and imparts a
higher nature to each. This higher vibration emanates from its

connection with the divine light. Thus the aura of the body is an energy field comprised of the emanations of each power center under the influence of the Divine Center.

On a physical level these centers function to maintain the body and its organs. The Energy Center governs the reproductive organs. The Personal Center governs general health and specifically the liver, pancreas, and spleen. The Power Center governs the adrenal glands. The Emotional Center governs the thymus gland. The Vibrational Center governs the thyroid gland. The Psychic Center governs the pineal gland. The Divine Center influences both the pituitary and pineal glands.

There are two currents of energy, the god and goddess currents, flowing through these centers within the body. The currents issue forth from the Energy Center and cross at the Emotional Center, then cross again at the Psychic Center. They directly influence our sexuality and gender preference through the "frequency" of their energy patterns, and they define our inner nature. In Judaic-Christian cultures usually only one of these currents is fully functional, rendering people either heterosexual or homosexual. Both currents operating in balance align one with the natural bisexual state. It is interesting to note that the medical symbol of the caduceus, symbolizing perfect health, is itself a symbol of the god and goddess currents flowing in balance along the spine.

GLANDS AND THE ENDOCRINE SYSTEM

In the Mystery Teachings, the endocrine system is a glandular system associated with seven sets of glands; in turn these glands are themselves associated with the seven power centers of the human body. In this system we see the relationship between the physical body and the etheric body. The endocrine system is designed to produce and release various hormones into the blood stream as needed for the full function of the body. Endocrine secretions regulate body activity, control growth, and coordinate the relationship between nerve impulses and responses within the body as a whole.

On a metaphysical level the glands function to disburse the astral and divine emanations channeled through the Divine Center into each of the other power centers. The occult function of the pineal glands is to regulate the incoming emanations of etheric light from the Divine Center as they collect within each of the power centers. On a metaphysical level the pineal glands also serve to regulate the energy that the etheric body draws from each center (in order to maintain its own form).

The thyroid gland regulates sensitivity to physical, psychic, and etheric sensations. The thymus and pancreatic glands coordinate the flux and response to energy currents associated with the solar plexus. This plexus serves as a web of energy sensing the stimulation of energies upon it, and is regulated by the spleen. The adrenals maintain the relationship between base instincts and higher spiritual principles. When stimulated we are flooded with signals to fight or to take flight. We respond to this according to our spiritual nature. The gonads influence the relationship between our physical and psychic drives. The energy of this center therefore affects our creativity on both a physical and mental nature.

It is interesting to note that occultists associate the solar plexus with clairvoyance. Through this center the body is fed with etheric energy from the sun, moon, and stars. The astral body is believed to be connected to the flesh body at the liver. The liver serves to filter elements from the bloodstream and also from the energies passing through its etheric counterpart. It was for this reason that ancients used the liver in divination. Abnormalities within the liver reflected the patterns contained within the cosmic energy flowing through to the astral body. In occultism all manifestations in the physical plane must first take place on the astral plane. Therefore the physical appearance of the liver reflected astral patterns not yet manifested. Perhaps more than any other civilization the Etruscans had developed this type of divination to an art of which they were masters.

THE MAGICKAL
ARTS

*Magic has power to experience and fathom
things which are inaccessible to human reason.
For magic is a great secret wisdom, just as reason
is a great public folly.*

—Paracelsus

M agick is the art of causing changes to occur in accordance with one's desires. It is the power to manipulate, channel, and direct sources of energy to empower one's mind. The mind creates mental images or sigils of its desire which can be empowered by those sources of energy to which the practitioner has access. The abilities that can be obtained through a working knowledge of magick are neither good nor evil. It is only the application of one's abilities that constitute such natures.

In the Wiccan Mystery Tradition, magick is viewed as a metaphysical science. The laws of physics are viewed as reflections of divine principles operating behind and within the forces of Nature. All works of magick and spell casting are founded upon time-proven formulas and metaphysical principles. True magick has little relationship to superstition or simple folk magick beliefs. The latter are based on fragmented pieces of ancient traditions, and the magickal formula has been forgotten leaving only the outcome of the spell as a result. An example of this would be the belief that a certain herb placed in your shoe can provide you with a specific power (such as winning a court case). The required methods of charging the herb, not to mention growing and harvesting it, have been forgotten in folk magick. The only thing remembered is that the herb is placed in the shoe and success is assured.

To employ magick, the conscious mind must be developed and controlled. The ability of the mind to concentrate and visualize must be cultivated to the highest degree possible. Magick requires mental discipline more than it does anything else. You must keep your word whenever you give it, and always follow through with everything you undertake. To do otherwise is to negate your own *will*. We often see in Wiccan magick the phrase "and as my word so mote it be." If your word means little to yourself or others, then it will reflect in your magickal ability.

The art of magick is one of creation. The material that we use is the astral substance. The power to create from *thoughts* is linked to the divine spark within us. We create in accordance with the divine formula that created all things (see chapter seven). The stronger the emotion, or the more exact the thought, then so too is the corresponding astral response or formation. The astral plane is the link between the divine world and the physical. It is where energy-forms from the physical world become empowered by higher principles. It is where divine energy can manifest as substance or form. Whatever manifests on the astral plane will eventually manifest on the physical plane.

In order to cause changes to occur in the physical dimension, you must first cause them to appear in the astral dimension. This is the purpose of magick and ritual. The symbols, gestures, colors, and so forth are all methods of astral communication. Each aspect conveys its own vibration or energy pattern to the astral substance. These all set in motion the subtle waves of action and reaction upon the planes. Stress lines and flow lines are formed by the operative rites. Thought-forms begin to appear in the astral material, which then become vehicles for the spirits or deities that have been invoked (through which they will respond to the desire of the magickal intent). The ritual energizes these forms, channels open, like responds to like, and the forces become potent and animated. Then, according to the nature of the work, raised energy will ascend to the astral, or drawn energy will descend to the physical.

There are essentially two types of magickal practice in Wicca: *raising power* and *drawing power*. The first is the art of personal power wherein one draws upon his or her own abilities. The latter is concerned with drawing power from spirits or deities in order to empower a spell or other work of magick. In this chapter we will examine some of the more important aspects of magick as reflected in various metaphysical principles. For practical reasons I am presenting here only those aspects concerned with *raising power*. If you are interested in *drawing power* please see chapter ten.

THOUGHT-FORMS

A thought-form is a mental image created by the mind. It is given substance within the etheric astral material and is animated by the indwelling consciousness of whatever is invoked within it. This is the metaphysical basis of the *magickal servant* or *witches' familiar*. Basically, thought-forms are built up by a combination of raised energy from the physical body and mental images from the mind (concentration/visualization).

The thought-form must be routinely *fed* energy in order to continue its existence in the early stages of its creation. The danger here is that if the form does not receive energy from its creator then it may draw it from another source on the planes. This is undesirable because it may become possessed by a consciousness dwelling on the planes (or an earth-bound spirit) or it may become a type of incubus or succubus. In the latter case it will draw energy from its creator and may cause severe fatigue or even illness. Therefore, when a thought-form is created it should be performed in a manner that will determine the length of its existence and the method of its termination.

Through the creation of thought-forms, a person can transmit influences, establish temporary protection around a place, object, or person, and generally create a useful servant on the mental or astral plane (the spheres of influence). The basic procedure for creating a simple thought-form is as follows:

1. Make or obtain a statue or image that corresponds to the nature you wish your thought-form to possess (for example: a wolf for protection). Hollow out the statue and fill it with sand or liquid. As an alternative you can place a small vial of liquid within the base of the statue.

2. Place the statue in front of you and sit in a comfortable position. Then visualize a sphere of light above your head. The color of the light must be symbolic of the nature of your desired effect.

3. Mentally draw the light down into your head and bring it to rest directly between your eyebrows. Concentrate strongly on the statue and its nature. Use the *Odic breath* and *informing technique* described in this chapter to empower the thought-form.

4. Now give the thought-form a name that is appropriate to the work it will perform for you. Say out loud: "I name thee _____."

5. Verbally instruct the thought-form, telling it when to work (time of day and night), where to work, how long, and when to finish. Then instruct it to terminate its existence on a given day and time. Do not extend the existence of the thought-form beyond seven days.

6. Release the thought-form, instructing it to go forth. Tell it to return to the statue when it requires more energy, and when it is not working as instructed. Each day you will want to *feed* the thought-form by putting energy into the statue (see Odic breath following the next section).

7. When the time has come to terminate the thought-form, slowly drain the liquid or sand out of the statue into a hole dug in the earth. As you empty the statue, *feel* the thought-form dissolve and ebb away. Finally, verbally affirm that the connection is now severed and the thought-form is dissolved. This step is vital; do not omit it.

THE ODIC FORCE

Sometime between 1936 and 1939, a scientist named William Reich discovered *orgone*, the biochemical basis for the Mystery Teachings of sex magick (sexual and bioelectric energy). He isolated the libido and demonstrated its existence as a tangible biological energy, as reported in his work *The Function of Orgasm*. Kenneth Grant in his book *Cults of the Shadow* (Weiser, 1976) writes:

> *Reich's discovery is significant because he was probably the first scientist to place psychology on a solid biological basis, and the first to demonstrate under laboratory conditions the existence of a tangible magical energy at last measurable and therefore strictly scientific.*

Following Reich's work, a German named Baron von Reichenbach performed certain experiments with electricity and magnetism. In the course of these experiments he made a discovery which he called the *Odic force*. Reichenbach discerned that this force was the underlying principle behind the physical forces of electricity and magnetism (as well as light and heat). He called it "the odic garment of the universe," and concluded that it emanated from within stellar/solar radiation. Reichenbach also stated that the Odic force was more concentrated in crystalline formations and magnetic objects.

The essence of this discovery was nothing new to occultists, for the force that Reichenbach spoke of was known to the ancients long ago. In metaphysical terms, Od is the fabric of the universe, present in all things to varying degrees. The main difference is the concentration of Odic energy, measurable by its emanation. Generally speaking, liquids, metals, and crystals are the best conductors. They easily absorb Odic energy and retain the original charge. Oils are the preferred liquids for magickal Odic charges because they do not evaporate as readily as water. Silk has proven to be the only substance that will not absorb additional energy, and can be used to insulate objects charged with Odic energy. This way no energy will accidentally drain off into any conductive object placed in close proximity to the charged object.

The Odic force is a very refined etheric substance and can be controlled and directed by the power of the mind. Magickal thought-forms can be bound to an Odic charge and placed within a conductive object for spell casting or general works of magick. The Odic energy itself can be accumulated through deep breathing which condenses the energy within the lungs. Next the Odic energy is sent a thought-form through mental imagery and emotional intensity. The blood flowing through the lungs carries with it the electromagnetically charged imagery from centers within the brain. The blood in turn passes the charged imagery into the Odic energy accumulating in the lungs. In occult terms this is known as *informing*, impregnating an object or substance with a concept (such as *heal*) embedded within an electromagnetic charge.

THE ODIC BREATH

The energy described as *Odic* can be accumulated and condensed for magickal purposes through deep breathing exercises or sexual stimulation. The resulting product can be passed into the blood by a technique known as *Informing* (see section so named), which is then employed for magickal purposes. The technique is very simple and can be performed by following these basic steps:

1. Relax your body and allow your thoughts to become calm; still the mind.

2. Focus your attention on the desire of your magickal spell. See its outcome clearly in your mind.

3. Rouse the emotions in order to charge the blood. Fill yourself with the desire for the outcome. If employing sexual stimulation as a power source, begin during this phase.

4. Begin deep breathing through the mouth only, taking in and releasing four breaths in succession while drawing in the stomach muscles slightly. This will keep air out of the stomach and help you to fill the lungs only.

5. Hold the breath on the next inhale and mentally transfer the image of your desire to the heart area/chakra.

6. Slowly release the breath out on the object you wish to charge. As you do so, mentally transfer the image of the desire, seeing the image carried out on the breath. Your desire is now magickally transferred into the object and will vibrate with the energy of your desire (thus attracting it, like unto like).

MAGICKAL MAGNETISM

The elements of magickal magnetism are quite similar to the properties of a mundane magnet: attraction, repulsion, and a balanced polarization. When employing magnetic energy to charge an object, or raise a cone of power, the nature of mundane electromagnetic power serves as a guideline. A stationary charge will produce only an electrical field in the surrounding space, but if the charge is flowing then a magnetic field is also produced. This field occupies its own space separate from the currents with which it is related. Typically this is produced by ritual circle dancing to raise a cone of power, or by ritual gestures involving circular hand passes around the object to be charged. The passion (emotional investment) of the dancers or the magician is essential for the manifestation of energy. For magickal purposes we may equate emotion with magnetism and by stimulating the emotions we increase the magnetic flow.

In the Mystery Teachings all inanimate objects and all living things emanate a field of energy. This field has often been referred to as the aura, although as Franz Bardon says in *Initiation into Hermetics* (Dieter Ruggeberg, 1971), the aura is not identical to the electromagnetic field of the body. The aura is an energy field that reflects the astral nature or status of the body. It reflects the interaction of the soul with each of the seven planes to which it is connected (see chapter seven). From the formation, colors, and strength of the aura we can discern the general health of the body and the soul. The aura emanates from the soul whereas the magnetic field emanates from the body.

In Western Occultism the male polarity is positive/active on the physical and mental planes; negative/receptive on the psychic and spiritual planes. The female polarity is negative/receptive on the physical and mental planes; positive/active on the psychic and spiritual planes. The female genitals are magnetic, lunar, and receptive. The male genitals are electric, solar, and active. In both genders, the right hand is solar, active, and electrical. The left hand is lunar, receptive, and magnetic. This is why during rituals we always receive with the left hand, and present with the right hand.

All living creatures emit an energy that may be called a bio-magnetic field. The interaction of the four elements creates an astral matrix that connects the soul to the physical body. Elemental *earth* nourishes the soul and preserves its vitality, *air* provides balance and harmony, *fire* contributes what is constructive for the soul, and *water* animates. Without this energy, the soul would not be able to reside within physical matter for very long. This bio-magnetic energy is what also draws the soul back to the body in cases of astral projection.

The metaphysical energy of magickal magnetism is perhaps best illustrated below in the glyph of the Magical Caduceus of Hermes. In this symbol the polarity of forces of magickal magnetism are depicted as the currents of OB and OD. OB is the lunar current and OD is the solar. AOUR represents what is manifest in the balance of these two currents, the *fire* of polarity when the OB and the OD exist in harmony. The secret of magnetism in magick lies in the ability of the mind to control these currents in order to create the perfect equilibrium which manifests as the creative power of the AOUR.

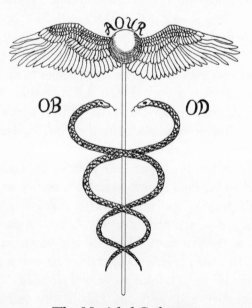

The Magickal Caduceus
(Based on an illustration in *Transcendental Magic* (pub. 1895) by Eliphas Levi.)

When viewed in context with the techniques of sex magick, the AOUR symbolizes the spinal column, the OB and OD are the left and right nerve currents running along it which influence endocrine gland secretions. When activated, these magickal currents arouse the serpent power residing at the base of the spine. This causes an awakening of this power center, which responds by forcing a current of energy upward along the OB and OD. This results in the manifestation of the flame burning in AOUR (the consciousness awakened).

INFORMING

Informing is the art of transferring mental images, through the will power of the mind, into target objects or substances. As human beings we all possess the creative spark of what created us. Therefore, on a lesser scale, we too can create by drawing upon the indwelling spiritual essence of our own being. All that is required is to bring one's will under control, and to employ it to build crystal-clear images. Added to this is the energy of *burning desire* to empower the image and transfer it.

The most effective method to stimulate the breath is to employ sexual stimulation. It is through such stimulation that the power centers of the body open in response, flooding the central nervous system and stimulating the endocrine glands. The blood becomes electromagnetically charged by the metaphysical *heat* created by the stimulation and quickened breathing. The essence of this charge is carried in the vapor emitted from the lungs, the breath of magick. Many ancient magickal texts employ the breath in spell casting and other works of magick.

Once the blood is magickally heated, then the mind infuses it with a mental image symbolizing the desired effect. This image is essential to binding the magickal charge so that it can be transmitted on the breath (see Magickal Sigils, page 148). The charge must be allowed to build within the blood until you feel a sensation of internal heat and pulsating blood. Once this point has been reached then the breath may be directed out toward the talisman that will contain it, or towards the target you wish to influence. To successfully wield energy you must be able to concentrate and project (fix and direct) with the power of your mind/will.

MAGICKAL SIGILS

Sigils are designs that condense a desire, concept, or aspect. In essence they encapsulate the desired goal or outcome of the spell in which they are employed. By creating a sigil, the practitioner places his or her desire into a drawing. Thus he or she will not have to think about the desired effect of the magickal spell while performing the spell. This frees the practitioner from having to think about why the spell is being cast, and allows him or her to focus totally on raising and directing magickal energy.

One of the most effective techniques for creating sigils is to condense the desired outcome into basic figures. For example, if I wanted to cast a spell to improve my concentration I would write out the wish: "I desire to increase my ability to concentrate." Then I would begin to condense the sentence by removing any letters that repeat (as I rewrite it): "I desr to nca my b". Next I take each remaining letter and incorporate it into a single design using my own imagination (see examples on page 149). This is called the Magickal Alphabet and is attributed to the great occultist Austin Spare who learned this art from a New England witch. By gazing on the sigil while raising magickal energy with which to empower the spell, the *desire* is transferred directly to the subconscious mind. This happens because the conscious mind no longer understands the sentence, therefore other levels of consciousness are brought into play in order to decipher what the eyes are seeing.

The following illustrations will provide you with excellent examples of how to create sigils from words.

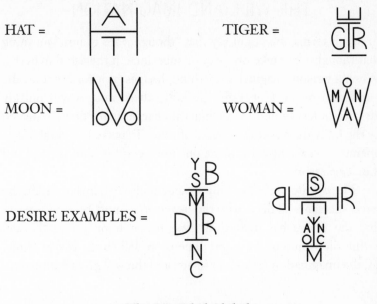

HAT =

TIGER =

MOON =

WOMAN =

DESIRE EXAMPLES =

The Magickal Alphabet

The secret behind how all of this works is really quite simple. We've all experienced a situation in which we are unable to remember the name of a certain person, or the verse from a certain song, and hours or days later it suddenly appears in our conscious mind. This is because the mind has been working behind the scenes to resolve the puzzle. It is the nature of consciousness to do so. Just as the conscious mind is connected to the physical dimension, the subconscious mind is linked to the astral dimension. When the conscious mind cannot interpret something, then the subconscious mind is tapped. Here, in our example, it goes to work behind the scenes to interpret the sigil. Because it is linked to the astral plane, it creates a thought-form as it unravels the sigil. What manifests upon the astral plane will then move toward manifestation upon the physical plane. Dreams are an example of how the subconscious mind works on various concepts that the conscious mind cannot. As Joseph Campbell once noted, the conscious mind is a secondary organ. It is only a part of our total consciousness, and yet we feel that it is in charge (however, it is not).

THE WILL AND IMAGINATION

In occult terms one might say that "thoughts are things," meaning that thoughts can take on form or substance in the astral material. When a person imagines something, images of it form within the astral dimension. Generally speaking, these images will quickly dissolve unless bound by a magickal charge or routinely repeated by the individual over the course of time. To make the astral image operative on the physical plane one must employ both the *will* and the *imagination*.

The *will* alone creates only a vague undefined image within the astral substance. This is why the *imagination* must be employed so that the image has definition. *Imagination* impregnates the *will* within the womb of the astral dimension. When the two are united, the imagination creates an image and the will gives it direction.

THE ART OF FASCINATION

Fascination is a magickal *binding* that is transmitted from the eyes of the spellcaster into the eyes of the target person. This art is the source of the Medieval fear that a person had been bewitched (was under the influence of another's mind). The magickal charge is the same one employed in *Informing*. Instead of using the breath, however, the vapor is poured out from the eyes in *rays* of energy directed by the mind through visualization. The vaporous rays carry the informed charge just as does the odic breath. The etheric charge enters through the eyes of the other person and passes into his or her blood in accord with the principles of contagion. This technique is more subtle than the breath method but also requires a greater degree of mental discipline. If you have ever glared back at someone who was staring at you, extending your neck slightly and sending them a mental message, then you have felt how this charge is launched.

The magickal intent is passed to the other person in a quick darting manner as though piercing his or her eyes. The charge contained within the vapor emitted from the sender is then transferred into the blood of the receiver. This in turn reverses the process that created it; the newly contaminated blood carries the charge to the lungs, which extract it and send in back into the bloodstream, which then carries the charge to the brain, thus influencing the mind.

So strong was the belief in this technique that people devised methods to ward off what they called the *evil eye*. Basically these techniques were designed to deflect or divert the focus of the spell caster. A quick hand gesture pointing downward would break the sender's concentration, as would a pair of dangling earrings. People put reflective objects on their horses to protect them from the evil eye. Colored glass balls similar to Christmas ornaments were hung in windows to deflect the power of anyone who practiced Fascination.

THE EIGHT-FOLD PATH

The eight-fold path represents the eight aspects of magickal and religious training, which must be mastered in order to become an adept or master of the Arts:

1. Mental discipline through fasting and physical disciplines.

2. Development of the Will through mental imagery, visualization, and meditation.

3. Proper controlled use of drugs (hemp, peyote, mescaline, alcohol).

4. Personal power, thought-projection, raising and drawing power.

5. The keys: ritual knowledge and practice. Use of enchantments, spells, symbols, and charms.

6. Psychic development and dream control.

7. Rising upon the planes. Astral projection and mental projection.

8. Sex magick, sensuality, and eroticism.

These traditional aspects of magickal/religious training within Wicca can be found in shamanistic traditions throughout the world as well as in the mystical disciplines of Eastern practices. In modern times many Wiccans no longer incorporate the use of drugs or sex due to social and legal issues associated with Judaic-Christian society and the laws that arose from its mentality. I list the eight-fold path here as a guideline to those who are interested in what the ancients believed were the necessary steps to personal power. A personal study of each of these aspects may prove to be most enlightening.

CHAPTER
TEN

WICCAN RITES

Seasonal rites are virtually as old as the hills they used to be practiced on by most of humanity, and even today they are kept up in very attenuated forms by a small minority of cultists. In principle, they afford an invaluable means of aligning our own natures with the essential energy behind creation itself through the cycles and changes that complete the great circle of cosmos which we simply term "nature." Put into absolutely basic language, if we can find a means of relating our little human nature with the incalculable divine nature, we shall have done something really worth doing. This was and is the aim of all true magical rites.

—William G. Gray, *Seasonal Occult Rites*

This chapter examines the main aspects of ceremonial and magickal ritual. In the Mystery Tradition every movement, act, and gesture is connected to time-honored occult principles that empower the work at hand. In essence, there is a momentum of energy from the past (a current) that is activated when ritual correspondences come into play. In other words, when a gesture or act meaning one specific thing is displayed time and time again over the centuries, then it begins to merge with the collective consciousness of the society to which it has meaning. Eventually the simple display of a gesture, or the directed movement of an object, can flood the ritual setting with the underlying consciousness of what the gesture or movement represents. This is why secrets exist in various covens and are made available only to those who have earned the trust of their initiators. Access to automatic sources of power without proper training and appropriate mentality is a very dangerous thing.

Charms, amulets, and talismans all basically fall into this category of time-honored symbolisms. They do not necessarily have to be related to what the person on the receiving end of their magick believes, or to what the user of such objects of power believes about them. Although this would certainly have a profound effect on the magick as well, such a concept is more related to the principles of folk magick. There is an old joke about whether a crucifix would work against a Jewish vampire. Let us look at this hypothetical situation. In folk magick the answer would be no, one would need a Star of David or a Pentacle of Solomon. According to occult principles, however, the answer would be yes, but not with the same immediate results as it would against a vampire from a Christian society. The symbol represents the occult principle and establishes its nature wherever it is displayed, regardless of cultural connections due to the Akashic influence (see chapter seven). Therefore the banishing power of light over darkness, heat over vapor, would still be evoked. Its effect would be to prevent the presence of a vampire from originally establishing its existence, and not one of fending off a vampire who suddenly appeared from outside the indigenous culture (for that you would need a pertinent cultural symbol).

Natural settings such as groves, hills, grottos, and the running water of streams and rivers appear to have universal meaning in all human cultures around the world. Natural objects such as stones, crystals, amber, and various metals all seem to have similar if not identical natures ascribed to them in Occult Traditions ranging from Egypt to the British Isles. The time-honored energies connected to elements of a cultural consciousness are often absorbed and preserved in such dense materials as stone, metal, and marble. This is why such places as the Great Pyramid in Egypt, Stonehenge, Rollright, and the temple ruins of Rome and Greece all generate occult energies. It is these energies that give a place that certain *feel* by which we know it as a sacred place. Regardless of the culture from which a person may originate, the *presence* of the place is still evident. To an individual whose bloodline goes back to the original culture that established the structure, the *presence* might be felt to an even stronger degree. (See "Ley Lines" in chapter eight for connective information.)

Let us look now at some of the main aspects concerning Wiccan rituals and examine their applications and inner meanings. Please bear in mind that we are looking at the Old Mystery Teachings; some modern traditions may not be employing these concepts (and the lack thereof is not meant as a judgment of any kind).

THE CIRCLE OF THE ARTS

The ritual circle is, in effect, a microcosm of the Universe. Properly cast, it becomes a place between the physical and spiritual world. Wiccans often refer to the ritual/magickal circle as *the world between the worlds*. Once established, the circle serves to contain the magickal and metaphysical energies raised within its sphere, so that they are condensed enough to accomplish the desired effect. The threshold of the circle, through which the celebrants enter and exit, is located at the northeast point of the circle. The north is the realm of the power of the gods, and the east is the realm of enlightenment. Thus to enter and exit at this point is to symbolically meet with the gods in power and enlightenment. In this sense the circle becomes a grotto for initiation and spiritual rebirth, the sacred womb of the Mother Goddess.

The circle is first marked out physically so that a vehicle exists wherein the elemental spirits can be invoked. The space is marked out to separate mundane from sacred, and the elements are called to each of the four quarters of the circle according to their correspondence. Traditionally, the element of earth is assigned to the north. Elemental air is placed at the east, fire at the south, and water at the west quarter. Depending upon the climatic conditions of the region in which any tradition abides, these elemental associations may vary.

The ritual or magickal circle should be visualized as a sphere of energy rather than a wall of energy enclosing the area. The sphere serves to seal not only the circumference but also the top and bottom of the sacred space that one has established. Traditionally the *Watchers* (see chapter five) are evoked to each of the four quarters of circle to magickally guard the sacred area against the intrusion of any forces not in harmony with the ritual itself. As noted in chapter five, the Watchers also bear witness to the rites and can exert a great deal of influence over the nature of the work at hand.

Movement within the ritual circle is always performed in a clockwise manner when creating sacred space or magickal workings. When dissolving the circle or negating magickal energy, the movements are always counterclockwise (unless you're in the Southern Hemisphere where everything is reversed from European associations). Wiccans refer to this as deosil (sunwise) and widdershins (or tuathal, against the shadows). According to the Mystery Teachings, however, the clockwise movement within the circle is symbolic of the lunar/feminine energies emerging from the left-hand side, and displacing the solar/masculine energies associated with the right-hand side. It is the moon rising to claim the heavens as the sun departs to the Underworld. Since Wicca is a matrifocal and lunar cult, it is only natural to find this association. The solar associations of movement within the circle stem from the Indo-European influences that usurped the matrifocal concepts, particularly in central Europe.

Once established, the ritual circle serves to accumulate energy. The participants within its sphere are emersed in the energies being drawn to, or raised inside of, the sacred sphere. Being attendant within the circle allows one to become aligned with the frequency or vibrational rate of the current of energy present within the circle. Aradia taught in ancient times that the power of a witch arose from an unbroken participation in the rituals of the year. Such participation aligned one with the natural flow of earth's energy. Becoming attuned with Nature freed one's psychic abilities and made available certain insights that helped one to develop magickal powers.

THE SEASONAL TIDES

The Seasonal Tides of the Earth are reflected in the eight festival occasions of the year—often referred to as the Wheel of the Year. In Wicca these are marked by each solstice and equinox. The quarterly tides fall under the influence of various *elemental rulers* as the seasons progress. The Spring Equinox, when the sun enters Aries, introduces the ruling element of fire. The Summer Solstice, when the sun enters Cancer, replaces this with the element of water. When the Autumn Equinox falls, the sun having entered Libra, then the ruling element becomes air. With the arrival of the Winter Solstice, as the sun enters Capricorn, elemental earth takes up the rule until the wheel turns again to the Spring Equinox. Through this ebb and flow of the elements the creative power of Nature is vitalized and can be tapped for magickal purposes. From equinox to equinox the magickal seeds planted in the astral plane at one equinox will germinate over the course of six months, manifesting at the next. The tides of the solstices maintain the balance between Light and Darkness, Form and Force, and Spirit and Matter in a rhythmical cycle contributing to the healthy cohesion of the metaphysical principles at play.

Centuries ago certain cults such as the Benandanti fought ritual battles over the harvests and herds during the Ember days in order to ensure their abundance. This was a period of three days that marked the change of one seasonal tide to the next. The term "Ember days" comes from an old Anglo-Saxon word meaning *circuit* and was used to indicate the connective points between each Solstice and Equinox. The number three has always held occult significance and often symbolizes the power of manifestation. It is also an aspect of lunar consciousness wherein the new moon is not visible for three days, indicating a mystical unseen force at play. In the Mystery Teachings the Ember days are periods when the approaching seasonal tides are most vulnerable to changes in their energy patterns. Therefore the magickal portals or thresholds of the equinoxes and solstices had to be protected.

The Spring Equinox is the season for planting new ideas and beginning studies that lead to spiritual enlightenment. What is begun at this time in a ritual sense will begin to manifest around the time of the Autumn Equinox. The Summer Solstice is a time of taking stock and celebrating all that is good in life. At this time we may wish to cultivate and care for those things that have come into our life in a special way. Rituals should include a celebration and an appreciation for the gifts we have received in life. The Autumn Equinox is the time of harvest when we can gather in the rewards of our labors. In a ritual setting it is a good time to work on mental imagery and new ideas for the coming year. Our desires and images will arise as new seeds come spring. The Winter Solstice marks the end of the vitality within the manifestations of what was planted in spring. It is a time to dispose of the *deadwood* of the year and to analyze what is healthy and unhealthy in our life and in our relationships. Rituals of winter should reflect personal purification and rebirth. Old debris is burned away and used to fertilize the ground for spring planting. In ancient times the ashes from the burning of the old year's effigy would be scattered over the fields to be planted in spring.

During the course of a year certain currents of energy flow across the surface of the earth. In Eastern Mysticism these forces are known as the Tattvic Tides. For purpose of discussion we will divide them into five aspects: Stellar, Solar, Planetary, Lunar, and Terrestrial. To understand how these tides influence us we need to first understand the terms *Bound Ether* and *Free Ether*. Free ether is an unseen occult medium in which solar systems orbit. In occultism this is the state of matter which is just above physical material in vibratory rate (astral material is slightly higher in rate, yet more plastic than ether). Bound ether is the occult counterpart of the magnetic sphere of our earth and other planetary bodies. It is sometimes referred to as the Odic Mantle (see chapter nine).

The stellar, solar, and lunar tides affect the magnetic sphere of the earth and produce currents of energy corresponding to the nature of each. As the earth orbits the sun, the gravitational pull creates centers of stress in the magnetic sphere of the earth (and thus within the bound ether). The earth's solar orbit causes a steady current of energy to flow from east to west across the surface of the earth. In other words, a tide of occult energy flows in the Odic Mantle of the earth, from east to west. As the earth spins on its axis during its orbit around the sun, a magnetic current is established, running north to south for half the year and then to the opposite poles for the remaining half. These energy flows are the seasonal tides that we associate with the solstices and equinoxes as follows:

The Tide of Destruction: December 23–March 21

The Tide of Sowing: March 21–June 21

The Tide of Reaping: June 21–September 23

The Tide of Planning: September 23–December 23

The Tattvic Tides are also connected with the four elements of creation as well as the fifth element known as spirit. As the sun appears on the horizon, the Odic mantle is stimulated as the elemental influences present themselves in response to the sun's energy. The elemental influences merge one into the other every two hours (every twenty minutes, according to Dion Fortune) as they pass through a repeating cycle until sunset. The first elemental influence of *spirit* begins with the sunrise. This is followed in order by Air, Fire, Water, and Earth. In Eastern Mysticism the five elements are Akasha, Vayu, Tejas, Apas, and Prithivi. Akasha is identified as spirit, and the remaining elemental terms are in the order listed here. Some traditions use these Tattvas as portals or doorways to the elemental realms (see appendix one).

THE WHEEL OF THE YEAR

Eight ritual Sabbats, four major and four minor, are celebrated during the Wiccan year. The major rites mark the agricultural year and occur on the solstices and equinoxes. The four minor festivals occur on the days that fall exactly between each major Sabbat, in May, August, October, and February. The rites of the festival year are based on the pre-Christian practices of the Old Religion which contain the inner mysteries of Nature and the Divine, collectively referred to as the Mythos. Within the mythos of the ritual year we find the names of various deities personifying the forces of nature. In this we find a symbolic mythos that serves to portray the life of humankind as well as the process of death and rebirth.

In essence the myths are a drama play, earth is the stage, and we are the players. In the Mystery Teachings of the Wheel we discover that we are the characters in the mythos. Everything is symbolic within each myth and represents various aspects of the encounters facing a soul as it passes from life to life. Through a study of the mythos, and routine participation in each Sabbat, one can gain spiritual enlightenment. Within the heroes and villains of the play, we find our own inner selves struggling with the forces of light and darkness. The Wheel of the Year represents the journey of the soul as it moves through the cycles of the natural and supernatural worlds. It is thought of as a spinning wheel, turning and weaving the patterns of life. On the physical level it is symbolic of the changing seasons. On the spiritual level it is symbolic of the "seasons of the soul." The mythos, which is an integral part of each rite, symbolizes the journey of the soul through a variety of existences.

RITUAL ITEMS AND OBJECTS

Wicca possesses a vast and rich legacy of mystical concepts reflected in the tools and ritual items incorporated into its ceremonies. In this section we will look at each item and ascribe its occult associations.

THE CORDS OF INITIATION

The cord of initiation originated from the bindings that once served to restrain the sacrificial king. Thus the red cord of first degree initiation symbolizes the *royal blood* and identifies the initiate as a follower (and therefore an inheritor) of the ancient Mystery Tradition. It has also come to represent the burning desire for knowledge within the new seeker. The green cord of the second degree symbolizes that one has been renewed by the blood of the Harvest Lord and has penetrated the mysteries. Therefore this individual is now a Priestess or a Priest of the Old Religion and wears the life-giving/fruit-producing green vine of the Harvest Lord. The blue cord of the third degree represents the wedding of initiate to the Goddess or God, the *hieros gamos* or divine marriage. Blue is the color of the day sky and only during the day can both the sun and moon be seen together in the blue sky. In the more matrifocal covens the third-degree cord is usually black, symbolizing the night sky and the womb of the Goddess from which all things issue forth.

THE DEGREE SYMBOLS

The inverted triangle symbol (point down) represents the vaginal area, the *Yoni* of the Great Goddess. This is a symbol of birth into Her cult. The upright five-pointed star represents the Great Goddess with arms and legs outstretched in ecstasy (it also represents *spirit* dominant over *matter*). This is also symbolic of the receptive posture in sex magic and is the manner in which a woman formed the altar in ancient times. This symbol indicates that one has penetrated the Mysteries of the Goddess, or has been granted permission to do so. The upright triangle is symbolic of the Divine light or flame (the presence of Divine Consciousness). In the third-degree symbol it appears over the five-pointed star. This indicates that the work one does, as he or she penetrates the mysteries, is under the sanction of one's deities. It also symbolizes the *Cone of Power* which is directed by the High Priest(ess).

First Degree	**Second Degree**	**Third Degree**

Degree Symbols used by Mainstream Wiccan Groups
These modern symbols show the influence of Hebrew Mysticism.

Some modern traditions influenced by Hebrew Mysticism (the Kabbalah) employ the reversed star or pentagram in their initiation symbols. This star represents the goat-foot god, and matter dominant over spirit. By taking sections out of the Hebrew Tree of Life this symbol (note the shaded area in illustration below) can be discerned, where it is rooted in the Kabbalistic concept of Yesod. Yesod represents the lunar realms as well as the realms of illusion.

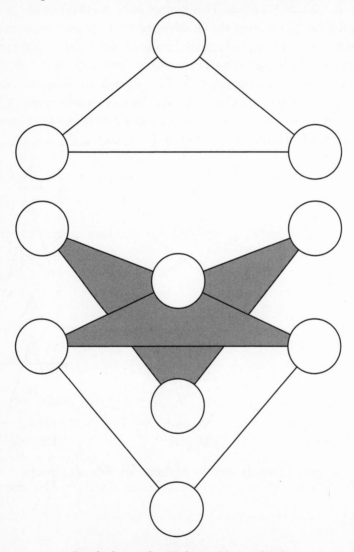

Symbols on the Hebrew Tree of Life

CAKES AND WINE

In the Mystery Tradition the wine and cakes represent the blood and body of the deities. In the early matrifocal associations of the hunter-gatherer era, the blood symbolized the menstrual blood of the Goddess and the cakes were the body of the God. As the cult evolved into the agricultural period and took on some of the patriarchal solar aspects, both the wine and cakes came to be connected with the God. In modern times some traditions still employ the older associations, while others embrace the solar god aspects, or blend the two together in some fashion. All are equally valid connections to the spirit of what underlies the rite, consuming the manifestation of the divine in order to become One with it.

The consuming of Divine essence is a very important aspect of the Transformation Mysteries. Ancient humans believed that the chemical effects of plants transformed the human spirit. The physical substance of the plant (or its extracts) gave renewal to the flesh, but intoxication was something spiritual and not corporeal. The mundane personality of the intoxicated individual was changed, thus (to primitive magickal reasoning) his or her spirit had been transformed. The feeling that a person has been transformed when he or she ingests intoxicants is one of the deepest and most intimate experiences of humankind. This is the basis for the rites of Bacchus/Dionysus as well as the rite of Communion among Catholics.

The solar aspects of the cakes and wine employ the Fermentation Mysteries covered in chapter twelve. Essentially they are concerned with the seed as a male symbol, becoming a plant-bearing seed (another male symbol). The seemingly magickal effects of psychotropic plants and fermented liquids created a belief in the indwelling consciousness of a spirit or a god within the plant or its fruit/seed. The spilling of seed and the dying of the plant became associated with men and thus did the blood symbolism pass to the God through the ritual use of wine. The crushing and grinding of plants and seeds to make cakes also reflects the sacrifice of the Harvest Lord who is cut down and dismembered, only to rise again.

RITUAL TOOLS

The ritual tools of Wicca are consistent with the tools commonly associated with Western Occultism. Two of the earliest known manuscripts to have influenced modern Wiccan tools and symbols are *The Key of Solomon* and the *Libri de Vita* (Book of Life). Both are fifteenth-century manuscripts reportedly based on much earlier works. The *Libri de Vita* was written in 1489 by Marsilio Ficino, a philosopher and physician in Florence. In it we see the symbol of the pentagram along with talismans depicting the four common ritual tools: the wand, cup, dagger, and pentacle. In the *Key of Solomon* we find these same tools, along with the hilt symbols common to Gardnerian Wicca.

Many Wiccan groups employ the sexual symbolism of the chalice and athame, or chalice and wand. The chalice is womb–like in appearance and the wand or blade is phallic. In a symbolic ritual gesture the wand or athame is lowered slowly into the chalice. This is meant to represent the union of the male and female, the divine marriage of Goddess and God. In the Mystery Teachings there is a connection between sexuality and nourishment, as represented by the chalice (nourishment) and the wand/athame (sexuality). The physical craving or desire for food is not unlike that for sex. Hunger and satiation, desire and fulfillment are elements of both realities. We often find food and drink present in settings associated with seduction, and in ancient times with fertility rites. The classic romantic date—a candlelit dinner with wine and a cozy fire in the fireplace—originates from primitive sex magick principles.

PRIESTESSES AND PRIESTS

The role of the Priestess and the Priest within a ritual setting is based on the interplay of the polarities of feminine and masculine energies. They are the facilitators of the rituals helping to keep things flowing smoothly as each rite progresses. As High Priestess and High Priest they may represent the Goddess and the God within the ritual celebration. An act such as *drawing down the moon*, where the Goddess is invoked directly into the mind and body of the High Priestess, is one such example.

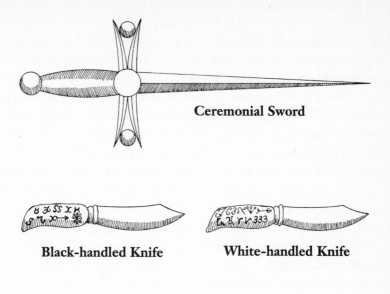

Ceremonial Sword

Black-handled Knife   **White-handled Knife**

Two Styles of Bolline

Ritual Tools
(Based on illustrations in the 15th-century manuscript, *The Key of Solomon*)

Wicca is essentially matrifocal and the Priestess and High Priestess typically oversee the religious practices. In most covens the High Priest assists the High Priestess during the celebrations. It is not uncommon for the High Priest to take on the mundane tasks of teaching newcomers and of taking care of the setup of the altar and circle. The High Priestess is then free to tend to more

spiritual matters and work on magickal aspects and ritual embell-
ishments. It is important that mutual respect and consideration
exist within this relationship. When polarities conflict with one
another then problems easily occur.

The role of teacher is very important within the Priest-
(ess)hood. It is the purpose of a teacher to lead the student to the
source of understanding and realization. Providing instructions
and exercises to develop the mind and character of the student is
essential, along with establishing situations through which the student can grow and evolve. A teacher cannot make one learn; he or
she can only reveal the setting, materials, and experiences that can
lead to enlightenment. Ideally the Priestess or Priest serves as a
source of redirection and reflection, providing the opportunity for
questions and clarifications (as the student seeks his or her own
understanding and connection).

The Priest(ess)hood is also concerned with the presence of
divinity within the ritual celebrations. In an attempt to communi-
cate with the Totality of Divine Consciousness, Wiccans divide
Deity into its feminine and masculine polarities or aspects, which
they call Goddess and God. We can break this down into the *Goddess-current* and the *God-current*. These currents also flow, to varying degrees, within the souls of all humans regardless of gender.
The Goddess-current tends to be more open and mutable while
the God-current tends to be more directive and fixed. The Goddess is the balance to the God, and He is the balance to Her. Without Her the God would be a judge without compassion, He would
be stern without understanding, He would control without loving.
Without the God, the Goddess would have compassion without
direction, understanding without foundation, love without form.
The God and Goddess complete each other, and together they are
the One True Creator and Maintainer of the Universe.

THE CELTS
AND THE
WICCAN MYSTERIES

*...the continental Celts, who had direct knowl-
edge of Greek and Roman culture, meeting their
insular brethren beyond the Channel and Irish
sea. All such ancient contacts push the problem
(doctrine origins) further and further back in
time; and our easiest and safest course is to
state—as we may of the similar problem of the
origin of the Celtic Otherworld—that available
facts of comparative religion, and myth, indicate
clearly a prehistoric epoch when there was a common ancestral stock for the Mediterranean and
pan-Celtic cultures.*

—W. Y. Evans-Wentz,
The Fairy Faith in Celtic Countries

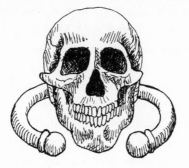

It may seem odd that a book on Wicca would need a separate chapter designed to link the Celts with this subject. Most people commonly associate Wicca with the Celts, and rarely think beyond that, but as I stated in the introduction, this book is not about Celtic religion, it is about the Mystery Tradition as a spiritual path within Wicca. Obviously it is impossible to not discuss both in the context of this book, for they are quite intimately connected. After all, religion grew out of early shamanistic beliefs and the mysteries formed around the basic truths of both perspectives.

In the Celtic Wiccan Mystery text known as *The Charge*, we find these words: "Nor do I demand sacrifice, for behold I am the Mother of all living, and my love is poured out upon the earth." It is difficult to reconcile this with what we know of Celtic culture up through even Roman times. The ancient Celts were headhunters who sacrificed humans as an integral part of their religious ceremonies. This we know from several Greek and Roman historians as well as from the writings of Julius Caesar during his campaign against the Celts in Gaul and Britain. Human sacrifice was still prevalent in A.D. 43 when the second Roman invasion of Britain took place, and continued for quite some time before the Romans were able to abolish it.

In this chapter we will sift through the facts and fallacies concerning the Celts and their influence on Wiccan beliefs. In this quest we will find that many Wiccan tenets come not from early Celtic beliefs, but rather from other cultural teachings later absorbed by the Celts. For example, the theme of the dying and returning god is much more prevalent in the Romanized areas of Gaul and the British Isles than in the unconquered territories. Jack-in-the-Green and other Green Man images can be traced in carvings from Britain to Gaul and then earlier to Rome and the Roman Rhineland. By comparison, what few images appear in Ireland and Scotland can be attributed to imported Pagan beliefs carried there by Christianity (not to mention contacts between various clans after the Roman withdrawal). What is most striking, however, is that in the areas not conquered by the Romans, harsh Indo-European elements are quite strong, while in the territories once held by Rome we find the merging of war-like Celtic deities with gentle and feminine forms reminiscent of the Aegean and Mediterranean deity forms.

There is a fast-growing trend among contemporary Wiccan authors to embellish both the antiquity and the achievements of the Celts. This is unnecessary because the facts alone are enough for us to sing their praises. Some authors erroneously place the Celts at around 3000 B.C. and a few even claim that the Celts laid the foundation for Western civilization. We know, of course, that Western culture inherited its basic philosophy and social standards from the Greeks, and it was the Romans who gave us our governmental and legal structure. In comparison, very little of Celtic culture survived to impact Western civilization. The wonderful contribution of Celtic culture to literature is, however, indisputable.

In this chapter we will not embellish any dates, or make exaggerated claims concerning any culture. We are interested only in the facts about when, why, and how the mysteries appeared from point A to point B. Each culture that we encounter becomes simply the carrier of the tradition, imparting its own mysteries as the teachings are passed along. It is not important, in and of itself, that the players here are Greeks, Etruscans, Romans, or Celts. It is only important in the consideration of what survived, what was connective, and why it was important to human experience in the first place. It is not my desire to elevate any specific culture, or to deny any other its rightful due.

As noted earlier, it is the premise of this book that the mysteries themselves originated in the region of Old Europe and later migrated west from southern Europe, eventually turning north to the British Isles. When the Mystery Tradition was carried into Gaul and Britain by the Romans, the Celts were involved in a mysterious form of worship unique to their own region in many ways. This was a blend of the beliefs of the early Britons mixed together with the Mediterranean Cult of the Dead. Eventually this earlier religion merged with Celtic beliefs, following the Celtic invasion of Britain, and evolved into what we know of these people from Greek and Roman historians.

In time, the headhunting nature of the warlike Celts was transformed under the incoming influence of the peaceful agrarian heirs of the religion of Old Europe. Clearly this came not from Imperial Rome, but from the simple Roman farmers sent into the occupied territories. It was the practice of Rome to turn occupied lands into productive resources for the Empire, passing on the technology of Rome to the indigenous peoples. Along with the mundane techniques of physical labor, Roman farmers also shared their shamanistic beliefs associated with plowing, seeding, and harvesting. Such beliefs are common to any people intimately involved with the cycles of Nature, as farmers would certainly be. These Romans carried into northern Europe not only advanced agricultural techniques, but also a Mystery Tradition inherited from the Neolithic Goddess cult of Old Europe, nurtured and refined over many centuries. This had a dramatic influence on celtic religion, laying the foundation for a Mystery Tradition that later became an integral aspect of Wiccan theology.

In chapter one we noted that the Celts first appear as a distinct people around 700 B.C. (during the Hallstatt period), but they were clearly the descendants of the earlier Urnfield people. The Greek historian Diodorus (first century B.C.) described the Celts as terrifying in appearance, with artificially bleached hair combed back from their foreheads "like wood-demons, their hair thick and shaggy like a horse's mane." He says they wore brightly colored clothes (shirts and trousers) with cloaks bearing designs of stripes or checkered patterns. Their clothing was made of spun wool, for they were not yet an advanced agricultural society capable of producing linen fabrics. The Roman historian Polybius wrote that the Celts of his time possessed unfortified villages with unfurnished homes. They reportedly slept on straw and their diet consisted mainly of meat. Polybius states they valued cattle and gold because these were easily transported and traded, suiting their nomadic lifestyle.

Diodorus and other Greek and Roman historians confirm that the Celts were headhunters and practiced human sacrifice. Strabo relates that the Celts built huge wood and straw enclosures in which they sacrificed humans and animals. The ashes were then spread over fields and poured into bogs as ceremonial offerings. This practice, he writes, was always overseen by "wise-men" known as Druids. Polybius says that the Celts relied on their superior height and "furor" in battle because their swords were made of an inferior metal that bent after the first blow. Author Gerhard Herm (*The Celts—The People Who Came Out of Darkness*) notes that although this was true of the common Celtic soldier, their commanders no doubt possessed swords of excellent quality (such as the one found in the excavations at Hallstatt).

The reported inferior metal work of Celtic weapons described by Polybius is certainly not reflected in the superior craftsmanship of their precious metal work. Although the Greeks and Romans considered the Celts to be uncivilized barbarians, their art work and beautifully colored clothing demonstrate a more cultured people. The Celts also left behind incredible stone work and intricate carvings clearly depicting a technology more advanced than what the Romans perceived. The Celts' love of a good brawl, the practice of headhunting, and their rambunctious style of battle (unsophisticated by Roman standards) no doubt undermined their general status in the eyes of southern Europeans. Since the Greeks and Romans looked down on the Celts as inferior barbarians, very little of their culture was assimilated in the Aegean and Mediterranean regions. Despite this bias perception, the Romans respected the Celts as warriors and did not take them lightly on the battlefield (at least not for long).

Ancient trade routes from northern Italy extended into several Celtic regions to the north and west. The Etruscans traded with the Celts through mountain passes to northern Europe and by sea routes to the southern Iberian coastline. It was through such early contact that the Celts first became aware of southern European religion and culture. Later (around 400 B.C.) the Gauls moved into northern Italy, attracted by the rich resources of the Po Valley. The Etruscans had sophisticated metal mining operations and an advanced agricultural system, both of which drew the Celts southward.

At the time of their arrival the Celtic Gauls were quite different from the people of Italy. They were a pastoral nomadic people organized into tribes, while the Italic peoples lived mainly in towns and cities dependent on agriculture. The Etruscans had already developed complex irrigation systems including reservoirs and artificial underground channels. They were famous in the known world for their techniques of extracting minerals and metal. Close to their mining tunnels they built complexes of smelting ovens that produced great quantities of metal. The Celts occupied a small area of northern Italy for approximately 300 years, absorbing both the technology and religious beliefs of the Etruscans.

The Celts soon began warring with the Etruscans and other peoples of Italy, and in 390 B.C. they even sacked the city of Rome. It wasn't until 82 B.C. that the Roman legions were finally successful in forcing them out of Italy. As the Romans moved on to conquer Gaul, they introduced advanced methods of farming there, designed to supply the growing Roman Empire with additional resources. Romans of all occupations and backgrounds soon followed the Roman Legions, impacting all facets of Celtic life. Essentially this same pattern was applied to the Roman invasion of Britain which soon followed the conquest of Gaul. This was but another step along the trail through which the mysteries were exported from southern Europe.

Although some writers refer to the pre-Roman Celts as an agricultural people, they were not in the true sense of the word. An agricultural society is one whose economy is dependent on farming and whose culture is clearly reflected in the lifestyle necessary for farming to thrive (and typically the religion of the people reflects aspects of their labor). Caesar noted during his invasion of England in 55 B.C. that the Celts possessed small family farmsteads grouped together, devoted to growing cereal grains and raising livestock. Meat was the main staple of the Celts' diet, supplemented by small portions of plant food—most of their crops were raised as food for their herds. Before the Roman era, the Celts were a pastoral people, not an agricultural people. Their culture was based on herding and the nomadic customs typical of a pastoral society. However, under Roman rule Britain was producing in a season up to 600 barge loads of grain for export to the Rhineland where their army was engaged in subduing that population.

In order to understand the Mystery Tradition as it evolved in Britain, we must look at some of the most powerful influences to shape Celtic beliefs in the British Isles: *Eurasian Shamanism, The Cult of the Dead*, the *Fairy Faith, Italian Paganism*, the invasion of the *Kurgan Culture*, and the *Cauldron Mysteries*. As will be demonstrated in this chapter, The Cult of the Dead, the Fairy Faith, and Italian Paganism all stem from southern Europe, and are themselves rooted in the earlier religion of Old Europe as a whole. Eurasian Shamanism is viewed as the basis for certain primitive forms of magick in the Wiccan Mysteries. The Kurgan invasion represents the arrival of patriarchal religion and the subsequent decline of the Goddess religion of Old Europe. Although the invasion predated the arrival of the Celts in Britain, it greatly influenced Celtic theology and therefore we must consider its contagious influence in the British Isles. The Cauldron Mysteries appear much more complex in Celtic beliefs than in other cultures, and may be largely an indigenous Mystery Tradition. Therefore, we shall now independently examine each of these factors.

EURASIAN SHAMANISM

In Carlo Ginzburg's book *Ecstasies: Deciphering the Witches' Sabbath*, we find an interesting connection between the magickal practices of ancient Witchcraft and those of Shamanism in central Europe. According to Ginzburg, their roots can be traced (in order) to the Scythians, Thracians, and the Celts. In all of these cultures we find very similar folk beliefs associated with ecstasy, magickal flight, and animal metamorphosis. These also appear in pre-Etruscan Mediterranean cultures as well. Concerning this, Ginzburg says:

> *To reconstruct the folkloric roots of the witches' Sabbath we set out from the evidence on the ecstatic cult of the nocturnal goddess. Its geographical distribution seemed at first to delimit a Celtic phenomenon. But this interpretation collapsed when confronted by a series of eccentric testimonies of Mediterranean origin. New hypotheses then emerged...beliefs that merged in the stereotype of the Sabbath, were encrusted much more ancient elements...such as the battles fought for the prosperity of the community or the seasonal rites which hinged on animal masquerades....*

The basis of this shamanistic cult was comprised of three elements: the ability to enter into a trance, leave the body in spirit form, and transform into the shape of an animal. More often than not, these practices were designed to engage the shaman in a battle against the forces of decline or decay. Sometimes these techniques were employed to recover a lost soul trapped in the spirit world. It was from such mystical practices that the legends of werewolves and other shapeshifters arose.

Herodotus wrote, as early as the fifth century B.C., of men who could transform themselves into wolves. Such themes are also found in the folklore of Africa, Asia, and all regions of Europe. Witches were also believed to have the power to shapeshift. Transcripts from Witch trials in the fifteenth century contain "confessions" describing how witches changed into wolves (in particular the Valais trials). Ginzburg says that such beliefs have a common origin traceable to the Indo-European peoples. Concerning things of this nature, Ginzburg relates:

> *To the contact between Scythians and Celts in the region of the lower Danube and in central Europe, we might perhaps trace back phenomena otherwise not readily explained, such as the massive presence in Ireland of legends linked to werewolves, the surfacing of shamanistic elements in certain Celtic sagas, the convergences of Ossetian epics with Arthurian romances....*

These are all elements found in Celtic myth and legend from the *Mabinogi* (the Celtic legends) up through the Arthurian texts. Although not native to the British Isles, these shamanistic beliefs influenced Celtic religion in general, and in turn the beliefs of the indigenous peoples after the Celtic invasion of ancient Briton. When the Celts arrived in the British Isles they encountered what is commonly referred to as The Cult of the Dead. The merging of these two cultures resulted in the creation of a religious structure unique to the Insular Celts.

THE CULT OF THE DEAD

From the culture of Old Europe there arose what is now called the Cult of the Dead. It is in this era that we find the emergence of distinctive burial customs, including the custom of placing personal items and tools with the corpse. From these practices we can conclude that early humans envisioned an existence beyond the grave in which the deceased would still require such things. In the earliest archaeological finds, these items are generally weapons or working tools related to the individual's status in the clan. Later we find the addition of jewelry and nonessential personal items such as combs and containers.

The Cult of the Dead produced certain cult objects appearing as universal symbols everywhere it spread and rooted. The main symbol of the cult was the human skull. At the Knowe of Yarso in the Orkney Islands, twenty-nine skulls were found in a neat pile, carefully positioned so that each viewed the passage way leading to the entrance of the tomb. The tomb entrances of this cult were aligned with the position of the moon at the Winter Solstice and both solar and lunar symbols associated with the measurement of time were found in the tombs. Typical also were depictions of serpents, plants, and the mystical forces controlled by goddesses. All of the tomb symbolism addresses the cult belief in the regeneration of life.

This ancient cult spread from southern Europe to the Mediterranean coast of Spain and across to Egypt sometime around 4000 B.C. From Iberia it moved into western Europe and was then carried north into the British Isles. This would have occurred sometime before 3000 B.C., which is when the same symbols appeared in Britain that were found earlier in the Mediterranean region. It is quite interesting to observe how the cult evolved along somewhat different paths as it became isolated in Britain, merging with the ways of the early Britons. In the Mediterranean it blended with ancient matrifocal practices and eventually faded into the religious fabric of Goddess worship. In Britain the cult became something of a separate patriarchal cult and was eventually overseen by Druid priests and priestesses.

The Celtic practice of head hunting is rooted in the Cult of the Dead's belief system. The severed head was symbolic of protection and regeneration, which is why the skulls always faced the opening of the tomb. The tomb's entrance represented the vaginal opening; the passage way symbolized the birth canal (from the Underworld). Therefore, skulls were also associated with fertility, which is why the Celts placed them upon pillars, forming a phallus-like symbol. In Celtic mythology we often find tales of severed heads associated with heroes and gods. One story in particular relates how Bran ordered that his head be buried in a certain location (facing Gaul), and that as long as it remained there no army could ever invade.

One aspect of the Cult of the Dead, unique to western and northern Europe, appears in the practice of "whitening the bones" prior to their placement within a tomb. Essentially, the corpse was left out to be picked clean by the birds. This is how the raven came to be associated with death in Celtic European folklore. The raven is also connected with battles, due to the many corpses lying on the field. Some warrior tribes in northern Europe were known to have carried a blood-red banner embellished with the image of a raven. This served as a warning to their enemies that soon the raven would clean their bones.

Another bird associated with death in Celtic Europe is the owl. Spiral symbols are often employed in owl motifs because of the circular patterns of their feathers, especially around the eyes. In *The Language of the Goddess* by Marija Gimbutas is a photo of a tomb with spiral symbols. The tomb, in Newgrange, Ireland, dates to around 3000 B.C. Also in the book is a drawing of a tomb at Castel-lucio, in southeastern Sicily on which this same motif appears.

The spiral itself symbolizes many things other than owls, including serpents and mystical forces. It is one of the symbols we find present everywhere we find the Cult of the Dead. Another aspect of the Cult's influence on Celtic religion were those tenets involving the spirit world. It was believed that the souls of the dead waited around for a chance to be reborn into the physical world. These spirits had to be appeased so that they would not manipulate the living or cause an early death. To this end, certain offerings were made and various ceremonies performed. This is all connected to the folklore of fairies and changelings, and to primitive beliefs concerning how souls were reborn. So let us turn now and examine the ancient beliefs of the Fairy Faith.

THE FAIRY FAITH

In the book *The Fairies in English Tradition and Literature* (University of Chicago Press, 1967), by K. M. Briggs, President of the English Folklore Society, who holds a doctorate on folklore from Oxford University, the author tells us that the earliest mention of fairies of any kind in England occurs in the Anglo-Saxon charms against elf-shot (from the *Anglo-Saxon Chronicles* circa A.D. 800). In chapter twenty of her book Briggs acknowledges that some fairies may have come into Celtic belief from Roman mythology and not from classical literature. We also learn in *The Fairy Faith in Celtic Countries*, by W. Y. Evans-Wentz (who also holds a doctorate in folklore from Oxford) that the words *fatua, fata* (respectively Greek and Roman for fairy) and *fee* (English for fairy) are all the same word. In this book we read in chapter three: "...the race of immortal damsels whom the old natives of Italy called *Fatuae* gave origin to all the family of fees...."

In the thirteenth-century manuscript *Lancelot du Lac* (Lancelot of the Lake) we find *Nimue*, the Lady of the Lake. The unknown author of this work calls the lake "The Lake of Diana" and refers to Diana as a Queen who reigned in Sicily before the time of Virgil. He says that the peasants believed her to be a Goddess, and that

she loved the woodlands where she was worshipped by the hea-
thens. The Medieval Sicilian Fairy Cult is well documented by the
Spanish Inquisition, and is linked to the goddess Diana, who the
Italians have long called "The Queen of the Fairies." Diana, in turn,
was worshipped in Italy at Lake Nemi where her temple once stood
(rebuilt around 500 B.C. on the site of her earlier temple). As noted
by Frazer in *The Golden Bough*, this ancient lake was called *Diana's
Mirror* by the Romans because the reflection of the full moon could
be seen on its surface from the temple. In the book *Ladies of the Lake*
(Aquarian Press, 1992), by Caitlin and John Matthews, we find that
Diana is associated with Nimue who had a consort named *Faunus*.
We also find that Nimue's father was Dionas whose name is curi-
ously close to Dianus.

The earliest origins for the stereotypical image of the fairy in
Western culture are in ancient Mediterranean art. The winged
creatures of the spirit world were first portrayed in ancient tomb
paintings. The earliest depiction of fairies as small winged beings
appeared in Etruscan art around 600 B.C., in the form of the *Lasa*,
who were spirits of the fields and forests. Images of fairies in Celtic
art do not appear until well after the rise of Christianity, following
the Roman occupation. Etruscan art also depicts the Lasa in
human size, usually when in the company of a god or goddess. The
small-winged Lasa are almost always pictured with humans and
typically hover over a container of incense or an offering bowl.
The Lasa were also associated with ancestor worship, and are
found in Etruscan shrines (a practice linking them with the ancient
Cult of the Dead). This is also true of the spirits known as *Lare*,
whom the Romans later absorbed and modified from Etruscan
Lasa beliefs.

The Mediterranean Cult of the Dead left its fairy imprint on
the Etruscan culture of Italy. We first see this in the Etruscan
story of Tages. As the legend goes, several farmers were preparing
to till a field when from out of the soil appeared a small elven-like
being who called himself Tages. Tages presented them with the
sacred teachings on which Etruscan religion was then established.
After this he seemingly died and disappeared back into the depths
of the earth.

A Lasa Figure
Drawing based on Etruscan art, circa 600 B.C.
(Illustration from *Etruscan Magic & Occult Remedies* by Charles Leland, 1895.)

It is in the Etruscan mythos that we encounter fairy creatures known as Lasa. These fairies are associated with vegetation and the secrets of Nature. In art they are depicted nude and winged, carrying a small vial of elixir. The liquid in the vials could produce any of three results. One drop could heal any malady, two drops opened the eyes to the secrets of Nature, and three drops transformed matter into spirit or spirit into matter. Such transformations were necessary in order to pass from the fairy world into the physical world and vice versa. Similar concepts also appear later in Celtic fairy legends.

Every European culture has a folklore involving mystical beings known as fairies. Sometimes they are viewed as benevolent and sometimes they are seen as creators of mischief. Although the beliefs concerning fairies do differ from culture to culture, there are two basic concepts universal in all fairy beliefs: the distortion of time itself, and the hidden entrances to the fairy world. These themes are more prominent in Celtic mythology. The "trooping" of fairies appears in Celtic legends and also in the Fairy Cult of Sicily. It does not, however, appear to have been an Etruscan mythos. However, the trooping of fairies is quite common in Italian folklore today.

In the book *Early Modern European Witchcraft* (Oxford Univ. Press, 1990), edited by Bengt Ankarloo and Gustav Henningsen, we find a chapter devoted to the Medieval Fairy Cult in Sicily. The chapter describes this cult as being comprised of an odd number of individuals, headed by a Queen. She bears such titles as *La Matrons* (the Mother), *La Maestra* (the Teacher), and *Dona Zabella* (The Wise Sybil). Sicilian fairies formed groups called companies, such as the *Company of Nobles* and the *Company of Poor*. These fairies had the power to bless fields, cure illnesses, and bestow good fortune. If ill treated, however, they were also capable of causing harm. Only after offerings were made to appease the fairies would they release the offender from their enchantment. Both humans and fairies belonged to "companies" that were essentially matriarchal (although some males were included). Only the human women could free an offender from a fairy spell, and they were highly revered among the peasantry.

Common to fairies of all regions is the belief in the distortion
of time. A night spent in a fairy realm often translated into several
years in mortal time. Secret entrances always guarded access to
these realms and were often found in mounds or tree trunks.
Fairies were believed to have a strong aversion to iron, and this
metal was used as a protection against them when the need arose.
Some folklorists feel that this legend is symbolic of the use of iron
to plow fields and fell trees, all of which addressed the power of
humans to assault Nature. Thus, to the fairies iron was an abomination. One legend tells us that when entering a fairy realm, the
person should stick a piece of iron in the door to prevent it from
closing. The fairies will not touch the iron, and thus cannot prevent the person from leaving at their will.

A Lasa Hovering Over an Ofering Bowl.
Etruscan art circa 600 B.C.
(Illustration from *Etruscan Magic & Occult Remedies* by Charles Leland, 1895.)

In the Cult of the Dead, wells, bogs, and all openings in the ground were considered sacred passages into the spirit world. These sites were often marked as sacred by erecting standing stones or stone enclosures at their location. This was especially true if the offering site was known to be effective for bringing about the desired results. This is why we find Celtic offerings in such places as bogs, pits, and wells. Many sacred stone sites of Britain were erected by the Mediterranean Iberians, whom historians refer to as the brown-skinned builders of the dolmens. As we have said earlier, these were the people who brought the Cult of the Dead to the British Isles. The burial mounds of Old Europe, connected to the Cult of the Dead, were also imported to the Celtic lands and eventually evolved into fairy mounds (see chapter thirteen).

The invading Celts appear to have originally feared the Cult in Britain, as noted by Lewis Spence in his book *The Mysteries of Britain* (Newcastle Publishing, 1993). Their main concern appears to be connected with Druidic practices associated with the souls of the dead. The Druids came to be revered by the Celts because these priests and priestesses knew how to control the spirit world through ritual and offerings. These practices evolved into the Sabbat known as Samhain or All Hallows, when food offerings were set out for a feast to honor the spirits of the dead. This practice from the Cult of the Dead still exists today in Sicily and the British Isles.

To partake of offered food is to enter into a relationship with those who offer it—a most ancient aspect of human culture still in use today. To invite someone to have dinner with us, or to be invited, has less to do with eating than it does with relationships. In the case of spirits it is the etheric substance of the food that is being offered and consumed. We see this reflected in the writings of Porphyry from ancient Roman times. He tells us that all gods and spirits enjoy as "nourishment" the odor of burnt offerings. It is the essence and not the substance that is important in an offering. By offering food to the spirits of the dead, the Cult of the Dead remained on good terms with them.

As mentioned earlier, fairies were originally thought to be souls of the departed. It wasn't until much later in the Cult of the Dead that they became associated with the elemental kingdoms of Nature. It was believed that the souls of the dead could enter into a living human and possess him or her. Out of this concept arose the tale of fairy changelings left in the crib of a human infant. Concerning the relationship between fairies and human souls, Lewis Spence writes:

> *The belief in the sidhe or fairies, the dead awaiting a return to mortal life, was essentially a feature of Druidic belief, as early Irish and later Welsh literature shows, and this in itself suffices to demonstrate that Druidism was a Cult of the Dead. How far the idea of the sidhe was Keltic and how far aboriginal or Iberian is a problem the answer to which is not far to seek, for we find the sidhe constantly associated with burial chambers in Ireland and Scotland which were originally of Iberian or "aboriginal" origin. That they were accepted and used as Keltic and Druidic burial-places is certain enough, indeed they were probably employed in many cases as graves by successive generations in Ireland and Britain for centuries, as excavation has abundantly proved.*

The Celts were quite aware of the mystical relationship between humans and Nature, and had a strong belief in the spirit world, evidenced by the many offerings found in archaeological excavations. We also know from ancient Greek and Roman historians that the Druids were well respected for their knowledge in such areas. In fact, Mediterranean historians of the time stated that the Druids possessed such a high degree of occult knowledge that they were surpassed only by the Etruscans. The Druids guided the Celts in these matters and maintained a mutually beneficial relationship with the Fairy Kingdom.

In later folklore a great many tales remind us to always acknowledge the good deeds performed by fairies. It was believed that fairies could both help and harm human beings. Therefore it was always important to thank them for good fortune. Out of this mentality arose the practice of saying "knock on wood" when speaking of one's good fortune. This was an acknowledgment that the woodland fairies were being kind. If a person failed to do so, the fairies could withdraw their aid, with disastrous results.

There exists today a predisposition to connect the Tuatha De Danaan with the Fairy Kingdom in Celtic lore. This is due, in part, to their mystical origins and disappearance in the British Isles. Legend tells us that the Tuatha De Danaan came from out of the mist when they arrived in the British Isles. Here they encountered the Fir Bolg people and defeated them in battle. Later, when the Celts invaded Britain (600–500 B.C.), the Tuatha De Danaan disappeared into the hills and forests. Some people believe that this is the origin of the belief that fairies dwell in rural areas. We know historically that at least as far back as 600 B.C. the Mediterranean people held such beliefs, as evidenced in Etruscan/Roman mythology and art.

Two problems are encountered when trying to connect Celtic lore with ancient origins and historical references. First, the Celts left behind no written record of their beliefs or mythology. Much of what is known comes from Greek and Roman historians. The Celtic myths and legends we do know about were passed along through the Bardic tradition of singing stories. The second problem is that while these Bardic tales were finally recorded in writing, it was not until around the fourteenth century A.D. that the task was completed. How much was added, modified, or deleted over the centuries no one can know.

The tales of Celtic myth are now largely preserved in such texts as the *Mabinogi*, the *White Book of Rhyderch* (1300–1325), and the *Red Book of Hergest* (1375–1425). Some scholars believe that these texts were based on fragmented manuscripts dating back several centuries earlier (circa A.D. 1100). The tremendous impact of Romanization followed by Christianity no doubt heavily modified the public writings we have today. It is highly unlikely that the Christian monks who set these Bardic tales in writing felt any loyalty to Pagan traditions, and since there are no original documents to compare against we can only speculate about the accuracy of their written accounts. Clearly their goal was to convert Pagans to

Christianity, and not to preserve Paganism. This was accomplished through such techniques as associating Saints with Pagan symbolism and festival dates, as well as constructing cathedrals upon ancient sites of worship.

THE KURGAN/INDO-EUROPEAN INVASION

The Old Religion in northern Europe differs from that of the Mediterranean due largely to the impact of the Indo-European invasions of Europe. One of the main invading forces, according to Gimbutas, were the Kurgans. They were a war-like pastoral society who rode horses and possessed ox-drawn wagons. Most scholars agree that they came out of the Volga-Ural region and spread quickly into eastern and central Europe. It is commonly believed that the Indo-European expansion covered a period from 4000 to 2000 B.C. and encompassed a vast region, including parts of northern Italy and southeastern Europe. With their appearance in Old Europe, we see a drastic decline in the indigenous goddess images, along with a rapid disintegration of fine ceramic work.

Gimbutas tells us that the Kurgans were responsible for the collapse of the matrifocal religion of Old Europe. In the book *In Search of the Indo-Europeans* (Thames & Hudson, 1991), by J. P. Mallory, we find partial confirmation of this, as he speaks of the Kurgans as a warrior society whose religion was focused on warlike sky-gods and sun worship. As the Kurgans spread across Europe, there is an abrupt decline in the Goddess cult indigenous to the invaded territories. Symbols of the axe, spear, arrow, and dagger begin to appear upon stone stellae erected by the Kurgans. Along with these symbols we find the sign of the new religion, the sun.

As we noted earlier in this book, Gimbutas tells us that the Mediterranean area withstood the invading patriarchal influences to a much later date than did other regions of Europe. She states that by 2500 B.C. the Kurgans had thoroughly transformed the Neolithic Goddess religion in central Europe. Gimbutas tells us that the Goddess religion in the Mediterranean flourished for another 1500 years after its demise in central Europe. This creates another problem for us in associating the Celts with the ancient

Goddess Mysteries that became Wicca. The Celts originated in central Europe, rising as a culture over a thousand years after the Indo-European patriarchal transformation of the Goddess religion. Therefore, once again we must turn to southern Europe in our quest for the Mysteries of Wicca.

ITALIAN PAGANISM

It is important to understand the Pagan beliefs from Italy when speaking of the Wiccan Mysteries because of the conquest and long Roman occupation of Celtic lands. The Romans shaped the beliefs and practices of those they conquered not only by use of the sword, but also by influencing their religious practices. This is one of the reasons the Romans identified foreign gods of a similar nature as their own, so that Roman beliefs could be introduced into the foreign cults. Share things in common with an enemy and you make a friend or ally.

Prior to the rise of the Etruscan civilization, the inhabitants of Italy were a mosaic of people distinct in origin, language, and cultural development. They consisted of ethnic groups at different stages of development. Among the main groups were the Latins, Sabines, Samnites, Etrusci, and Umbrians. Despite their lack of unity, the groups had in common many of the Neolithic beliefs of the Great Goddess cult. The insular territories of Sicily, Sardinia, and Corsica are keys to understanding the adaptations that later developed on the mainland due to the influence of other cultures such as the Greeks, Phoenicians, and Carthaginians.

In the book *Roman and European Mythologies*, compiled by Yves Bonnefoy, we find an interesting passage concerning the survival of prehistoric beliefs among the ancient peoples of Italy:

> *...traces survived of primitive conceptions and practices so distant from the rationality of the classical world that they sometimes provoked the astonishment and incomprehension of writers in the Hellenistic and Roman periods. Most striking are the suggestions of an animistic conception of the supernatural; the omnipresent importance of divine signs and divination; the high*

social and religious status of women (in Etruria and even in early Rome), which have been interpreted as survivals of matriarchy, and the tenacious belief in the material survival of the dead in their place of burial, and all the rites implied in such a belief (house-shaped urns and tombs, portrait images, rich funerary apparatus, funeral games, etc.).

The Etruscans appear in Italy around 1000 B.C. and according to Gimbutas are the heirs of the surviving remnants of the Neolithic Great Goddess religion. Some scholars have theorized that the Etruscans were not indigenous to Italy, but were an Indo-European people. However, a linguistics study of the 10,000 inscriptions left by the Etruscans has convinced the majority of linguists that these people were not Indo-Europeans. In the book *In Search of the Indo-Europeans* (Mallory), the author writes:

Nevertheless, the present tendency in Etruscan research is to adopt the most economical thesis: the Etruscans were a non-Indo-European people native to Italy who adopted many items and styles of east Mediterranean provenance by way of trade.

The Etruscans believed in the ultimate power of supernatural forces. The central focus of their religious beliefs was on the relationship between humans and a host of deities. All acts of Nature were seen as initiated by a god or a spirit and had to be discerned. Therefore a special class of priests developed to interpret various signs and omens for the people (not unlike the Celtic Druids who later appeared in western and Northern Europe). The Roman historian Seneca commented on the mystical nature of the Etruscans by saying that the Romans believed that lightning is emitted because clouds collide, but the Etruscans believed that clouds collide in order for lightning to be emitted. They believed that lightning only appeared when there was something the gods wished to indicate to humankind.

Connected to the belief in the power of omens and signs is the ancient myth of the animal guide or ancestor. This prehistoric concept was widespread throughout Italy and remained linked to pastoralism and transhumance as evidenced in the archaeological studies of the Apennine Bronze Age. The early nomadics of Italy believed they were guided by an animal spirit.

For example, the Piceni tribe believed their guide was a woodpecker, the Sabellians a bull, the Lucani a wolf, and the Ursenti a bear. The people of this era practiced a custom known as *Ver Sacrum*, the "sacred Springtime." This required a portion of each tribe to leave and settle in another area each spring. This is one of the reasons the animal guide was important to such a pastoral-nomadic people.

With the rise of agriculture, the spirits of meadows and forests were transformed into spirits of the plowed and seeded fields. These were the Lasa spirits, and later the Lare spirits which we encountered earlier in our discussion of fairies.

The Etruscans further developed and refined these early pagan beliefs, creating a mystical and magickal tradition famous throughout the classical world. They worshipped the Great Mother Goddess Uni and her consort Tinia. These deities oversaw a host of spirits and demi-gods who wielded power over the forces of Nature and human destiny. The pantheon of the Etruscans was not unlike the Olympic gods of Greece, although they worshipped another set of gods who were above them. These gods were called the Involuti or *gods of the mists* (the Tuatha de Danaan are also said to have appeared from out of the mist). The names of these particular deities have never been discovered, nor have any myths been associated with them. In time the Romans would absorb the Etruscan civilization and carry off the ancient beliefs of the Great Goddess cult into Gaul and the British Isles.

THE CAULDRON MYSTERIES

Cauldrons play a principal role in Celtic mythology and are connected to themes of *Quest*. There is almost an obsession with the cauldron among the Celts, and this mythos later appears in the Arthurian legends connected with the Quest for the Holy Grail. The cauldron also appears in other European myths and is found in several Witchcraft traditions from Britain to the Mediterranean.

Among the Celts, however, it often seems to represent something lost or just out of reach within the Celtic psyche. Almost without exception their cauldron myths are tales of Quest and Transformation. The cauldron itself is almost always located in a distant mysterious castle or a secret realm.

I offer here a personal theory on why this may be the case. First, we know that cauldrons represent the womb of the goddess in European Witchcraft. Second, we know that the Great Goddess cult in Celtic Europe was transformed by the patriarchal Indo-Europeans centuries before the emergence of a people identifiable as Celts. Third, we know that the Celts had early contact with the Greeks, Etruscans, and Romans, all of whom still worshipped the Neolithic Great Goddess of Old Europe in one form or another. The continental Celts by comparison appear to have worshipped primarily goddesses of war.

I suggest that the Celts somehow recognized this former element of their own spirituality within the Great Goddess-based religions of southern Europe (perhaps from remaining fragments of her earlier Cult). Something within the Celtic soul awoke to the ancient memory of the Goddess who once reigned supreme in central Europe before the Kurgan/Indo-European invasion. Thus, for the Celts, the quest to reclaim the cauldron was born. I believe there is a connection here between the warrior/knight who must seek out and find the grail. Perhaps this mythos arose from a need to reconcile the nature of the aggressive Celtic warrior with that of the comparatively peaceful Agrarian worshipper of the Great Goddess. After all, the early Celtic deities were gods *and* goddesses of war and death. The Mother goddess herself is not historically traceable in Celtic religion prior to contact with the peoples of the Mediterranean (see chapter three).

One problem we encounter in this theory is connected with the Tuatha de Danaan. These are the children of the Goddess Dana, and in the Celtic pantheon she is a Mother Goddess. The Tuatha de Danann are described, in Celtic mythology, as an advanced people with superior weapons. Bardic tradition would seem to date the myth of the Tuatha de Danaan prior to Roman contact; legends claim they were already in Britain when the Celts invaded. This appears to contradict the statement by author Miranda Green (*Symbol & Image*) that the Mother Goddess is not traceable in Celtic religion before the Roman era, although as we investigate further it becomes evident that the Bardic timeframe is simply off by several centuries. This is not surprising, however, because Celtic myths and legends were never intended as literal historical or chronological events (although many are intentionally based on actual incidents or individuals). They serve as cultural memories of ancient deeds and heroes, some real and some symbolic.

One indication of the nonhistorical accuracy of mythic history is found in the legend of the Tuatha de Danaan themselves. Among this race we find Govannon (in Britain) or Goibniu (in Ireland) who was the god of the forge, supplying his people with the necessary weapons of war and self-defense. However, he was also the god who brewed the *beer that confers immortality*. As we noted in chapter three, beer was not brewed in the British Isles (or in Gaul) until after the Roman occupation. Tacitus dates the brewing of beer in Britain to around A.D. 100 when it was introduced by the Roman armies. The Irish credit Goibniu as the architect of the high round towers, which did not appear until well after the Roman era. The inclusion of a god of beer in the mythos of the Tuatha de Danaan may be a later addition to an older myth. Likewise it is possible that the Mother Goddess may have also been added at a later date, displacing or modifying an earlier deity (most likely a warrior goddess).

In the book *The Druids*, by Ward Rutherford (Gordon & Cremonesi, 1978), we find an association between the Irish goddess Dana and the Mediterranean goddess Diana. The author notes a connection between the prefix of both names (indicating divinity); Dana is D-ana and Diana is Di-ana. The name Diana is derived from the Latin *Diviana* (the literal translation would be "the divine Ana," and Dana would translate as "the goddess Ana"). Diana was a mother goddess in Ephesus and at Nemi, as was Dana among the Irish. Even in her chaste aspect (inherited from Artemis) Diana was a goddess to whom offerings were made for an easy childbirth. This practice recalls her earlier aspect as a mother goddess, and she was also known as Diana Triformis: maiden, mother, and crone.

Robert Graves, in his book *The White Goddess* (Farrar, Straus & Giroux, 1974), maintains that the Tuatha de Danaan were Bronze Age Pelasgians who worshipped the Greek goddess Danae. According to Janet and Stewart Farrar, in *The Witches' Goddess* (Phoenix Publishing, 1987), this coincides with Irish tradition as reflected in the *Lebor Gabala Erenn*. It is also interesting to note that the word "Danaan" was a term used for all the Greeks (from Rhoda Hendrick's book *Classical Gods and Heroes: Myths as Told by the Ancient Authors*, Morrow Quill Paperbacks, 1974). Robert Graves (*The White Goddess*) uses the spelling "danaan" (Tuatha de Danaan) for the race. The contemporary usage is Tuatha de Danann.

The Italian people worshipped Diana as early as 500 B.C. and passed on her mystery cult under this name. The Roman Dianic cult was influenced by the earlier Etruscan goddess Atimite and the Greek and Ephesian Artemis. The Latin name Diana would have been employed in Britain over the course of almost 400 years of Roman rule. Logically it would have been in common usage when the Bardic tales were first set down in writing. Therefore what we may have here is an ancient Bardic account of the arrival of an advanced people who worshipped a Mediterranean/Aegean goddess. We know historically that, at a much earlier date, the civilizations of the Mediterranean were more technologically advanced than those of northern and western Europe (which would explain the superior weapons of the Tuatha de Danaan). If what I propose is accurate, then it is possible that the Tuatha de Danaan were actually a Dianic-like cult who migrated to the British Isles from the Mediterranean or Aegean region. Diana is Queen of the Fairies in Italian mythology, and the Tuatha de Danaan are associated with the origins of fairies in Celtic mythology.

Most myths depict the Tuatha de Danaan as a race from the north who settled in the British Isles. This, of course, is in direct conflict with what I have proposed. However, it is not surprising that post-Roman Bardic tales would disassociate the Tuatha de Danaan with anything connected with southern Europe (Roman rule having been something less than welcome). In addition, the north is a place of great power in Celtic cosmology and it is not unlikely that this association is simply designed to identify the race with a place of mystical power. Also, the Tuatha de Danaan did not appear in any traceable source until the eleventh century A.D. in such Irish texts as *The Four Branches of Mabinogion* and *The Book of Invasions*. In any event, if what I suggest is correct, then it only means that the mythical history of the Insular Celts is simply what the term itself denotes, and is largely unrelated to any historical chronology. This, in turn, would explain why the Mother Goddess seemingly appears in Celtic mythology prior to the arrival of the Romans.

Transformations of all kinds are an integral part of Celtic mythology, whether it occurs with names, heroes, events, or settings. At the center of this mystical element we find tales of various cauldrons associated with certain deities or heroes. In the Mystery Tradition there are three particular types of cauldrons: the Cauldron of Transformation, the Cauldron of Rejuvenation (or Rebirth), and the Cauldron of Inspiration. In the Wiccan Mysteries the cauldron of Cerridwen symbolizes the joining of all three aspects into one cauldron. Cerridwen is a Celtic moon goddess who, in modern times, possesses the three aspects of Diana: Maiden, Mother, Crone.

In Celtic mythology the cauldron is associated with various aspects of the Mystery Tradition. These are: abundance, rebirth, transformation, germination, and womb symbolism (as in womb of the Goddess). It is also employed to represent the powers of the Other World, symbolized as the Cauldron of Annwn. Annwn is the Welsh Underworld, the abode of departed souls. In *The Spoils of Annwn*, composed by the Bard Taliesin, a group of adventurers descend into Annwn to recover the cauldron of Pwll (the Lord of Annwn). The cauldron is located in Caer Sidi or Caer Pedryan, the four-cornered castle. Symbolically this is the meeting place of the four elements of creation, existing in stable harmony as reflected in the castle structure itself.

This legend is the basis for the Arthurian quest for the Holy Grail. The ancient lunar cauldron of the Goddess was transformed by the patriarchy into a solar symbol, the chalice used by Christ at the Last Supper. Very little of its mystical symbolism was changed however, and it is still a symbol of enlightenment and spiritual transformation. As I stated earlier, what is unique to the Celtic

Tradition is the elusiveness of the Cauldron/Grail. In the Mediterranean Traditions the cauldron appears in this world, and even in the case of Hecate the cauldron could be accessed through a cave. The magickal cauldrons of Circe, Medea, and Demeter/Persephone (in the Eleusinian Mysteries), although associated with the powers of the Other World, were tangible in the physical dimension. Symbolically they were the connective vessel between the worlds from which potions, spells, and miracles issued forth.

Another aspect unique to the Celts is found in the use of the cauldron as a symbol of nourishment. In various legends it is told that the cauldron would not boil meat for a coward, and in some accounts not for a liar. It was said that such a person could not even approach the cauldron without great risk to their very lives. The role of personal virtue becomes an essential element in the Grail legends appearing later in northern Europe (see chapter fourteen). Here it is linked to the transformation of the warrior/knight. All of these aspects of the cauldron mysteries are covered in further detail in chapter twelve.

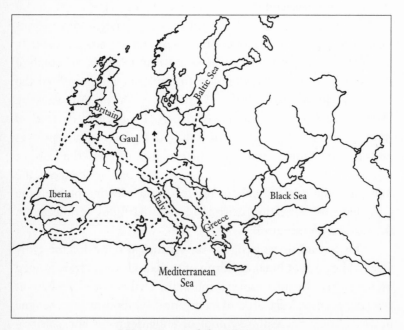

Migrations of the Mysteries

MYSTERY ROOTS TIMELINE

DATES	EVENTS
6500 B.C.	Beginning stages of food production and village formations in the Aegean and Mediterranean.
6000 B.C.	First temples in the Aegean region. Full-fledged Neolithic culture in the Aegean and Mediterranean, producing pottery, cultivating wheat, barley and other crops. Villages of mudbrick and timber.
5000 B.C.	Sacred script emerges for use in religious cults.
4200 B.C.	Mediterranean Iberians migrate to Britain and the Cult of the Dead becomes rooted in the British Isles.
4000 B.C.	Neolithic culture of Old Europe producing painted pottery, tombs cut in rock, and religious shrines. Voyagers from Sicily and southern Italy known as the people of Partholon settle in Ireland. They introduce crude, primitive farming to the island.
3500 B.C.	Transformation begins from Matrifocal cults to Patriarchal systems in central Europe. Demonstrated by a reduction in Old European matrifocal figurines and art work. Matrifocal cults still flourishing in the Mediterranean and western Europe. Court tombs and passage graves appear in Britain and Ireland.
3000 B.C.	Temples, subterranean tombs and tomb-shrines appear on the Mediterranean islands of Malta and Sardinia.
2500 B.C.	Minoan Civilization maintains Mystery Teachings of the Great Goddess Neolithic Cult. Cult no longer exists in central Europe.
2000 B.C.	Greek Civilization inherits Mystery Cult from Minoans.

DATES	EVENTS
1000 B.C.	– Etruscan Civilization inherits Greek aspects of Mystery Tradition religion and blends with indigenous beliefs of the Neolithic Great Goddess Cult in Italy.
700 B.C.	– Romans begin to absorb Greek and Etruscan elements. Hesiod's Theogony addresses the concept of three worlds in the creation mythos, and instructs farmers on the Mystery Teachings.
600 B.C.	– Lasa/fairy images appear in Etruscan art as small winged beings with magickal powers.
525 B.C.	– Pythagoreans establish School of Mysteries in southern Italy (Crotona).
400 B.C.	– Celts invade northern Italy and come into contact with the surviving elements of the religion of Old Europe.
155 B.C.	– Greek philosopher Critolaus formally introduces Greek philosophy in Rome.
50 B.C.	– Romans carry the Mystery Teachings into Gaul.
43 A.D.	– Romans carry the Mystery Teachings into Britain.
150 A.D.	– Celts conquered by the Romans. Roman farmers spread the Mystery Teachings of Old Europe among the common Celtic people.
410 A.D.	– Romans withdraw from Britain. Celts blend Mediterranean beliefs with indigenous beliefs. Clans spread Romanized Celtic religion throughout the British Isles.
600 A.D.	– First written Mystery texts appear among the Celts by this date, attributed to such poet/bards as Taliesin.

CHAPTER
TWELVE

THE MYSTERY
TRADITION

*We have not even to risk the adventure alone.
For the heroes of all time have gone before us.
The labyrinth is thoroughly known. We have
only to follow the thread of the heroe path. And
where we had thought to find an abomination we
shall find a god. And where we had thought to
slay another we shall slay ourselves. Where we
had thought to travel outward we shall come to
the center of our own existence. Where we had
thought to be alone we shall be with all the
world.*

—Joseph Campbell,
The Hero with a Thousand Faces

To early humans the world around them was a total mystery, and they themselves were a part of that mystery. Each day a hot sphere of light arose from below the horizon and darkness departed. Later the light sank beneath the horizon and darkness returned again. In the night sky appeared an even more mysterious sphere of light, changing its shape as the nights passed, only to disappear and once again return. Among themselves, humans were also caught up in mysterious events. Women's bellies occasionally swelled like the shape of the moon and from their bodies there issued forth another human being.

Out of the earth, plants would spring up, but where were they coming from? Frightening sounds occasionally pounded the heavens, sudden streaks of light flashed about, and water would fall down from the sky. The ground itself would shake and rumble and everything seemed at the mercy of some mysterious force. As humans began to seek out the causes of these events, a pattern of relationships within Nature came into human consciousness. They did not yet understand how a seed became a plant, for example, but they knew that burying one led to the eventual appearance of another. The key to the mysteries was close at hand, and the early shamans guarded these powerful secrets of Nature.

The word "mystery" is derived from the Greek verb *myein* meaning "to close" and refers to closing one's lips as in remaining silent. It can also refer to closing one's eyes, which is reflected in the use of a blindfold in the first degree initiation ceremonies of many Wiccan traditions. The removal of the blindfold opens the eyes of the initiate to behold the sacred tools and symbols of Wicca, highlighted by the flickering candles and accented by the magickal fragrance of burning incense. This action imprints upon the initiate's psyche and serves to activate the dormant psychic nature sleeping within the subconscious mind. The Wiccan Mysteries are often discussed in modern times and just as often misunderstood. Today many people associate to the mysteries aspects of Wicca that in fact have little, if anything, to do with a Mystery Tradition. In this chapter we will explore the inner teachings of Wicca rooted in the Mystery Tradition of Old Europe. Where there is a definite relationship we will also include certain aspects of the Oriental Mystery Tradition, essentially because of the Universal "Truths" contained in all esoteric teachings.

It is in the Mystery Tradition that an individual comes to discover his or her own role within the Wiccan spiritual path. The experiences and teachings of those who have gone before form what is often called *the well-worn path*. Where the path ends is the threshold through which the individual must pass, and from there discern his or her own place in the Universe. This is the quest that one must make to obtain enlightenment, and to gain liberation from the Cycle of Rebirth.

As human beings, we are creatures who are naturally gregarious. The need to belong within a family, tribe, or clan is part of our nature. We are healthiest when we are part of a loving and supporting group (however one wishes to define it). Yet within ourselves there is also a striving toward self-fulfillment. The Mystery Tradition exists to teach individuals how their individuality can serve not only themselves but the group as well. It is a map by which a person can come to realize his or her full potential.

Essentially the mysteries can be divided up into two main aspects. First is the understanding of the inner mechanisms within Nature. To this category would belong such knowledge as the inner teachings of magick, rituals, spell casting, divination, and so forth. Second is the understanding of the soul and its relationship to Divinity and the Universe. In this category we would place things like personal power, the Cycle of Rebirth, personal enlightenment, the gods, astral dimensions, the Three-Fold Law, the journey of the soul, the Summerland, and others.

Before we can begin to grasp the Mystery Tradition, we must understand its origins in order to comprehend the mentality from which the Mystery Teachings themselves arose. It is essential to always consider the cultural aspects of any teaching in order to fully understand its application. This is one reason for the problems encountered today in religions such as Christianity, because the majority of Christians know little if anything about the times in which Jesus taught. Therefore the context of his teachings is wide open to misinterpretation and misunderstanding.

To avoid this in the Wiccan Mysteries we must look back to the cultural flavoring of our tradition, from which we can discern the context of the teachings and their relevance for us today. Once we understand the old ways as well as the mentality that produced and maintained them, then we can apply the teachings to ourselves. Thus we walk the well-worn path that leads to the beginning of our own *spirit quest*.

MENTALITY OF THE OLD WAYS

The ancients believed that all physical objects contained magickal or mystical power. The divine spark of the Creator(s) dwelled within everything on the earth. From this basic tenet we view crystals, stones, herbs, feathers, and such as *objects of power*. The world of Nature appeared ordered and cyclical—something sentient was clearly at work. Observing cause and effect in Nature, humans concluded that something Conscious was involving itself in the environment. All life was connected and interdependent, thus humankind had to determine its own relationship to Nature. This led to belief in the value of offerings, prayers, chants, and ritual observances of the seasons of Nature.

Omens were quite important to ancient peoples. They believed that the gods revealed things through the actions of certain creatures, the appearance of natural phenomena, or the sudden manifestation of storms. It is from this tenet that we accept the role of *synchronicity* within our lives. This is when many things connect us together with another person or event, seemingly running a parallel course to our own lives or actions.

Signs and omens from the gods came also in the sudden appearance of a specific bird. Birds were particularly magickal because of their ability to fly; thus they were associated with the gods who dwelled in the heavens. Some of the earliest Neolithic deities were depicted as part human and part bird. Later their images evolved into birds that accompanied a goddess or a god. In Teutonic lore we find Odin or Woden and his ravens. There are also Athena and the owl, Diana and the stag or hound, Blodeuwedd and the owl, Epona and the horse, Morrigan and the raven, along with a host of others. This aspect of Paganism is also linked to the belief in an animal guide or guardian—in turn this is associated with the witches' familiar. All of these aspects serve to link humankind with the Source of Divine power itself.

Magick, as a Wiccan tenet, originates from Paleolithic and Neolithic times. The effects of consuming certain plants containing psychotropic elements or poisons would certainly have appeared magickal. The signs associated with the seasonal migration of animals would have been originally perceived as magickal as well, foretelling or announcing the return of various animals. The act of dreaming, the occasional coincidence, and other aspects of human experience all contributed to the concept of some mysterious power. Out of this we draw our practice of magickal symbols and sigils, representing the power of an intangible element at work.

The duality of all things is another Wiccan tenet. In Nature we see this divine principle at work within the physical world: hot and cold, wet and dry, abundance and scarcity, and so on. We see also the masculine and feminine principles that must unite in order to produce or make manifest. It is a Wiccan belief that the imprint of the Creators can be found in whatever they create—from this tenet we discern the *Source of All Things* to be both male and female, God and Goddess.

THE MYTHOS IN WICCA

The essential mythos contained within Wicca is centered on the Wheel of the Year. This is the foundation of the belief in ever-returning cycles, an aspect of which encompasses the belief in reincarnation. Death and the survival of the soul or spirit are important elements of the Mystery Teachings. Wicca is essentially an Agrarian Mystery Tradition wherein the aspects of plowing, planting, growing, and harvesting are all symbolic of the journey of the soul.

The Agricultural Mysteries are involved with loss, return, death, and rebirth. This is best depicted in the myth of Demeter and Persephone (see appendix six). They are also involved with the transformations associated with changes in states of consciousness. This incorporates the use of psychotropic plants such as hallucinogenic mushrooms, or various fermented liquids. We refer to this aspect as the Fermentation Mysteries. These teachings also include the Harvest Mysteries, which symbolically reveal the mysteries through various myths of dying gods.

The Slain God or Divine King is an integral part of the Wiccan Mysteries. He is intimately connected to the life cycle of the Plant Kingdom and shares the attributes associated with planting and harvesting. His blood contains the same vital life-giving principle as does the seed, and therefore must return to the soil in order for there to be life and abundance in the coming year. The Slain God mythos retains the earlier Lunar Mysteries of the Great Goddess cult. The Divine King reflects the Solar Mysteries of the Indo-European cults. In Wicca these have blended together into one mythos (covered in more detail in chapters thirteen and fourteen).

In the Wiccan mythos, the seasonal cycles of Nature comprise what is known as the *waxing* and *waning* tides of the earth. These are the forces of growth and decline, the old making way for the new. There are two sets of mythical figures (depending on the tradition) that represent these tides. The first set is the Oak King and the Holly King, common to traditions in northern Europe. The second is the Stag and the Wolf, found in many traditions of southern Europe. Their myths are tales of life and death, one succeeding the other in an ever-repeating cycle (chapter fourteen).

THE MYSTERY PATH

When a person follows the ways of the Wicca, forces come into play that can change one's life in a variety of ways. Whether these forces possess consciousness or are simply metaphysical principles is best left up to the person experiencing them to decide. What is clear, however, is that situations, objects, and realizations begin to present themselves at the most appropriate times. Wiccans soon discover that the seemingly random occurrences of life now take on discernable patterns, and synchronicity meets them at every corner and crossroad.

An impulse to stop by a bookstore turns into the purchase of a book which is later found to have the exact information you've been looking for. You pass by a street bearing the name of a long-lost friend, who just happens to get back in touch with you later that week. Lessons and spiritual connections present themselves under the most mundane circumstances. You think of someone, the phone rings, and it's the person you thought of. In all of these things the mysteries are touching the conscious mind. From this point on, the path you walk is ever ancient and ever new, for you walk the well-worn path that leads to crossroads yet unexplored.

The mechanism of the mysteries is reflected in beliefs concerning fairies, Nature spirits, and other entities. To believe in such things is part of the magickal consciousness of the Wiccan. This empowers the forces that maintain and direct synchronicity in our lives. Nature spirits are the vitalizing and animating forces working within Nature, whether it is the spirit of a plant, rock, stream, river or whatever. They draw energy from our offerings, ceremonies, and our beliefs about them, and in turn they help to align us with Nature. It is from such alignments that psychic and magickal powers arise, for both abilities are simply manifestations of specific levels of consciousness within the individual Wiccan.

The recognition that some unseen force is active can be seen in many folk beliefs. To knock on wood after recounting one's good fortune is rooted in the belief that woodland fairies aid humans; thus we thank them with a ritual knock. Tossing a pinch of spilled salt over one's shoulder, not stepping on a crack, and other such folk beliefs are all derived from ancient beliefs about the influence of various spirits upon human lives.

What this all means is that there is a directing force behind the synchronistic events of our lives. We never walk the path alone for by our side are our spirit guide, our familiar spirits, and a host of Nature spirits. Through them we are connected to the very source of the mysteries; we are linked with other worlds and other Beings. Ultimately we are connected to the source of our own existence (that which created us and to which we shall all one day return).

In the Mystery Teachings a religious structure represents the body. It is the material form in which Spirit can manifest in the physical dimension. Our free will and our intuition is the soul that gives life to the body. Rituals are guidelines that help us focus and they are proven formulas on which we can rely. Our own spirits give life and animation to Wicca as a religion and a spiritual path. We are not bound to it as servants. Thus we find these words in the Mystery Text known as *The Charge*: "And you shall be free, and as a sign that you are truly free you shall be naked in your Rites."

TRANSFORMATION MYSTERIES

The magickal ability to physically change shape, or to fly, is found in almost every legend and fairy tale associated with witches. This power to transform and transcend the laws of physics is an integral aspect of the Mysteries of Wicca. In some cases a potion, ointment, or elixir of some kind is required to bring about the desired effect. Transcripts from witch trials during the Middle Ages mention the so-called *flying ointment* of the witches, said to contain powerful drugs and grotesque ingredients.

The origin of such potions and ointments stems from the use of hallucinogenic plants by shamans of the early Witch Cult. Ergot mold (*claviceps purpurea*), found particularly on rye grains, was used for shamanistic journeys of the mind. The active component *ergonovine* survived the process of making the flour that was an ingredient used in Sabbat cakes. LSD is a synthesized product made from ergonovine. Mushrooms such as the *amanita muscaria* (toad mushroom) also produced a state of intoxication. The toxin is highly concentrated in the urine of anyone drinking the mushroom's juice, and we find urine is an ingredient in some very ancient potions. Another ingredient known as *bufotenina* comes from the secretion of certain frogs, also another ancient ingredient associated with witches.

The ability to shapeshift, turning into an animal form such as a wolf, is still claimed as a power by witches of the Old Ways. Some people believe this to be a thought-form projected by the mind under the influence of trance or intoxicants. Others believe it to be a form of mimetic magick, wherein one romps about as a wolf would (the experience heightened by hallucinogenics). Some witches of the Old Family Traditions maintain that shapeshifting is an actual physical transformation.

The Transformation Mysteries include other experiences such as initiation and psychic development. In modern Wicca, wine is used during these rites; in ancient times the wine would have contained a psychotropic ingredient of some kind. Psychic centers of the body are activated and the person is aligned with occult energies. This allows the person to access certain planes or dimensions through employing both the conscious and subconscious mind. In the Bacchic mysteries of Italy this was the divine intoxication that brought one into the presence of the Divine. Chapters thirteen and fourteen provide additional information on the Transformation Mysteries.

THE FERMENTATION MYSTERIES

The Mystery Tradition associated with fermentation is an essential element of the Transformation Mysteries. I separate them here simply for clarification of references made in other chapters. The reader can isolate these teachings here and reflect on their context in other chapters. The *Teachings of the Grain* are intimately connected to the Fermentation Mysteries and are probably best reflected in the Eleusinian Mysteries.

The dry seed being planted in the soil is symbolic of death, the descent into the Underworld. The mystical meeting beneath the soil with the inherent properties of decay eventually results in the awakening of new life within the seed. This is the meeting of the Goddess with the Lord of the Underworld. The emergence of physical life from the seed, pushing up toward the surface, is symbolic of the process of rebirth within the Underworld. It is the beginning of the ascent of the Goddess, her return to the World of the living.

The appearance of the young sprout, having broken through the soil, is symbolic of rebirth into the physical dimension, the return of the Goddess. However, the plant itself is the god, the *Child of Promise*. The spiritual/mystical process described here is itself the Goddess. She is the spirit; he is the body. Thus, in time, this newborn god will become the Harvest Lord. His life energy will be returned to the earth where it will impregnate the Goddess. His seed will be sown in her womb and new life will issue forth once again.

The *essence* of the God is contained in the seed or grain (or in the grape: the blood) as is the case with Dionysus. The intoxicating power of fermented grain was believed to be the presence of the God within one's body. This ancient concept is the basis for the Wiccan rite of cakes and wine, and the Christian rite of Communion. To consume the God was to take on his nature. To take on the nature of the God was to align one's self with him, and thus inherit his power of resurrection. Through union with the God, death lost its power and rebirth was assured.

THE CAULDRON MYSTERIES

The cauldron appears in almost every tale associated with European witchcraft. In myth and legend the cauldron brews potions, aids in the casting of spells, produces abundance or decline, and is a holy vessel for offerings to the powers of the Night, and to the Great Goddess. Its main attribute is that of transformation, whether of a spiritual or physical nature. As a symbol of the Goddess it can bestow wisdom, knowledge, and inspiration.

In the tale of the Cauldron of Cerridwen we find many associated aspects of the Mystery Teachings. The basic story recounts how Cerridwen prepared a potion in her cauldron designed to impart enlightenment to her son. The potion had to brew for a year and a day. This is symbolic of Wiccan Initiation and reflects the teaching that each degree requires a year and a day of training. In the tale of Cerridwen the brew is accidentally tasted by Gwion, for whom it was not intended. This angers the Goddess and she pursues Gwion; both of them transform into various cult animals during the chase (see appendix six).

The Mystery Teachings tell us that the potion of Cerridwen consisted of yellow flowers known as the Pipes of Lleu (cowslip), fluxwort (Gwion's silver), hedge-berry (the borues of Gwion), vervain (Taliesin's cresses), and mistletoe berries mixed with sea foam. The dredge of this brew was poisonous and had to be handled properly. In the earlier Greek tradition, the cauldron used was the Cauldron of Ceres whose potion's residue was likewise a poisonous substance, the herbal ingredients of which were also mixed with sea water. This is all connected to one of the greatest Mystery Teachings, that of the *Blood Mysteries*. A potentially deadly potion was prepared for the willing initiates to ingest, whereby their consciousness could retrieve the genetic memories of their ancestors. This is related to the teaching that trauma or extreme introversion can bring about a dramatic increase in psychic abilities. In the case of near death, survival mechanisms engage to tap into the cumulative knowledge of our genetic material, searching for a way to escape from the impending death. Surviving this experience can result in a conscious merging with the atavistic collective consciousness of our ancestors, as retained in our DNA (the cauldron hidden in the Underworld).

In the Celtic myth, recorded between A.D. 500–600, the Cauldron of Cerridwen was warmed by the breath of nine maidens and produced an elixir that conferred Inspiration. It is easy to see here the earlier Greek influence of the nine Muses who gave Inspiration to humans (depicted in Greek art as early as 800 B.C.). In line 27 of the "Taliesin riddle" (from the Celtic work *The Tale of Taliesin*) we find the words: "*I have obtained the muse from the Cauldron*

of Caridwen." The Muses freed mortals from the drudgery of physical reality and provided access to Eternal Truths. The music of the
Muses was likened to the sound of a stream pouring over rocks;
this in turn was likened to the sound of wine being poured, thus a
connection with Dionysus. The intoxication of wine was also
likened to the intoxication of the lyre, a nine-stringed instrument
sacred to the Muses.

It is noteworthy to consider the association of the Muses and
Dionysus. The Druids, according to Strabo (the Greek historian),
worshipped Dionysus. As the teachers and priests of the Celts, they
taught a form of the Cauldron Mysteries in Gaul and Briton. In
chapter two of *A Celtic Reader*, compiled and edited by John
Matthews, we find this association:

> *The Druidic mythology and culture consists mainly of Greek
> traditions...It was the worship of the mysterious Cabiri. In this
> was retained an ancient sacramental and initiatory system,
> inherited from the Pelasgi. The centre of this worship was not
> the mainland of Greece, but in the island of Samothrace. To the
> priests of the Cabiri repaired all the great heroes and princes of
> Greece and the surrounding countries, to be initiated into the
> mysteries. The Eleusinian mysteries were something similar,
> instituted at a place called Eleusis in Attica on the mainland of
> Greece. These mysteries centered on the figures of Ceres, Pluto,
> Proserpina and Bacchus.*

The Pelasgi were a people from mainland Greece, and their
association with the Druids would give more credence to the view
that the Tuatha de Danaan actually came from either the Mediterranean or Aegean regions. In Greek mythology the followers of the
Greek goddess Danae fled in ships to an island off the coast of
Greece. This island was Samothrace, where the Cabiri lived. As we
saw in chapter eleven, Robert Graves (*The White Goddess*) describes
the Tuatha de Danaan as Bronze Age Pelasgians who were expelled
from Greece. The Cabiri were a people of the Greek islands and
maintained a priesthood centered on Samothrace, accounting for
their connection to Dionysus and the Muses. If the descendants of

the expelled Pelasgi carried the cult of Dionysus to Briton, this would have allowed the Celts in Briton to more readily accept the Roman Mystery Cult of Bacchus/Dianus (having been already acclimated; this also provides us with another theory of why the Celts were so eager to trade for wine prior to the Roman occupation). In turn, this acceptance under Roman rule would account for the lesser degree of violence in the Druids' version of the cult; as we saw in chapter three the cult of Dionysus merged with the peaceful agrarian cult of Bacchus/Dianus in Italy. The Romans then carried it into the Celtic lands where they established the Grain and Fermentation Mysteries.

In the Celtic legends that later evolved out of the Mediterranean Mystery Tradition, Cerridwen's Cauldron was said to have a ring of pearls around its rim. It was located in the realm of Annwn (the Underworld) and, according to Taliesin's poem *The Spoils of Annwn*, the fire beneath it was kindled by the breath of nine maidens, and oracle speech issued forth from it. This is another association with the Greek Muses who were connected to the Oracle at Delphi. What is of interest to us here is the association of the Cauldron in the Underworld. Ceridwen was a moon goddess in Celtic mythology, yet her cauldron appears in Annwn under the title of *the cauldron of Pwyll, the lord of Annwn*. To understand this connection, we must examine the Grail Mysteries.

THE GRAIL MYSTERIES

In Taliesin's poem *The Spoils of Annwn* we encounter the tale of a group of adventurers who descend into Annwn to recover the missing cauldron. In the Mystery Tradition they locate it in Caer Sidi or Caer Pedryan, the four-cornered castle, also known as Castle Spiral. As we noted in the Cult of the Dead, the spiral was a tomb symbol representing death and renewal. It is here in the center of the spiral, itself within the center of the castle, that the adventurers find the Cauldron of Ceridwen.

The tale is representative of many Mystery Teachings. One aspect concerns itself with the Lunar Mysteries. Here the missing cauldron of Ceridwen represents the waning of the moon and its disappearance for three days (prior to the return of the crescent in the night sky). To the ancients, this was a time of dread, for the moon was gone. It had to be retrieved from the Underworld into which the moon seemingly descended each night. The quest to retrieve the cauldron of Ceridwen is a quest to retrieve the light of the moon. The Cauldron is the source of that light and belongs to the Goddess. In a metaphysical sense, this is the enlightenment residing in the subconscious mind. The subconscious is free from the constraining influences of the five senses on the conscious mind. It is directly linked to the astral dimensions, the dream worlds, and therefore to the spiritual or nonphysical dimensions. To retrieve it from the Underworld is a Holy Quest.

Some people believe that the cauldron of Cerridwen was a solar symbol, most likely derived from the tale that Ceridwen's brew had to be protected from moonlight falling upon it. Actually this reference means that the power of Darkness was required to bring forth Ceridwen's Inspiration. In the Mystery Teachings, Night (or Darkness) is the Mother of the moon. The moon is symbolic of enlightenment appearing in the dark of night. Darkness is the state of procreation, the void from which all things spring forth. It is the dark womb of the Great Goddess. This womb is the gateway to both death and life, as we saw in chapter three.

In the book *The Celts—Uncovering the Mythic and Historic Origins of Western Culture* (Jean Markale, Inner Traditions Inc., 1978), the author states that the cauldron foreshadows the Grail and that the Grail itself is a feminine solar symbol. She further states that the sun was a feminine aspect in Celtic mythology (chapter eleven of her book). Personally, I doubt that this was originally the case; more likely this is a transformation due to the influence of the patriarchy and Christianity. I say this because the lunar-based matrifocal cult of the Great Goddess predates Indo-European cultures in central Europe. Therefore the solar goddesses of the Celts were quite likely lunar goddesses prior to the decline of the Great Goddess culture of Old Europe.

There is little doubt that the adventurers in *The Spoils of Annwn* are Arthur and his Grail knights. In the Arthurian legends we encounter a mixture of Paganism and Christianity. Clearly the

Mystical traditions associated with Arthur are not founded on Christian teachings but on ancient Pagan concepts. The old European Goddess is left peeking out of such female images as Guinevere, Morgana, and the Grail itself. Arthur himself represents the ancient leader of the hunter-gatherer society, including the wound that breaks faith with the community and threatens the wasting away of the kingdom. This is the "lame god" who was once the greatest hunter/warrior in the clan. Once wounded, he resided with the female shamans and became a priest of the Moon Cult.

To the Solar Cult, this event brings about what is called the Wasteland. The kingdom declines: crops fail, hunting is poor, and the community no longer thrives. It becomes the Time of the Wolf in which the Group Consciousness unravels and the individual rules supreme. This is followed by lawlessness and a complete disregard for fellow human beings. In the Solar Mysteries, the moral and spiritual nature of the King must be restored (his right to bear the sword excaliber, see chapter fourteen). Thus he sets into motion a Quest for the Grail. From the perspective of the Lunar Mysteries he is seeking rebirth through the Cauldron of the Goddess. In the solar mentality he is seeking renewal of his inner nature through a cleansing by the power of the Sun (or Son). To drink from the Well of the Sun is to restore one's spiritual nature.

In a metaphysical sense, the King's decline is the failing of the seed. His seed has gone bad and he is no longer at his prime. The time of ripened grain is past and he was not harvested. His virility has left him. The King is without a sword and the land is without a King. This is devastating to an agricultural society and the power of the King must be renewed or another King must be chosen. In the lunar cult, the King would have been replaced. In the solar cult he wishes to remain past his natural time, and thus he seeks a magickal solution to avoid becoming the Slain God of the Harvest. Therefore he remains as the Divine King of the solar mythos. However, as we see throughout Europe, the sacrifice of the Harvest Lord is still a living part of European folk practices.

THE THREE MYSTICAL REALMS

In the Celtic Mystery Tradition there are three realms comprising the Universe. These dimensions are known as Annwn, Abred, and Gwynvyd. In some Wiccan Traditions they are called Abred, Gwynvyd, and Ceugant. Annwn (the Welsh Underworld) is then placed either in the center with the three worlds revolving around it, or depicted as surrounding and enclosing the three realms. The Circle of Ceugant is the realm of Divinity where only the deities may dwell; this is why many traditions do not include it as a dimension through which humans will pass. Confusion over the Celtic view of the planes stems from conflicting passages in the *Book of Dwyfyddiaeth* as to the order of the planes. According to Lewis Spence this can be rectified through the following assignment: the Circle of Abred is the earth plane where souls work off the impurity that is attached to them. The Circle of Gwynvyd is the place of justified spirits, the so-called realm of heaven. Annwn is the abode of souls not in either of the two other realms, for a variety of reasons relating to their spiritual condition. It is also the realm from which souls reincarnate into Abred.

The existence of three realms in mystical cosmology actually appears earlier among the ancient Greeks. Hesiod wrote in his *Theogony* (circa 700 B.C.) of the three realms comprising the Universe. He called them Chaos, Gaea, and Eros. From these realms there issued forth the earth, the heavens, and the Underworld. Hesiod describes the inescapable lot of humankind assigned to interplay of the gods and Cosmic Forces. He outlines the ways in which humankind can progress through a series of guidelines he sets forth. It is interesting to note that these guidelines apply mainly to farmers. It was largely through Roman farmers that the mysteries were passed into northern and western Europe.

The Celtic teachings from the *Barddas* also provide a set of teachings setting forth guidelines for the progression of the soul. The Barddas first appeared in 1862 under the auspices of the Welsh Manuscript Society at Landovery. In 1858 a request went out for authentic sources of material relating to the Bardo-Druidic system of the British Isles. Only one manuscript was received, bearing the author's name Plennydd. Upon inspection it was deemed to be an authentic account of earlier beliefs, similar in nature to *The Sentences of Bardism* written in 1450 and the writings of the bard Llywelyn Sion, circa 1560.

According to the teachings, humans are subject to *suffering*, *change*, and *choice*. Men and women may attach themselves to objects and situations in the physical plane, or may liberate themselves from these things as they so choose. The Western Mystery Tradition does not reflect fatalism as does the Eastern Tradition. Death brings on forgetfulness in the realm of Gwynvyd, where there is no recollection of sorrow. Annwn and Abred both require the recollections of sorrow in order for the soul to progress beyond the root causes of these experiences. The *Blue Book* of the bards relates the optimism of Celtic spiritual views:

> *There will be no transgression which will not be set right, no displeasure which will not be forgiven, and no anger which will not be pacified, and thence will be obtained the three excellences: first, there will be nothing ill-favored which shall not be adorned; secondly there will be no evil which shall not be removed; thirdly, there will be no desire which shall not be attained....*
>
> —Lewis Spence, *Mysteries of Britain*

Essentially, humans may fall back from Annwn into Abred many times during their Quest for Gwynvyd. This is a purifying process that prepares one for the state of spirituality necessary to remain within the higher dimensions of nonphysical existence. The Bardic teachings tell us that three things exist everywhere: God, Truth, and the Circle of Gwynvyd. To reach Gwynvyd one must have experienced all things and shed the limitations that caused attachment within physical existence. It is also taught that one must retain the knowledge of these former existences. This appears to contradict the concept of "forgetfulness of sorrow" in Gwynvyd. However, the teaching means that one remembers without emotional attachment to the memory; in other words the pain and sorrow of former experiences are not evoked in their recollection.

Very few Wiccan Traditions currently employ the Celtic view of the Three Worlds. This is most likely due to the many influences on Celtic culture from Indo-European and Roman civilization. In addition to these we find the influence of Eastern Mysticism in Wicca, a popular import during the 1930s up through the 1960s. Most Wiccan Traditions today derive their basic structure from Gardnerian Wicca. Some, like the Faery Tradition, have developed along more traditional Celtic lines.

WOMEN'S
MYSTERIES

The vessel of Transformation—viewed as magical can only be effected by the woman because she herself, in her body that corresponds to the Great Goddess, is the cauldron of incarnation, birth, and rebirth. And that is why the magical cauldron or pot is always in the hand of the female mana figure, the priestess and later the witch.
　　　　　　　—Erich Neumann, *The Great Mother*

Wicca is, among other things, essentially a lunar cult in which the Women's Mysteries of Old Europe reside. The Women's Mysteries can be broken down into three main categories: Triad Mysteries, Blood Mysteries, and Dark Mysteries. Each of these contain within themselves other related aspects of the associated mythos in which they reside. In this chapter we shall examine these levels and explore their relationships to Wicca as a living Mystery Tradition.

The Women's Triad Mysteries are comprised of the following aspects: Preservation, Formation, and Transformation. These are related to the mundane mysteries wherein women traditionally hold dominance over the home, the table, and the bed. In days of old the symbols of a woman's power were related to these facets of human life. The broom, cauldron, hearth, and the pillow were all signs of her domestic reign. In ancient times women were honored for their gift of nurturing the family. The home was a place of stability and sanctuary. Women controlled, either directly or indirectly, all facets of family life and played a vital role within the community.

The Blood Mysteries are associated with the teachings and rites connected with menstruation, rebirth among the same clan, contagion magick, sex magick, and atavistic resurgence. These are all extremely ancient concepts originating from at least the Neolithic era. The Blood Mysteries are largely unique to women and served to elevate them in the early clan structure. The inherent power of these mysteries compelled men to become acquiescent within the early matrifocal cults. Out of this Mystery Tradition arose the matriarchal priestesshood of Wicca.

The Dark Mysteries involve things of an occult nature. Under this category we find such things as lunar magick, the worship of Diana, Hecate, and Proserpine, death and regeneration, astral magick, dream magick, and generally things of an "Otherworld" nature. This is one of the most dangerous, and perhaps most powerful, aspects of the mysteries. No doubt the resulting personal power associated with a mastery of this tradition underlies some of the fears concerning witches during the time of the Inquisition.

The Women's Mystery Tradition arose from the fact that primitive women saw themselves as a mystery. There was a natural need to understand such things as menstrual bleeding, pregnancy, and childbirth. Clearly these things separated them from the men whose bodies displayed no such powers. To primitive humans there must surely have been a magickal force at work, and apparently it was only concerned with the women of the clan. This mentality served to elevate women and established a sense of awe among the men.

Originally the clan operated as a group of individuals, a collective consciousness. During this period the Women's Mysteries consisted mainly of fertility rites involving the clan as a whole. The change of consciousness wherein the individual (and individual relationships) held importance gradually evolved, giving rise to various inner cults. These cults were extensions of the mysteries overseen by women. Within this new structure arose rules concerning sexual intercourse and menstruation. Women were the first to perceive the connection between sexual intercourse and conception. Female initiates were taught methods of preventing conception along with the secrets of love magick.

Over the course of time, individuals began to stand out due to special skills or unique qualities. This shift is quite evident in the hunter/warrior cult of the Men's Mysteries where the bravest and strongest individuals held special roles. Among women this developed more along the lines of shamanistic practices. Certain individuals displayed a unique affinity with the natural world of plants and animals, and possessed a high degree of magickal and psychic abilities. These individuals then became the facilitators of tribal rites, some secret and some public.

THE TRIAD MYSTERIES

The transformation from hunter-gatherer tribes to agricultural communities (primitive to cultural) was a process instituted by women. Women tended the fires and prepared the meals; they were the very center of life. Women were also essential to the construction and maintenance of shelters. They were the weavers, knotting and binding, creating patches for roofing and other essential parts of the home. They also created vessels for food gathering and transporting water.

During times when food was less abundant, women controlled the dispensing of food by hiding it in storage pits beneath the soil. The men, who were usually hunting, fending off enemies of the tribe, or involved in manual labor were unaware of the women's activities. It was from this practice of hiding food that women learned about the cycles of plant life. Tubers and various grains buried in the soil began to sprout or take root, providing women with the first observation of farming. The ability to transform clay into pottery and seeds into plants was the basis for the Transformation Mysteries. Out of this evolved the knowledge of brewing, whether herbal potions or intoxicating beverages.

Such discoveries and associations stimulated the minds of women and they developed modes of consciousness that differed from men's. Women began to think along more expansive levels, breaking out of the mold of primitive thinking. Men were more focused on immediate connections; the fresh track of an animal meant its presence, the distance at which a spear could be thrown with accuracy, and so forth. This stimulated different modes of consciousness for the men, and they evolved along separate mental pathways than did the women (see chapter fifteen for the development of different mental pathways concerning sexuality). Each was a mentality necessary for the well-being of the clan; without this balance we would most likely not be here today.

The fact that women usually were responsible for the children of the clan meant that they remained in close proximity to the village. The village was relatively safer than the wilderness where the danger of wild animals and nomadic intruders was a real threat. Out of this setting, women naturally initiated the formation of social systems. In the Formation Mysteries the social structure was matrilinear. It wasn't until men realized their role in procreation that this system began to change. However in some parts of the world today, such as Africa and South America, matrilinear societies or the remnants of them still exist.

Women set into place certain social factors designed to control the naturally strong sex drives of the men. In the book *Blood Relations—Menstruation and the Origins of Culture* (Yale Univ. Press, 1991), by Chris Knight, there are many interesting examples of such social structures. Knight theorizes that women went on sex strikes in order to force men off to the hunt. Returning with fresh meat meant an end to the strike, an exchange of sex for food. So that the men would not worry about younger males having sexual privileges in their absence, the women created taboos against intercourse between brothers and sisters, mothers and sons. Women also nurtured a relationship between brothers and sisters, so that the sexual interests of other males remaining in the village would be fended off by the females' brothers. Just as women controlled the fires that cooked food and transformed clay, so too did they control the *fire* of men's sexual nature.

Thus we find in the early role of women within clan life the mysteries of preservation, formation, and transformation. Out of this essential role for women arose inner traditions associated with their private and personal needs. The taboo system was originally initiated by women in order to withdraw from the demands/needs of the community and focus on the mysteries that came upon them: menstruation, pregnancy, and childbirth.

THE BLOOD MYSTERIES

In the book *Sacred Pleasure—Sex, Myth, and the Politics of the Body* (HarperCollins, 1995), by Riane Eisler, the author tells us that the BaMbuti pygmies of the Congo forest call menstruation being *blessed by the moon*. Within this culture there do not appear to be any negative associations connected with the time of menstruation. A woman's first menstrual blood is celebrated through a festival called *elima* involving the entire village. After her first menstruation, being blessed by the moon again in the future is simply viewed as a natural part of the woman's life and no further ceremony is associated with it. No taboos are connected to a woman's time of menstruation among the BaMbuti, and this perhaps best reflects the ancient non-Judaic-Christian mentality.

The flow of blood and its ceasing are both intimately connected to the Women's Mysteries. Menstruation, pregnancy, childbirth, and menopause are aspects of the life cycle of all women. Blood, or its absence, naturally marks the transformational stages of a woman from the breaking of the hymen, to the blood of childbirth, to the cessation of bleeding at menopause. In ancient times the manner in which a woman wore her girdle was an outward sign of what stage in life she had reached.

In *Blood Relations—Menstruation and the origins of Culture*, Knight tells us that primitive forest-dwelling humans slept in treetops beneath the night sky. The light cycles of the moon influenced the menstrual cycles of women accordingly. Knight's research indicates that the majority of women begin menstruation during the new moon phase and ovulate at the time of the full moon. Luisa Francia, in her book *Dragon Time—Magic and Mystery of Menstruation* (Ash Tree, 1991), also states that women who live and sleep outdoors (away from artificial lights) are in tune with this cycle.

Knight presents some interesting findings compiled from the research of A. E. Treloar, W. Menaker, and Gunn, well-known researchers in women's biology. A study of 270,000 cycle lengths of women representing all ages of reproductive life revealed the following. The highest single percentage (28%) of women in the study menstruated during the new moon. The second highest percentage menstruated during the first quarter (12.6%) and only 11.5% menstruated during the time of the full moon. Knight's research also indicated that 28% of women in the study showed a menstrual cycle length of 29.5 days. This cycle was also shown to be the most fertile. The study further presented a finding that heterosexual women who engaged in regular weekly sex had cycles more closely related to the moon's cycle than women whose sex life was either sporadic or celibate in nature. The study also indicated that male pheromones may be involved in aligning a women's menstrual cycle to the so-called *normal* cycle commencing with the new moon.

In the Mystery Teachings we find that menstrual blood was more than the indicator of a woman's fertility cycle. The vagina was viewed as a magickal portal through which life issued forth from a mysterious inner source. In matrifocal religion it was a portal of both physical regeneration and spiritual transformation. Women are more attuned to their psychic nature during menstruation. Because the flow of menstrual blood tends to absorb astral energy, women are better at healing others during this time. Illness is first reflected in the astral body and lingers in the energy field of the aura. Thus a menstruating woman can absorb another's astral energy and *ground* it through her own physical bleeding. Once the blood is put into the earth, the energy is neutralized and healing can begin within the aura of the unhealthy person.

Menstrual blood was also used to fertilize seeds for planting, passing the essence of the life force into them. Fields were sometimes sprinkled with a mixture of water and menstrual blood to encourage growth. The seeds and plants absorbed some of the energy before the soil neutralized the etheric charge. Female shamans also passed magickal charges into the planted fields through menstrual blood, designed to influence the group mind of the community feeding on the harvest. During the Middle Ages witches were often accused of bewitching crops.

Another function of menstrual blood was to anoint the dead. This was believed to assure their rebirth due to the life-giving properties of the blood that issued forth from the portal of life itself. During the Neolithic period and early Bronze Age in Old Europe, the Aegean region saw the creation of round tombs with small openings oriented to the east, the quarter of the rising sun. These tombs represented the womb of the goddess and the opening was her vagina. Sacred blood bowls were used to collect menstrual blood for the anointing of the dead. These were sacred vessels of fertility, light, and transformation. The dead were anointed with menstrual blood and placed in the tombs. The light of the rising sun was a symbol of renewal and regeneration as it penetrated the opening of the tomb (the solar phallus entering the lunar vagina). Later in history these earthen tombs evolved into fairy mounds, remnants of the Cult of the Dead (see chapter eleven).

In *Sacred Pleasures*, Riane Eisler recounts how prehistoric funerary rites and ceremonies included sexual acts. Such acts were designed to connect the tomb with the energy of procreation. Spiral symbols were often marked upon Neolithic tombs as symbols of regeneration. They also symbolized the shamanistic transformation of consciousness which employed hallucinogenic mushrooms. Mushrooms have a reputation as an aphrodisiac and their similarity to male genitalia was certainly obvious to the ancient Europeans. The quickness with which mushrooms swell up and then ebb away also contributed to their association with the phallus. Thus we can easily equate ecstatic dancing with the burial rites of blood magick.

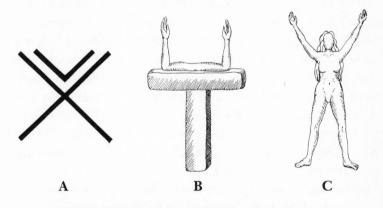

A   B   C

Mediterranean Roots of the Goddess Posture
Neolithic Old European Goddess Symbol (A), Egyptian Ka symbol representing "the Spirit Double (B), and Wiccan "Drawing Down the Moon" posture (C). Note the similarities.

In the Mystery Teachings blood magick is connected to the phases of the moon. The full moon initiates ovulation and is symbolic of the transformational powers of lunar energy (and therefore feminine energy). Because of its fertile aspect in a woman's cycle the full moon is the *time of the mother*. During this phase it is best to formulate and visualize whatever is desirable in one's life. Magickal images take root during this phase and the blood is charged with whatever thought-forms may be directed into it (see chapter nine). The waning moon moves what was conceived during the full moon toward manifestation. It is a time to make those connections with the physical world that will assist the flow of related energy toward one's desires. The new moon releases the charged blood from the magickal cauldron of the womb. The magickal energy is now spent and it is a time for reflection and turning inward. The waxing moon is a time of potential, a time to read and study, preparing the fertile soil of the womb for the magickal seed that will be planted by the full moon.

THE DARK MYSTERIES

The Dark Mysteries are concerned with the occult nature of things, and the secret essence of both physical and spiritual things. The mythos of the Dark Mysteries is reflected in such myths as Demeter and Persephone. In this ancient myth we find the theme of the Goddess meeting the Lord of the Underworld, resisting him at first and then submitting to his love for Her. Here Persephone represents the seed going down into darkness beneath the soil where its fertile energy is awakened. The Underworld represents the mysterious force that pushes the sprout upward toward renewal. Demeter represents the energy that nourishes the growth of the new plant. This Greek/Roman mythos is typical of the descent myths that first arose in Mesopotamia, migrated through the Aegean/Mediterranean, and eventually were embraced by the Celts.

The Dark Mysteries are connected with several creatures commonly associated with witches and magick in general. The raven was associated with death and the Underworld because of its link to the Cult of the Dead (chapter eleven). The souls of Scottish witches were believed to leave the body in the form of a raven during trance. The pig was an animal sacrificed to Demeter and also appears in myths connected to the Greek witch Circe. In ancient times pig's blood was thought to be the purest of all animals and had power to cleanse the soul of hatred and evil. It was linked to the Cult of the Dead and many burial sites included pigs as offerings to the deities of the Underworld. Another creature associated with the Dark Mysteries is the toad. The secretions of certain toads contain *bufotenina* which is a powerful psychotropic drug causing hallucinations. Its secretions were used in the making of potions and salves employed for trance inducement and astral travel. Certain mushrooms such as *claviceps purpurea* and *amanita muscaria* (toad mushroom) were also employed in conjunction with toad secretions. It is interesting to note that *claviceps purpurea* establishes itself on rye grain and survives into the flour where it is called ergot (containing ergonovine, from which LSD was synthesized). Here we find a connection to the use of cakes and wine at the ancient witches' Sabbat.

As distasteful as it may seem to modern sensitivities, the ancients discovered that the hallucinogenic properties of the toad mushroom were highly concentrated in the urine of anyone who consumed the mushrooms. As odd as it may seem, this was the beginning of the Mystery Teachings of distillation and fermentation. Through shamanistic experimentation other body fluids were explored for occult properties as well, including semen, vaginal secretions, and menstrual blood (see chapter fifteen). The employment of body fluids for magickal purposes was one of the aspects of witchcraft that became distorted by Judaic-Christian principles into perverted obscenities.

The connection of fluids to magickal properties also extended to the juices of plants, fruits, and vegetables. The moon was believed to have influence over the growth of plants and therefore over the spiritual or magickal nature as well. The effects of poisons, medicines, and intoxicants were at first believed to be the magickal power of the spirit dwelling within the plant. The transformation process from fruit to juice, by fermentation to intoxication, was performed by female shamans under the auspices of the moon. From this arose the ancient images of witches at their caul-drons stirring magickal brews.

In the Dark Mysteries the Goddess can appear as the Bringer of Life and Death, the Creator and the Destroyer. She brings storms, rain, and dew which can be both beneficial and destructive, especially to an agricultural community. In the same manner in which the Goddess sends forth moisture so too does she send forth the flood of menstrual blood. The moon governs the tides of the earth as well as the tides of women. Liquids have always been sym-bols of the mystical presence of the Goddess. Her shrines were often established in grottos where water trickled forth from the rocks. Ceremonies involving the drawing and pouring of water are typical in Her rites, where vessels having phallus spouts were employed in Her service. In her book, *The Women's Mysteries* (Harper Colophon Books, 1976), Esther Harding recounts the ancient rain-making ceremonies of the matrifocal cults (which men were forbidden to observe). The women gathered nude in a stream and poured water over each other's bodies. Often this involved focusing on a priestess who represented the Moon Goddess.

The essential connection of the Mysteries of the Goddess to women is always through fluids, whether symbolically or physical-ly. The subconscious mind is associated with the element of water, as are emotions in general, and these in turn are associated with the feminine nature (whether in men or in women). Where the Female Mysteries do not reflect the psyche in some manner, they can be found in magickal associations of women's body fluids. One of the aspects of the Old Religion was that objects were blessed through contact or insertion into the vagina of a nude woman laid upon the altar. This ancient practice later became debased by Satanic prac-tices. However, from an occult view, what is desecration from one perspective can be consecration or transformation from another perspective. See chapter fifteen for connective information.

CHAPTER
FOURTEEN

MEN'S MYSTERIES

For the primitive hunting people the wild animals were the manifestations of what was alien. The source of both danger and sustenance became linked psychologically with the task of sharing the wilderness with these beings. An unconscious identification took place and this manifested in the half human half animal mythic totems of the ancient tribes. The animal became the tutors of humanity. Through acts of imitation the separate natures of humans and animals became shattered and the relationship of Oneness was realized. The same was true of the later agricultural community which saw the cycles of human birth life and death reflected in the cycles of the crops.

—Joseph Campbell, *Primitive Mythology*

The Men's Mysteries arose out of the matrifocal cult of the Neolithic period. They have their basis in the formation of hunter and warrior cults which were necessary for the survival of the clan as a whole. These sub-cults were uninfluenced by the women of the clan who remained in the villages while the men went off to hunt or engage an enemy. This was a time when men were alone together without the responsibilities of family or village community. Thus freed from the constraints of the social structure established by women, men developed a subculture of their own, reflecting needs and drives that are uniquely masculine.

The Men's Mystery Tradition can be divided up into four categories: the Hunter/Warrior, Satyr, Divine King/Slain God, and the Hero. These mysteries associated with men best sum up the aspects of masculine mentality and behavior. Therefore we can separate most men into one or more of the types listed above. As with all generalizations (and stereotypes) these aspects of behavior or mentality will not apply to every individual.

Initiations involving tests of courage, physical strength, endurance, or tolerance for pain were all aspects of initiation into the ancient male cults. These were essential traits for operating within the male society, mainly due to the fact that hunting animals was dangerous, enemies were common, fights were inevitable, and physical injuries were expected. Thus, at the onset of puberty, when male hormones were magickally transforming boys into men, the first rites of manhood commenced.

The first step in this transformative initiation was to encounter the Monster (whatever that might be to any given community). One of my favorite tales involves a clan whose village was subjected to the horrible sounds of a monster dwelling in the woods surrounding the village. Only the warriors/hunters ever left the safety of the village, and then only fully armed. The rest of the village listened in fear to the sounds of this incredible beast. The men would often return with frightening descriptions of this dangerous monster.

When a boy reached puberty he had to go with the men into the woods and face the beast. During the journey the men would gradually disappear into the woods unnoticed until the boy was left with just one man, his initiator. As they neared the place from where the sounds were emanating, the boy was given a spear. Then the man took the boy by the arm and, screaming a war cry, he ran with the boy dragging him into the clearing to attack the creature. There in the center sat a man blowing into a large horn from which emanated the horrible cries of the monster. The boy had now slain the monster of his childhood and had become a man.

It was a practice of the Men's Mysteries to create stories of haunted woods and dreadful monsters. This served not only the example I cited, but also served to secure private ritual sites. This was particularly important during the time of the Inquisition. The average villager was not about to go out into the woods where supernatural forces were at work.

THE HUNTER/WARRIOR

The early human clans survived due, in a large part, to the hunters and warriors of the tribe. Deer were hunted, providing food, clothing, and tools fashioned from horns and hooves. The stag became a symbol of provision, and in its nature of leading and protecting the herd, the early hunters saw something of their own clan. The rivalry of the stags for the does was in many ways symbolic of the passions with which the men themselves struggled. Among the deer early men beheld their own herding and sexual instincts joined together within the fervor of the hunt (in modern times various sports serve this important social function for men). Watching the stags fend off predators with thrusts of their antlers taught humans the use of the spear. Out of the intimate relationship between the hunter and the hunted evolved a certain reverence and likeness of spirit. Men were probably the first to sigilize concepts, the track of an animal became a symbol of it; seeing the symbol meant the possibility of seeing the animal (the prototype of evocation). By reversing the process you produce the symbol and thus create the possibility of seeing the animal associated with it. From this primitive association magickal thinking was born and we see ancient wall paintings and carvings intended to evoke the presence of various animals for the hunt.

In ancient times the bravest and strongest member of the clan held a high position in the hunter/warrior cult, just as the great stag did among his harem of doe. These were the attributes that best ensured successful hunting and fighting. Dressed in the horns and skins of his prey, primal power passed into his spirit and he became the Master of Animals, Lord of the Forest. One of the most curious aspects of the Hunter/Warrior Mysteries lies in the codes of conduct that formed around a basically violent society. As men became less barbaric they established various rules relating mainly to fighting. This applied to how captives were to be treated, when an unarmed enemy could or could not be slain, and so forth. This code of personal honor eventually became the cornerstone of male societies.

A man who was respected for his physical prowess and fighting skill would quickly lose the respect of others if he displayed a lack of personal honor. This marked a time when the inner man became more important than the outer man. A modern example of this would be the sports heroes who display poor sportsmanship on the field. The true strength of a man lies not in his physical power, but in his personal restraint. Knowing when not to employ his physical attributes (either directly or by implication) is the mark of a man of honor. Examples of this would be the physical and psychological abuse of women and children.

It is popular these days to view men as an evil patriarchy that all but eradicated the ancient Goddess cults, and continues to consciously subjugate women even in modern times. However, this is not reflected in the long-standing tradition of the Men's Mysteries, and men often demonstrate selfless sacrifice for others, especially the oppressed and those who are unable to defend themselves. This is best summed up in the code of chivalry befitting a knight. Despite the modern opinions of certain political groups, true men do not as a whole consciously oppress or abuse women. It is, however, natural for men to compete and maintain social leadership roles stemming from the ancient drives that first formed the Hunter/Warrior cults.

Combat is an experience that, although not unique to men, is experienced by men in greater numbers than by women. In modern society it is the one time when men may openly cry and hold one another without social disapproval. In combat men readily and willingly sacrifice their lives for the life of a friend, in defense of their nation, or for their beliefs and principles. This is the true nobility of men, emerging from the inner self in the midst of chaos and fear. However, it is also true that atrocities are committed in war and that this too comes from the nature of humankind. It is important to understand that this is not instinctive behavior; it is the manifestation of hate, prejudice, frustration, and revenge. It must be nurtured and cultivated, unlike those traits that I have spoken of as noble which are inherent in our souls.

There is some speculation that feelings of anger and resentment toward women arose within the male societies during the transition from hunter-gatherer to farmer. It was women who established the Slain God mythos involving men. The ancient god-forms of the Master of Animals and Lord of the Forest gave way to goat-foot gods and Harvest Lords. Women maintained the religious structures, organizing and directing the domestic lives of the people within the village, and men began to labor in the fields. Where once he was a great tracker, the man now walked along furrows planting seeds. Where once he wielded a spear against his prey, now he scratched the earth with a stick.

Some historians and archaeologists believe that marauding bands of male warriors set out on a crusade against the matrifocal cults in an attempt to destroy them (a theory largely reflected in the work of Marija Gimbutas). It is more likely that patriarchal tribes simply expanded into regions held by matrifocal societies due to changes of weather, famine, and/or lack of game to hunt. These were the Indo-Europeans who were known to be war-like and they simply took what they needed or desired, putting any and all resistance to the sword. It is unlikely that the matrifocal societies were without weapons and the ability to use them as needed for survival, but in the end they were simply no match for the invading armies and their culture became absorbed by the conquerors. The religious concepts and icons of the *vanquished* were replaced with those of the *victors*, for by ancient logic the gods who granted victory must be greater than those who allowed defeat.

THE SATYR

The ancient images of the satyr and the centaur symbolized the division within men of their higher and lower natures. The animalistic lower half of the body represented the sexual nature as well as the desire to be untamed or uncontrolled. The upper half of the figure represented his intellect and spiritual nature that sought to balance and govern his base instincts and desires. For many modern men this is still the dilemma in which they find themselves. The struggle for men is with what psychologists label the *libido* or *Id*. This basic urge is connected to the three fundamental instincts: self-preservation (survival instinct), reproduction (sexual instinct), and companionship (herd instinct). Unlike the other animals, humankind seemingly merged all three into a fourth instinct, that of the religious instinct. It is through religion that humans have developed ways of dealing with their natural desires and fears.

In modern society the male instincts have been channeled off into sports and other forms of competition. In ancient times they were incorporated into rituals that empowered the land and the community. These rites, as well as men's sexual drives, were controlled and directed by women. Many women today still seek to control the sexual instincts of men by protesting against men's adult magazines and videos. Men are inherently visually oriented to sexual stimulation. Mental pathways were formed long ago in this area stemming from the natural exposure of women's genitals before humans walked fully upright. The genitals gave off sexual signals, some associated with menstrual bleeding. The *normal* intercourse position was rear entry, requiring a visual focus. The female, facing away from the activity, formed mental pathways wherein the imagination was required for sexual stimulation instead of actual viewing. In modern times men are often attracted to large breasts and red lips, reminiscent of the exposed vagina and buttocks from a rear entry perspective.

In ancient times women did not equate a man's sexual pleasure within a ritual as something negative. His semen was magickal and life-producing and therefore was employed as one of the sacred ritual and ceremonial fluids. Unfortunately in modern times many people look on any ritual that includes sexual pleasure for men as something perverse, manipulative, or abusive to women. This repression of the dynamic power inherent in men has created a rift between the conscious and subconscious mind. Thus the satyr image symbolizes men as caught in the middle between their higher and lower natures. In some cases this can manifest in a man as an inability to understand his own feelings, and so he turns to physical outlets in order to maintain or discover his sense of identity.

THE DIVINE KING/THE SLAIN GOD

In ancient times, the law of "only the strong survive" was a very true and common reality. Today, with modern medicine and technology, we as a society keep alive those who Nature would have allowed to perish. (This is not meant as a judgment but simply as an observation.)

In early tribal settings, hunters and warriors held a very significant place in the social structure. The bravest and most cunning of these was honored by the tribe, and was looked on as a leader. In many cases, the *well-being* of this individual affected the *well-being* of the tribe. This is a theme that we openly find in the King

Arthur Mythos of northern Europe. Merlin tells Arthur that if he succeeds the land will flourish, if he fails the land will perish. Arthur asks, "Why?" and Merlin replies, "Because you are King!" Even today our own national leaders' ailments are downplayed and they are always "recovering quite nicely." To understand this intimate relationship, we must look at certain aspects and connections. As Merlin tells Arthur, "You are the Land, and the Land is you," so let us continue our journey back into the past to uncover these ancient roots.

Before humans learned to farm and to herd, the hunt was essential to life. Without successful hunters, the clans would perish. Hunting was dangerous, for humans had not yet removed themselves from the food chain. Early weapons required that the hunters be quite close to the prey, and personal injuries were common. Many hunters lost their lives or were made lame as a result of the hunt. In time, the hunter became the warrior, risking his life for the sake of his tribe. The needs of the tribe, whether it was for food or defense, required sending out the best hunter or warrior the tribe had to offer.

In time, this concept evolved along with humankind's religious and spiritual consciousness. The concept of Deity, and its role in life and death, took shape within ritual and dogma. Eventually the idea arose of sending the best of the tribe's people directly to the gods to secure favors. This was the origin of human sacrifice (those who went willingly were believed to become gods themselves).

Offerings were nothing new to our ancient ancestors; many times food and flowers or game were laid out before the gods. To offer one of your own was considered the highest offering the tribe could make. Among human offerings, the sacrifice of a willing individual was the height of all possibilities. Surely, it was believed, the gods would grant the tribe anything if someone willingly laid down their life.

In his book *Western Inner Workings* (Weiser, 1983), William Gray addresses many aspects of this Cult theme. One of these has to do with blood lines. Here he writes:

Something drove them toward Deities not from fear or for seeking favors, but because they sensed a degree of affinity between themselves and the invisible Immortals. In a remote way they realized they were distantly related to those Gods and wanted to improve that relationship. This trait in specific members of the human race shows some evidence of genetic lines leading back to the "Old Blood" which originated from outside this Earth altogether.

Gray shows how eventually kings or rulers were sacrificed (being the "best" of the clan) and how blood lines were an important consideration. The rulers of ancient Rome and Egypt were considered by their people to be descended from the gods, or even as gods themselves.

In a chapter titled "The Cult of Kingship," Gray gives an account of how the blood and flesh were distributed among the clan, and into the land. Parts of the body were buried in cultivated fields to ensure the harvest. Small portions of the body and blood were added to ceremonial feast of which Gray writes:

They gave their late leader the most honorable burial of all—in their own stomachs.

This kind of sacrifice can also be found in Christian mythology, where the body and blood of Jesus is the focus of the rite of Communion. After these practices ended, Gray notes that the custom remained to burn the body in a funeral pyre.

In the Divine King/Slain God Mythos, sacrifice is only part of the story. Sacrifice is the sending of your best, but what about getting them back? In Craft verse we find a passage that reads: "*...and you must meet, know, remember, and love them again.*" To this effect, rituals were designed to bring about the rebirth of these *Slain Gods* and blood lines were carefully traced. Special maidens were prepared to bring about the birth, usually virgins who were artificially inseminated so that no human male was known to be the father.

As human consciousness matured and evolved, human sacrifice turned to animal sacrifice (the *scapegoat* ritual of killing an animal) and eventually to plant sacrifice. The same mythos applies to plant sacrifice, and we find the "eating of Deity" in the cakes and wine (flesh and blood) of Craft rituals. Although the meaning and preparation has been lost in most *reconstructed* Systems, they have still been preserved by many of the Elder Traditions of Wicca.

In the ancient tradition it was through the connection of the body and blood of the Slain God that the people were made one with Deity. This is essentially the concept of the Christian rite of Communion or Eucharistic Celebration. At the "Last Supper" Jesus declares to his followers that the bread and wine are his body. He then declares that he will lay down his life for his people, and bids them to eat of his flesh and drink of his blood (the bread and the wine).

Blood was believed to contain the essence of the life force. The death of the king freed the sacred inner spirit, and by the distribution of his flesh and blood (in the people and the land) heaven and earth were united, and his vital energy renewed the Kingdom. Remnants of these practices can still be clearly seen in the Old Religion, although they are veiled and highly symbolic.

The Divine King/Slain God appears in various aspects throughout the Ages. His image manifests as Jack-in-the-Green, the Hooded Man, the Green Man, and the Hanged Man of the Tarot. He is the Lord of Vegetation, he is the Harvest, and in his wild (or free) aspect he is the Forest. He does not take the place of the Earth Mother, nor does he usurp her power—he is the complement to her, and her consort.

The Green Man image probably best symbolizes the Divine King/Slain God. He is the Spirit of the Land, manifesting in all plant forms. He is the procreative power and the seed of life. His face is obscured within the foliage, but he is always watching. The Green Man signifies the relationship of man to Nature. Author William Anderson, in his book *The Green Man*, writes:

> *He sums up in himself the union that ought to be maintained between humanity and Nature. In himself he is a symbol of hope: he affirms that the wisdom of man can be allied to the instinctive and emotional forces of Nature.*

He is, in effect, our bridge between the Worlds. He is One with Heaven and Earth, and to be One with him is to be One with the Source of All Things.

THE HERO

I wish to make it clear that the path of the hero is not specific to gender. I include it here among the Men's Mysteries simply because the vast majority of surviving myths and legends associated with the hero involve men. It is now part of our Collective Consciousness as a Western culture, thus it is here that we enter in upon the mysteries. Where we choose to go from here is up to us. In ancient times the hero path included women; remnants of female heroes still exist in such tales as Persephone and Demeter, Inanna, Isis and many others. The journey of the hero is one of challenge and sacrifice for others. Whether a man risks his life in combat, or a woman in childbirth, both are acts of courage worthy of the hero path. The Way of the Hero is one of self-sacrifice for the well-being of others.

The hero embodies the traits to which the culture that produced him or her aspires. The hero preserves what is noble, inspirational, and valuable to a society, all woven into tales of Quest, challenge, and resolution. Joseph Campbell calls this *the one deed done by many*. Clearly we do find that the deeds of the hero of any one culture are not unlike those of another. In this we find that the nature of the Hero is indeed universal within human culture.

On the outward levels the Hero leaves the safety of his or her village or tribe and journeys off to face a monster or perform a task, both of which will serve the needs of his or her community. On the inward level, each of us is a hero figure who must leave the safety of what we have been taught and venture off in our Quest of knowledge. The hero must leave one condition and face a challenge through which he or she can raise his or her own consciousness. Sometimes this is done deliberately and sometimes it occurs quite by accident or as a simple reaction to a situation. In any event, the elements of the hero path are three: departure, fulfillment, and return.

In Celtic lore the hero is often lured into the wilderness by a creature of some kind who later transforms into a fairy or a goddess. The hero adventure begins at this point of the story. In Aegean/Mediterranean lore the hero typically sets off on a pre-established Quest with defined parameters. As the spiritual and intellectual consciousness of the culture matures, the hero adventure transforms along with it. The legend of King Arthur is an excellent example of a mythos that has evolved along with the consciousness of the culture from which it sprang. As we noted in chapter twelve, the earlier lunar aspects can be found disguised in later patriarchal solar symbolism.

In the Mystery Tradition we find some very interesting similarities between the sword of King Arthur and the staff of the King at the sanctuary of Diana at Lake Nemi. Only a person bearing certain strengths could draw the sword from the stone or break the branch from the oak tree at Nemi. To do so in either case bestowed kingship. The Sacred Oak represented the sun god and was under the protection of the Guardian of the Grove. At Lake Nemi there dwelled a magickal water nymph known as Egeria. She was associated with the stream that flowed from Diana's grotto into Lake Nemi and with the lake itself. Egeria at Nemi and the Lady of the Lake associated with the Celtic legend of Arthur may be one and the same.

The well-being of the King of the Woods was attributed in part to his relationship with Egeria. According to Frazer (in *The Golden Bough*) Egeria's stream bubbled up from the roots of the Sacred Oak at Nemi. Oak was the wood used to heat the forge from which swords were produced; oak produces higher temperatures than most other woods. Thus the spirit of the Oak God was passed to the flames and thus to the sword carried by the King of the Woods. This mythos may well underlie the Celtic legend of King Arthur and the sword Excaliber. Arthur's magickal sword was rooted in the stone from which he drew it, and was returned to him by the Lady of the Lake after it had been broken in a foolish challenge of combat. The branch broken from the Oak at Nemi was a challenge of combat to the Guardian of the Grove. It was part of the tree rooted in the earth, filled with the water bubbling up from

Egeria's stream. It is not difficult to see the sword Excaliber rising from the Lake, and the Oak Branch ascending from the Sacred Tree within the stream of Egeria as one and the same image.

Sometimes the hero is a spiritual person rather than an adventurer or warrior. He or she teaches *transformation of consciousness* which is the true goal of the Hero Quest. The Quest itself represents the trials and revelations that are required in order to gain enlightenment. The dark times of our lives, in mythic symbolism represented by being trapped in the belly of the whale, are the times of personal ordeal. In the Wiccan first degree initiation ceremony the initiate is told that he or she must face an ordeal and that only through suffering can one obtain knowledge and enlightenment.

Water represents the unconscious mind and the whale represents what lurks therein. It is an important part of the Hero Quest that the hero must face this monster. A common element in the majority of such tales is what Campbell calls supernatural aid. This is where the hero is provided with a mystical weapon of some type or another in order to meet his enemies. Arthur pulling the sword Excaliber out of the stone is one such example. The monster must be defeated in order for the hero to accomplish his or her Quest. In other words, the hero must vanquish what is symbolized by such creatures as the dragon (typically fear, insecurity, or egotism). Once the dragon no longer blocks the path (or guards the *treasure*) then the hero may proceed toward the goal.

It is the work of the hero, externally and internally, to discern the personal relationship to the society in which he or she lives. The hero must also learn how to relate that society to the world of Nature in which it functions. Further, he or she must discern the relationship of all of this to the Great Cosmos. The hero must begin this Quest from within, and *as above so below*, he or she will discern the Macrocosm through the examples found and resolved in the Microcosm. This is what the myths of all ages have addressed since the first Bardic tales were sung.

CHAPTER
FIFTEEN

SEXUALITY AND MAGICK

Witchcraft does not need to apologize for involving sex magic. It is other religions which need to apologize for the miseries of puritanical repression they have inflicted on humanity.
—Doreen Valiente, *Witchcraft for Tomorrow*

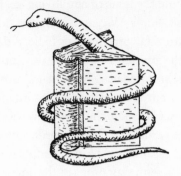

Picture for a moment a couple sitting down to an intimate dinner for two. Lighted candles are on the table; a small vase of flowers adorns the setting. Music plays in the background and wine is poured into glasses. These are familiar elements that we associate with love and sexuality. It is interesting to note that they are also the elements incorporated into Wiccan rituals. Here we see that both settings are in fact acts of reverence for the Feminine. Wine and flowers are time-honored offerings to the Goddess. Candlelight reveals that the setting is special and magickal, it is neither day nor night, light nor dark. The moment is sacred, far removed from the concerns of mundane life.

In order to understand the function of sexuality within the Old Religion we must step away from our modern views and personal politics for a few moments. We must return to a time when the community as a whole viewed sex as healthy, natural, and desirable. It was an age when men were not held in contempt for their sex drive and visual orientations to sexuality. Women were not degraded for their sexual desires or sensuality; the Judaic-Christian moral concept of *whore* had not yet evolved. Sacred prostitutes served the gods in holy temples, homosexuality and heterosexuality were nothing more than definitions of sexual preference (as evidenced in ancient Greece).

The Old Religion of pre-Christian Europe was based on fertility rites designed to ensure the propagation of animals, plants and human life. One of the most controversial aspects of Wicca today revolves around the issue of employing sexual activity for ritual or magickal use. Some Wiccan Traditions do not incorporate sexual elements into their practices (or beliefs) due in part to personal politics, inhibitions, and various health concerns. The social pressure of living in a Judaic-Christian culture has also caused some traditions to omit sexual elements in order to negate allegations made by many Christian churches that witches participate in orgies and perverse sexual practices. In order not to offend Judaic-Christian sensitivities, many Wiccans compromise the Old Ways by creating symbolic representations of the ancient fertility aspects of Witchcraft.

In ancient times, sexual energy was the most powerful energy that humans could experience through their own physical senses. The seemingly magickal ability of this energy to create other humans must have had a profound effect on the ancient human psyche. In the Mystery Tradition, this aspect of magick involves the use of sexual energy as a source of power. The Pagan concept of sexual activity is totally different than the Judaic-Christian concept. Sex is seen as a natural and pleasant experience. It can be a part of one's expression of love, or it can simply be a sharing of pleasure or lust with another person. For magickal and ritual purposes it can simply be the energy source that empowers the rites.

WOMAN AS SACRED ALTAR

In the text of the Great Rite we find that the ancients employed a woman's body as the sacred altar for their religious ceremonies:

> *Assist me to erect the ancient altar,*
> *at which in days past all worshipped;*
> *The great altar of all things.*
> *For in times of old, woman was the altar.*

It is only natural and logical that a matrifocal society would view the female form as sacred and employ it as the focus for religious and magickal rites. Here the living altar itself possessed the ability to give birth and to nourish new life. Menstrual blood, called the blood of the moon, was used for ritual markings in initiation ceremonies and rites designed to return departed souls back into their clan.

The concept of mixing blood together, as in the American Indian *blood-brother* ritual, dates back to ancient times. To join one's blood with another's forever bound the two together. Thus the High Priestess of the clan could join the souls of all members through her menstrual blood. Due to Indo-European influences ritual wine is often viewed today as the blood of the God. In its oldest associations it was the blood of the Goddess, wherein the wine contained three drops of menstrual blood magickally uniting the celebrants in this life and the life to come. Hunters and warriors were often anointed with ritual paint containing menstrual blood in case they were killed while away from the village. To anoint the dead with the blood of the moon was to ensure their return to life again. In the next reincarnation they would meet again and renew their love.

The triangle or pyramid shape is a sacred symbol associated with female anatomy. It reflects not only the pubic area but also denotes the nipples and clitoris which are linked by neural pathways. There is also a neuropsychological tract connecting the nipples to the pituitary gland. Stimulation of the nipples can cause the pituitary gland to secrete a hormone that triggers uterine contractions. This in turn causes the outflow of certain fluids containing various elements of glandular secretions. In the Wiccan Mystery Tradition the magickal Triangle of Manifestation is invoked by the High Priest who kisses the nipples and clitoris of the High Priestess during the rite of Drawing down the Moon. This rite of the triangle is also performed during the Great Rite. Some traditions shy away from this ancient practice and employ a modern version of the invocation wherein the kisses are placed upon the feet, knees, navel, breasts, and mouth.

The sacred altar is formed by a chosen woman who lies nude upon her back with knees bent and legs drawn up and parted (heels touching, or almost touching, the buttocks). A bowl or chalice is

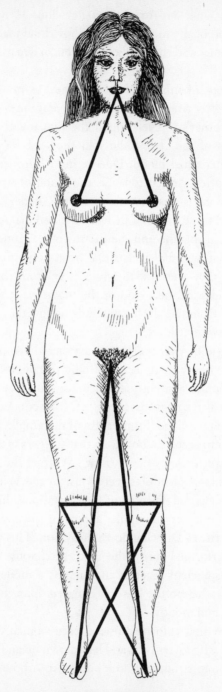

The Five-fold Kiss

set directly upon her navel, connecting the vessel to the etheric umbilical cord of the Goddess who is invoked within her body. The wine is poured into the bowl or chalice as the altar woman holds the vessel in place. The High Priest then dips his fingers into the vessel and anoints the woman's nipples and clitoris with three drops of wine each. This is followed by a kiss to each point as the invocation is recited. When performed with reverence this rite is quite beautiful.

PSYCHIC MASSAGE

In Sex Magick the art of creating bioelectromagnetic charges to stimulate and activate various psychic centers of the body is called psychic massage. It bears this name because it empowers the Chakras from which psychic abilities are maintained and generated. During the physical massage Odic currents are passed through each Chakra in the same fashion as is employed in the art of informing (see chapter nine). By combining Odic breath with magnetic passes the physical massage becomes etheric as well. Thus both the astral body and physical body are refreshed and invigorated.

In occult terminology the left hand is magnetic and the right hand is electric, when in close proximity to one another they create a flow of energy between them. This energy can be used to *patch* or strengthen weakened areas in the body's aura. It can also be used to balance the Chakra centers and restore the smooth flow of energy between each. This is accomplished by massaging along the areas connecting the Chakras and various nerve pathways.

The massage is begun at the forehead, moving downward to the feet and back up again. At each Chakra point the zone is massaged in a spiral fashion. The nipples and genitals are gently massaged as the hands pass through the Chakra zone associated with these areas. Nerve endings connecting the triangle (nipples and genitals) carry impulses to the third eye, heart, and base Chakra, activating a very powerful occult current that serves to empower the Chakras and aura. In some Wiccan Traditions this may be employed as a prelude to second degree Initiation (when generally the power is first passed to the initiate).

SEX MAGICK AND BODY FLUIDS

For the purposes of magick, sexual stimulation produces both energy and *charged* liquid *condensers*, both of which can be employed towards any given goal. The male's semen is channeled energy and always moves toward the manifestation of material form (whether it enters the womb or any other receptacle). In the case of fellatio, masturbation, or sodomy, the energy is absorbed by one of the planes and vitalizes entities that dwell there. These entities may be thought-forms or pre-existing beings.

When the usual conclusion of sexual intercourse is avoided, the discharge of energy is absorbed and forms an astral image of the mental image in the mind at the time of orgasm. This image becomes *alive* and is a functioning link between the subconscious mind and the astral plane. The incarnation of these images is one of the goals of sex magick. Another goal is to raise a form of power from the base of the spine. In this area resides the *Kundalini* or *Serpent Power* which has been suppressed for centuries by the Christian church. The goal is to bring this energy up to the *third eye* where it will give the person almost unlimited power. This system of sex magick is known as Tantra.

Two currents (or channels) of energy exist within the human entity. These currents are associated with the central nervous system and the spinal cord. We can refer to these currents as Lunar and Solar, or Feminine and Masculine (receptive/negative and active/positive). These polarities indicate bioelectromagnetic energy and are not meant to refer to gender natures. The Lunar and Solar currents are manifest within the body as the left and right branches of the ganglionic nerve structures. The left side is feminine/lunar and the right side is masculine/solar. Unfortunately, for centuries sexuality has evoked feelings of guilt and shame, due largely to Judaic-Christian morality. This mentality has served to negate (in most people) the natural function of the lunar and solar currents. One of the aims of sex magick is to free one's expression of sexuality from negative and inhibiting feelings. Once accomplished, the natural harmony of these currents can be restored.

Within the average person today, only one of the energy currents is open and flowing. The counter current is usually inhibited and suppressed, causing disharmony (dis-ease) within the physical body. This also causes a negative influence on the endocrine balance. In the untrained female only the lunar current flows uninhibited, and in the untrained male only the solar current is truly free. In the case of homosexuals this situation is reversed. The lunar and solar currents flowing in harmony within the body are symbolized by the ancient symbol of the Caduceus. This natural state eliminates disharmony (dis-ease) within the body and thus the Caduceus has come to symbolize health in our society today.

In the Mystery Teachings the natural sexual state is one of bisexuality, wherein both currents flow together in harmony. The indwelling soul inhabiting the physical body is neither male nor female, and so our gender is merely a circumstance of the physical dimension. The attitude that we display concerning the polarity of gender in which our souls reside is fashioned largely by our social environment. We must bear in mind, however, that gender may also be a manifestation of Karma for the individual soul.

THE MAGICKAL CHILD

The magickal child is a term used in sex magick for a magickal form or image. This aspect of sex magick involves the inhibition of orgasm for prolonged periods, allowing intensified mental/astral images to take shape. Sexual energy is not *grounded* as it is with mundane intercourse, but instead directed by the mind to manifest in a magickal thought-form. The channeled energy forms a subtle astral image of the concept dominant within the mind at the moment of orgasm.

The ejaculated semen of the male is unabsorbed, concentrated energy (a fixed charge). It always moves toward the creation of a manifested form, for it is the essence of creative energy. This is true of semen deposited in a vagina or any other receptacle. When semen enters a womb it is focused on a physical manifestation. Its magickal influence on the astral plane is annulled. When semen is not received by a womb (as in masturbation, oral copulation, or sodomy) its energy is drawn by entities existing on the astral levels.

Vaginal secretions are equally valuable fluids for the purpose of sex magick. They contain secretions from the endocrine glands which are charged by sexually activated lunar and solar currents. These secretions possess elements from the cerebrospinal fluid and the endocrine glands. Nerve pathways associated with bladder function through the third ventricle can initiate various secretions. Once roused, the currents flowing to the genital area stimulate nerves, which cause reactions within the entire body. The pituitary glands and pineal gland are stimulated, as are nerves affecting urination. The energy of vaginal secretions carries (to varying degrees) some element of all of these aspects. Vaginal fluids can be used in a similar manner to semen, or can be mixed with it for magickal purposes.

The mental state of Consciousness established during sex magick forms a *portal* to the subconscious and therefore to the astral. Visualized (and/or sigilized) images or concepts are vitalized and become *alive* (empowered). It is essential that the practitioner

Symbol of Renewal and Transformation

Virgin Symbol

Mother Symbol

Spirals: Death and Renewal

Net: Symbol of "Becoming," Emerging

Symbol of Women's Body Fluids: Milk, Blood, and Secretion

Life and Birth: the Power to Give

Women's Symbols

has developed the art of concentration/visualization and has a firm control over personal will power. There must be nothing in the mind at the moment of orgasm except the image (or sigil) of the desired *child* to be born or created. If the mental image is not complete or becomes distorted by interruptions in the mental imagery, then it is possible that very negative thought-forms can manifest. The inherent danger here is that these forms may begin to possess their creator and increase his or her sexual appetites. In such cases the individual may become obsessed with sexual release, as the entity demands more and more sexual energy to feed on. This is the basis of the incubus and succubus legends.

SEXUALITY AND MODERN WICCA

Many Wiccans who still wish to employ sexual energy, but for whatever reasons wish to avoid actual intercourse, have incorporated nonphysical aspects of sexuality into their rites. This can include anything from provocative and seductive dancing, to erotic verses or suggestive body language and demeanor. Theses elements within a ritual setting can indeed evoke strong sexual currents.

As we saw in chapter ten, some Wiccans employ ritual tools to take the place of human sexual participants. Holding and manipulating tools representing the phallus or vagina/womb is meant to raise the sexual energies through mimetic magick and make the symbolic connections to the fertility aspects that once empowered ancient rituals. Some Wiccans feel that this serves their purposes quite well and others feel a definite lack of power associated with such symbolic acts.

In ancient times sexual union was part of the initiation process and power was passed from teacher to student through the bioelectromagnetic currents aroused by sexual stimulation between opposite genders/polarities. Functional and beneficial sexual initiations date back to antiquity, and can still be found in tribal practices from South America and Africa. This is still seen in the vast majority of Hereditary and Family Traditions. Many modern Wiccans feel that this is improper. Especially when the man is the teacher of a woman, many Wiccan women see sexual initiation as abusive and manipulative. However, the presence of men in any sexual initiation involving women may negate the validity of the rite. Clearly this view stems from sexually abusive behavior toward women perpetrated by a minority of men. This need not be the case as Wiccan men traditionally hold women in very high regard.

Sexuality, like most things in Wicca, is an aspect that Wiccans must individually examine and arrive at their own assessment. What is useful for one person may not serve the needs of another. Therefore I leave the reader to discern the teachings of this chapter as the spirit leads.

CHAPTER SIXTEEN

———————

LIVING THE MYSTERIES

Of that place beyond the heavens none of our earthly poets has yet sung, and none shall sing worthily. But this is the manner of it, for assuredly we must be bold to speak what is true, above all when our discourse is upon truth It is there that true Being dwells, without color or shape, that cannot be touched; reason alone, the soul's pilot, can behold it, and all true knowledge is knowledge thereof...

—Plato, *Phaedrus*

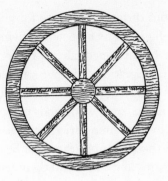

Now that we have seen the Mystery pattern in myths, legends, and rituals we must turn to the application of these tenets within our own lives. The Mysteries exist in order to lead us inward through an application of outer teachings. There are essentially five stages that we may incorporate into our lives to align ourselves with the Wiccan Mysteries. Through them we can set into play a flow of energy that will open channels upon the higher planes allowing us to connect with the essence of the Mysteries. These are covered in this chapter under the subheadings: Nature, Ancestors, Deities, Mythos, Rites, and Death.

At this point in the book you should be familiar with the concepts being discussed here under each subheading. If you find that you do not understand the associations being discussed then it is likely that you have missed an important point in the related chapters of this book. Go back, using the index and chapter titles, and read through the text again. It is good training in discipline and will help you to make the mental pathway connections required for a sound understanding of the Mysteries. *Everything in this book is connected to everything else.* It is your Quest to assemble them and integrate them into your consciousness. Answer all the questions contained in this chapter and you can create your own Mystery Tradition from any eclectic or traditional sources. You have already read the answers if you have truly read rather than skimmed this book, so now it is time to consider the questions raised here.

NATURE

Nature is the syllabus through which we formulate the beliefs and principles of our religion. The first step to living the Mystery Tradition is to observe Nature, meditate on Her and merge ourselves with the beauty of Creation. Simple camping trips or walks through the woods can become teachings in and of themselves. Sit on a hilltop and look out over woodlands or open fields. Let your mind drift back to another time period—imagining how this scene might have looked thousands of years ago. Such thoughts will be sensed by the life-forms in the area and their genetic memories will be passed back to you if you remain open and reverent. *What metaphysical mechanism or principle could account for this?*

It is very useful to become involved in planting a garden, especially a vegetable or herb garden. Many nurseries even carry small portable greenhouses that can be used in an apartment or a home with little yard space. Failing this, even a flower-yielding plant of some kind will help connect you to the living cycles of Nature. Caring for a garden creates a vibration in your aura that can be detected by life-forms in the wild. Through this they will sense your reverence for living things and aid you in your meditations and attempts to relink with Nature. *From where would this be sensed and how is it transmitted?*

To help personify the forces working behind Nature, it is useful to employ a figurine, usually of an elven or fairy image. This can be a yard statue or a simple figurine standing next to your portable greenhouse. In mythology the fairy is associated with fields and woodlands as a magickal entity involved with the life forces of plants and animals. By creating a mental link with this concept through emergence in the life cycles of Nature (and your Nature hikes) you can more easily align yourself with the Nature spirits. *How would this work in relationship to the astral plane and the concept known as Egregore?*

ANCESTORS

Though not essential to the practice of any Wiccan Tradition, a person's genetic link with ancient cultures can prove beneficial in establishing currents of energy associated with various deities and spirits. Remember that you are the direct descendant of an ancient Pagan who knew what you now desire to know. Ancestral shrines can be erected to activate genetic memories. In some traditions Initiates are taught to memorize their lineage, reciting the names of departed relatives in order to open mental pathways into the past.

Another effective technique is to light a candle at your ancestral shrine and read myths or legends associated with your heritage out loud. The spoken voice creates vibrations that carry upon them into the ether the passion of your blood. This creates a ripple through the astral plane and connects you with times long forgotten. On the shrine you should place symbols or icons typically associated with your nationality (past and present if possible).

It is also useful to take on a name of the type that may have been used in ancient times in order to further connect yourself with energies of antiquity. Reading books and viewing movies that involve cultural heroes is also an excellent aid to alignment. These tales often reflect the Collective Consciousness of the ancient peoples who created them. Therefore, by incorporating them into your own consciousness you become a part of the spiritual heritage of your people. *What connection does this have with the Blood Mysteries?*

AN ANCESTRAL RITE

The purpose of this basic rite is to connect you with the spiritual currents that have been carried in your genetic makeup, aligning you with the ancestral memories sleeping within you.

REQUIRED ITEMS:

1. An oil. This should be something from the mint family. Pennyroyal is excellent. In the absence of oil, anything "minty" will do. What you want is the scent on you so that you can smell it throughout the ritual. The smell of mint stimulates memory centers.

2. A candle. This should be of a symbolic color associated with your ancestors. If nothing comes to mind, then use a red candle as this carries the association of the blood link.

3. Incense (if performed outdoors use a lunar incense that employs camphor, which has a catalytic influence on astral material). Do not use incense indoors for this rite as it will negate the mint scent. The smoke of the incense should rise into the ether, "carrying" your words into the astral plane.

4. A myth or legend: something connected to your ethnic heritage. Choose a favorite myth or legend—there is a metaphysical reason that tale holds meaning for you.

5. Icons, symbols, or something reflective of the culture with which you desire to awaken memories. A picture or painting is good, even a book cover is fine. Place this object in plain view, next to the candle.

6. An offering. Typically this is a mixture of red wine and honey, in equal parts. This will be poured as a libation at the conclusion of the ritual. You can also offer flowers or herbs associated with your ancestors, in which case you would plant them in the ground or in a pot as an offering.

THE RITUAL

1. Now you are ready to begin. This ritual is best performed outdoors at night, under the stars. The night of the full moon is excellent, of course. Sit in a quiet place, state that your purpose is to align yourself with the ancestral memories within, and then light the candle. Next, anoint yourself with the oil, in the pentagram pattern: * forehead * right breast * left shoulder * right shoulder * left breast * forehead.

2. Then sit by the lighted candle and visualize a time period with which you seek to connect. See the type of clothing that was worn then within your mind's eye. Bring any other images into your mind that will help "fine-tune" the alignment. If there are traditional foods or drink available, connected to your ancestors, you can enhance the rite by consuming them as you go along (you are what you eat).

3. Next, begin to read out loud from your myth or legend. Read to the flame of the candle as though it were a person, looking up into the flame as you finish a sentence here and there. The flame is the portal, the animating etheric substance of this rite. Fire is symbolic of passion and energy; passion and energy are terms we associate with blood, the link, the portal to the past, within you and outside of you.

4. When you have finished your tale, hold the libation in your hands, close your eyes and take three deep, slow breaths, exhaling fully between each breath (into the libation). Open your eyes and then pour half of the libation out on the ground as an offering and leave half in the bowl for the "Fairy Folk."

5. The rite is now completed, and all you need do now is allow the memories to come to you on their own. You will find that this rite enhances your ability to create rituals and to make various connections when you study and do research. Anoint yourself with the mind oil beforehand to enhance genetic memory recall.

Those of you with more experience may want to empower the candles and oil with your own charges, and pick a night when the moon is well aspected for psychic workings. Feel free to modify this rite as you please.

DEITIES

It is important to have a focal point for your alignment to the Mysteries. This can be served by obtaining a statue of a goddess or a god typical of the deity or deities worshipped by your ancestors. Enshrine this in a special place set aside for this purpose only. Each day, for a cycle of one full moon to the next, take a dry cloth and clean the statue as an act of reverence for what it represents to you. Place fresh flowers before the statue, or something else appropriate to its nature. Do a little research on the nature of the deity and decide whether grain, flowers, or other offerings might be best used. Take some time to talk to your deity, openly and honestly. No one can fulfill needs that are left unspoken. Your relationship with your deity is no different than any other of your relationships. All require communication, attention, and respect. If you ignore your deity you drift away from its sphere of influence. The gods never abandon us, and sadly it is we who come and go as we please.

Whether you choose to view your god or goddess as an actual entity or a metaphysical concept is up to you. Regardless of whether your heart or your mind leads you, it is important to follow the guideline as given. There will be plenty of time for you to modify your focus after the first full lunar cycle has passed. Give yourself a chance to be child-like and innocent once again.

MYTHOS

It is vital to embracing the mysteries that you understand the mythos of your ancestors and their deities. In order to do this you must grasp the thread running through the Wheel of the Year as reflected in the rites of your tradition. If you're creating your own tradition, then it is even more important that you have a sound understanding of the seasonal mythos. You will need to outline the aspects of your goddess and god and their connections to rites of the year.

Let us now consider the God. Does he represent the Animal Kingdom or the Plant Kingdom (or both)? Is he a Harvest Lord and if so what represents him in your rites? *Is he the cakes/bread or is he the wine (or both)?* If he is only of the Animal Kingdom what represents him and how do you merge with him? *Does the god take on different forms/aspects representing the waxing and waning parts of the year?* If so, what forms are they and why those particular forms? In other words, how do they relate to themes of growth and decay? Does he have a relationship to the Goddess and if so what is it and why? Remember, the rites are designed so that you may become one with his essence. You will need to understand what you are merging with, why, and what you will consume to bind the connection.

Next we will consider the Goddess. Is she a Moon Goddess, and if so does she reflect various lunar phases or all of them, and why? Is she an Earth Goddess and does she represent specific life-forms or all life-forms, and why? *Does she have a relationship to the God, and if so what is it and why is it needed or desired?* What aspects does the Goddess possess? Is she creator and destroyer, is she maiden, mother, and crone? *If so, why is she these things, what is served by these aspects of her being?*

How is the Goddess reflected in your Wheel of the Year? Does she age and grow young again with the seasons? Does she descend into the Underworld at the Fall Equinox and ascend again at the Spring Equinox. If she does, why, and what does it serve? Lastly, do you see yourself in her? What does she bring to you and your ritual circle that is nurturing and empowering?

RITES

Last we must consider the mysteries and how they relate to various aspects of the rites you practice. One of the most significant acts performed in Wiccan rites is *Drawing Down the Moon*. This involves the invocation of Goddess consciousness into the Priestess or High Priestess. *How does this relate to the astral plane and the Egregore concept? What is it that you are actually merging or sharing consciousness with?* The ritual posture for this invocation is very ancient and elements of it can be found in Neolithic and early Egyptian times. In some traditions it is referred to as the Star Position because it represents the Totality of the Goddess, the Goddess as the Universe. In the case of ritual, the posture establishes the Goddess Consciousness within the Universe or microcosm of the circle.

It is a very ancient technique to take on the sacred postures that reflect aspects of various deities. The wearing of masks and animal skins was also employed to merge the human consciousness with that of other beings (whether spirits or deities). In Western Occultism such organizations as the Golden Dawn established a series of ritual postures for opening portals to other dimensions and for merging with various aspects of divinity. Many of them were based on Egyptian forms, Egypt being another Mediterranean Mystery Cult. The Cult of the Dead and remnants of the Neolithic Bird deities (reflected in bird-headed gods and goddesses) are very common elements of Egyptian religion.

The seasonal rites that comprise the Wheel of the Year are very important rituals for aligning one's spirit and energy patterns to the natural flow of earth's energy. It is important to see the patterns of your own life within the cycle of the year. How are your moods and actions like the seasons? When do you feel most empowered during the year, and least empowered? See the seasonal rites of the waxing year as opportunities to plant new ideas and goals. Incorporate this into your rituals. See the rites of the waning year as opportunities to cast off the chaff in your life and to gather in the harvest. *Who are you in the myths and legends that are integral parts of your rituals and why?* How is it useful to align with these powerful ancient currents of energy?

DEATH

We conclude this chapter with perhaps the greatest of all mysteries known to the human experience, that of dying. All religions deal with this topic in one way or another. Death is an integral part of life and yet many people dread and fear it. In part this is due to our natural instincts as physical beings: our will to survive. As spiritual beings we may also fear it due to confusion about what awaits us, or due to actions we took that may have Karmic consequences.

The Mystery Teachings tell us that death is a fading away into temporary unconsciousness, from which we awaken in a new world as full of opportunities for personal growth as was the physical world when we were first born. *As above, so below.* Death may be as much a struggle to emerge into a new existence as was physical birth—a brief and intense experience not without its own anxiety, but ending in the comforting arms of those who await the birth.

To the Wiccan the realm of Death is a time for rest and renewal. Death is a portal to rebirth and eventually to release from the Reincarnation Cycle. The ancient Aegean/Mediterranean Mystery Cults taught that the soul would inhabit three temporary boides and one eternal body. The first body was one of flesh made from the dust of the earth. The second body was one of astral form made from the light of the moon. The third body was a body of light cast from the sun. The fourth and final body was made of starlight. Thus a soul journeys and lives many lives within the physical dimension, lunar and solar realms, eventually rejoining the stars wherein dwell the community of higher souls.

CHAPTER
SEVENTEEN

SUMMARY

*...we find the ancient continually confirming the
extreme antiquity of the modern. Be it a tract
here, a small observance there, now an herb in
an incantation, and anon a couplet in a charm,
they continually interlace, cross, touch, and coin-
cide. I find these unobserved small identities continually manifesting themselves, and they form a
chain of intrinsic evidence which is as valuable to
a truly critical scholar as any historical or directly traditional confirmation.*

—Charles Leland, *Etruscan Magic*

Because much of the ancient Celtic beliefs and practices have been lost to us due to Roman and Germanic conquest, it is difficult to say with certainty what they truly were. Fortunately we do know a great deal historically about those cultures with which the Celts had prolonged contact. By comparing those beliefs that have been passed on to us in the Wiccan religion with those related to foreign ones that we can historically document, it is possible to make a good case for the antiquity and validity of Wiccan claims to actual ancient practices and beliefs. This is above all the purpose of this book.

Much ground has been covered in the brief span of this book and it would be useful for us to now review what we have uncovered. Beginning with the Cult of the Dead we have seen that fairies evolved from primitive beliefs concerning departed souls and their burial sites. These burial mounds were themselves the basis for fairy mounds seen in later fairy lore. The burial mounds of Old Europe, like the fairy mounds, had entrances by which the spirit could leave or enter. This primitive cult migrated from Old Europe to Egypt and Iberia, and eventually to the British Isles. Here it became an integral part of Druidic beliefs that were later absorbed by the Celts.

The investigation of fairies led us to the Tuatha de Danaan whom we found were most likely exiled Pelasgians from Greece. It was also revealed that the Aegeans used the word "Danaan" as a term for Greeks as a whole, which seems to support the Aegean origins. The Pelasgi worshipped the Greek goddess Danae and we saw the similarities between the names Danae, Dana, and Diana. In Italy Diana was a Moon Goddess and Queen of the Fairies. Wiccans have long held the belief that the Tuatha de Danaan were the origins of the Fairy Race in Ireland, and it is interesting to note the Aegean and Mediterranean connections. We also noted that in legend the Tuatha de Danaan first appeared from out of a mist, and we saw that the earlier Etruscans called their highest deities *the shrouded ones*, or *gods of the mist*.

The Druids were very much influenced by Aegean concepts due to their contacts with the Greeks. In the book *The Celtic Reader* (Aquarian Press, 1992), edited by John Matthews, a well-known writer on Celtic themes, he tells us that much of their customs and beliefs were derived from Greek traditions. It seems likely that the Druids were descendants of an exiled people from Greece, or perhaps even an early Etruscan priesthood that migrated north (three bronze Etruscan statues discovered in Sligo, Ireland, are now in the Irish National Museum in Dublin). We also saw that ancient Greek and Roman historians noted the worship of Dionysus among the Druids. These historians also reveal to us that the Druids taught the Celts the doctrine of reincarnation, and were themselves instructed by the Greeks. According to Hippolytus of Alexandria, the legendary Thrachian Zalmoxis (circa 525 B.C., nearly two centuries before Celtic settlements appear in Thrace) taught to the Druids the Pythagorean theory of reincarnation. After the time of Zalmoxis, the Thracians eventually became a Celtic people. Some historians have mislabeled Zalmoxis a Celt because he came from Thrace, but the timeline does not support this.

Through an examination of the god Dionysus, and his transformation into Bacchus, we have discovered all of the aspects connected with Wiccan Horned God concepts. We noted Dionysus' aspects as a stag-horned god, bull-horned god, and goat-horned god, as well as his Green Man images. Upon further investigation we saw that he was also the Child of Promise and the Son/Lover of the Goddess, a mythos central to European Paganism. It is interesting to note that ancient frescoes depicted scenes of women directing blindfolded initiates, and that Dionysus carried the wand

and chalice, symbols common to Wicca today. These discoveries support the claims of antiquity concerning the beliefs within Wicca. No other single European god could be found who was associated with every one of these elements in Wiccan belief.

Artemis, wife to Dionysus in Homeric legend, appeared to be the origin of the Mother and Triple Goddess in Diana Triformis (seen still in her Mother aspect as Diana of Ephesus). The Romans had inherited the Triformis aspects from Hekate Triformis of whom Porphory wrote: "The moon is Hekate...her power appears in three forms: Selene in heaven, Artemis on earth, Hekate in the Underworld." Hesiod wrote in the *Theogony* that Hekate ruled over the three great mysteries: Birth, Death, and Life (we see the same association in the Wiccan Legend of the Descent concerning the *three mysteries in the life of Man*). It was from a study of these aspects that we discovered the origins of the Celtic Matres, stemming from the Roman concept of the Iuones.

An investigation of the Agricultural Mysteries revealed a long and ancient trail leading from the Aegean to the Mediterranean and up into western and northern Europe. Here we noted that the Harvest Lord and Slain God concepts were rooted in the Agricultural Mysteries of southern and southeastern Europe. These were passed from the Greeks to the Etruscans, and in turn to the Romans who passed them on to the Celts (see appendix six). The people of the British Isles absorbed the Agricultural Mysteries from which later sprang their own Harvest Lords, such as John Barley Corn.

Many other elements of Celtic Wiccan concepts were also traceable to Aegean and Mediterranean origins. We saw evidence that the Cauldron of Cerridwen and her nine maidens were almost identical to the Cauldron of Ceres and the nine Greek Muses. The Norns or Wyrrd Sisters of northern Europe were clearly based on the much earlier Greek Moerae (and Roman Fates) whose function and form was identical. We also found that the concept of the *Three Worlds* in the Celtic Cosmos had been a Greek philosophy appearing in the *Theogony* centuries before the arrival of the Celts in Greece or Italy. Surprisingly we also noted that the legend of

King Arthur and the sword Excaliber may have been rooted in the mythos of the King of the Woods at Lake Nemi in Italy. It is interesting to note that the earliest accounts of King Arthur place him near the southern Alps in the region of Lake Leman, not in the British Isles (as noted in *Ecstasies*, by Carlo Ginzburg).

The doctrine of the *four elements*, an integral aspect of Wiccan religion and magick, was first taught (in Sicily) by Empedocles in 475 B.C., as noted in chapter seven. The Wiccan verses appearing in the *Charge of the Goddess* are traceable to Italian witches as evidenced by the text appearing in Charles Leland's *Aradia—Gospel of the Witches* published over half a century before the Gardnerian version. *The Legend of the Descent* is clearly derived from Mesopotamia, relating to such myths as Inanna, and the *Legend* also bears aspects of the Roman Mysteries as practiced in Pompeii. These elements are dealt with in greater historical depth in my previous book *Ways of the Strega*.

Historical evidence is important when speaking of the Wiccan Mysteries mainly because it confirms the antiquity of Wiccan beliefs. There are too many complex connections and elements present within Wiccan theology to be a modern work created by a handful of individuals such as Gerald Gardner, Doreen Valiente, or even Aleister Crowley (as many people wish to claim). The historical evidence concerning origins is clear and abundant, but we are also concerned with history as revealed in the Mystery Teachings themselves. It was here that we saw the rise and fall of an ancient matriarchy. Out of this arose a blending of masculine and feminine aspects resulting in the formation of rites and principles that we now relate to as Wicca. The reverence for Nature and for the Great Mother were two of the most influential aspects of human consciousness in formulating Wiccan Theology. To acknowledge the Mother was to acknowledge Her lover and impregnator, the God. Fertility rites were formed around the primitive understanding of sexuality, and these rituals served to empower the ancient magickal ceremonies. The arts of magick were based on the ways of Nature, and to merge with the forces of Nature in order to discern the inner secrets gave rise to ritual observances of the Solstices and Equinoxes.

The Mysteries of Wicca are the very fabric of the Universe, woven by the Sisters of Wyrrd into the patterns of our lives. They are the forces within Nature that direct us toward a discovery of ourselves. The Mysteries reveal the connections and revelations that bring forth enlightenment. They are hidden and ever present, waiting for that receptive moment when we can embrace them fully. Sometimes they reside in myths and legends where the object of the Quest represents the teaching. The heroes are aspects of our own being, elements of our mind and soul. Sometimes they are reflected in a chance meeting, a heart-to-heart talk with a friend, or even an honest talk with ourselves.

To further explore the mysteries you need only look to those myths and legends that call to you. The adventure of your hero is your own hero path, and the adventurer is that part of you that has the strength to retrieve what you believe to be lost or beyond your reach. The stories speak to you because they contain the symbolic language of the subconscious mind. They know what you need to know. You naturally possess all the abilities required to meet the challenge. You need only accept the call of the hero. Whether you need to pull the sword from the stone, slay the dragon who keeps you from your treasure, or find the sacred Grail within you is known only to you.

Scott Cunningham wrote, in his book *Living Wicca* (Llewellyn Publications, 1993), that "if you wanted to understand the Wiccan Mysteries you should watch an ice cube melt." Perhaps it's time to pick up the ice cube and drop it into a glass of water, because there is a lot of thirsty work ahead before the mysteries are revealed.

In closing, I wish you a life filled with mysteries of wonder and exploration. May the teachings in this book be useful sign posts as you journey on your own Mystery Quest. And may your path be truly Wyrrd.

———————

THE ELEMENTAL DOORWAYS

The purpose of this technique is to create portals or doorways through which the practitioner can mentally explore other realms. The technique used here is based on the practices of the Golden Dawn. Place the appropriate symbol on a poster board or paint it on a full-length mirror with watercolor or poster paints (see illustrations). Off to one side place a large blank white posterboard (or something of that nature).

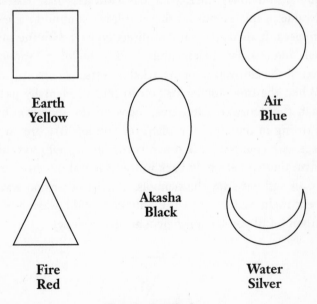

Earth
Yellow

Air
Blue

Akasha
Black

Fire
Red

Water
Silver

Tattvic Symbols

The colors should be as *true* as possible, the guides being that the colors have strength and brilliance. A fiery red is good for the triangle, sky blue for the circle, light yellow for the square, metallic silver for the crescent, and a deep black or indigo for the oval.

Sit comfortably in front of the selected symbol and relax while viewing it. Stare at the symbol with a deliberate fixed gaze until you notice a slight haze or halo effect around it. At this point look away at the blank white posterboard. Within a few seconds an illusion of the complimentary color will appear against the white background. Close your eyes and mentally visualize the symbol as a doorway through which you can walk. It is important to either mentally make the symbol as large as a doorway or yourself small enough to pass through the drawing of the symbol.

Mentally pass through the doorway. If you have any difficulty, try taking on a physical sense of the represented element and then try to pass through the portal. Once through, take stock of the setting. Mentally affirm that the doorway is now behind you and do not lose a sense of where it is in relation to where you are. You are relatively safe during this type of exercise and you mentally explore the dimension into which your consciousness has passed. The main value of this exercise is that it trains the mind in *other world* experiences. It also puts you into direct contact with the four elementals and associated elementals. In time building a rapport will aid you in the cultivation of magickal powers.

When the time comes for you to return, mentally pass back through the doorway. After this, focus on the sensation of your body sitting in the chair (or wherever you left it). Stretch, touch surfaces with your hands. In other words, allow your physical sense to affirm that you are fully back in the material dimension. Open your eyes and put away the symbols. Try the other doorways on a different night and always work only during the waxing phase of the moon (until you feel proficient at this exercise).

APPENDIX TWO

THE ASTRAL TEMPLE

Exploring the astral plane is an integral part of Wiccan practices. To this end Wiccans have developed various techniques for creating an Astral Temple from which to explore and influence the astral dimensions. Provided here is one such technique. Once established, the temple can be used not only for the purposes already given but also to channel energy to and from the astral. It can also be employed as a place to meet with Deity in personal sacred space.

First obtain a painting or drawing that depicts the appearance of the astral image you would like the temple to have. Some Wiccans use the image of an actual stone temple, some use a magickal room image such as in a castle, and others prefer a woodland scene. Ideally all of these settings should have an entry way whether it is a path leading into the woods, steps going up into the temple, or a doorway opening into a chamber.

Once you have found or created the setting, then the picture must be charged. Place the image in a picture frame with a clear glass cover (a nice oak frame is a good choice, or choose something else symbolic to you). Place the picture before you and sit or stand comfortably while facing it. On the floor in front of you place a bottle of a beverage of any kind (wine or mead would be an excellent choice). Cup both hands around the bottle as you perform the following. Using the technique of *informing* from chapter nine (incorporating the Odic breath), mentally pass images of yourself walking into the setting of the picture (ignore the bottle for now but keep holding it).

Let your imagination work freely and only redirect it if images become negative or silly. What you want to do at this point is to create quarter portals within the setting. These can be doorways, windows, archways, openings between trees, or whatever. Place protective pentagram symbols on both sides of the portals. Next mentally create an altar at the center of the temple. Imagine yourself building it or magickally forming it with ritual gestures (it is your own Universe and you are its creator and master). Pass an Odic breath charge into everything you create. You can then embellish the temple with any items or decorations you wish. Try to keep it simple because you will have to mentally recall the images of what you create in the setting for the first few times you enter the temple. Obviously the more appropriate images that are already a part of the physical painting, the less you will need to add.

Once you have finished adding the personal items it is time to look around at what you have created. Mentally walk about and take special note of everything. To exit the temple simply allow your vision of the picture to slightly blur, then close your eyes and clap your hands or snap your fingers three times. Turn your head away from the picture and open your eyes. The bottle you held during this exercise is now charged with the essence of all that you experienced. The next few times that you enter the temple, take a drink from the bottle first and it will empower your mental/astral work.

From this point forward the astral temple is there for you, until you mentally dissolve it or destroy the picture. Enter it for solitary rituals or mental spell casting. Use it to call on spirit guides or the goddess or god. There are many applications and you should feel free to explore them. Always wear a protective amulet of some kind and ask for the blessings and protection of the Goddess and God when you first enter the temple. Use common sense and basic courtesy when encountering any entities, should you choose to pass through the portals and explore the astral dimensions. More importantly, stay oriented to direction and remember the way of return to the portal.

THE WICCAN MYSTERY SCRIPT

Almost every Mystery Tradition has a secret alphabet or script of some type. The Egyptians used hieroglyphics, the Druids employed the Ogham, and in Wicca we traditionaly use either the Theban script or some types of runic alphabet. The use of mystical script serves to invoke a change in consciousness, employing levels of the subconscious mind directly linked to the astral plane. Pictured below is the traditional Wiccan alphabet.

A	B	C	D	E	F
G	H	I	K	L	M
N	O	P	Q	R	S
	T	V	Y	Z

APPENDIX FOUR

WICCAN SYMBOLS

Different Traditions employ the use of different symbols to represent various concepts. Shown here are the most common ones used in such Traditions as the Gardnerian and other Celtic Systems.

Athame and Sword: Top side, carve initial of witch name and:

The 8-fold Path to the Center   The Arrow of Magic Issuing Forth   The Perfect Couple

Underside, carve the following:

| Sign of God | Name of God | Scourge | Kiss | Sign of Goddesss | Name of Goddess |

Bolline: Top side handle, carve the following:

Top side blade, carve the following:

Underside handle, carve the following:

WICCAN RITUAL TOOLS

Pictured here and on the following page are the most common ritual tools employed for ceremonial and magickal uses. The earliest known depiction of a magician appearing with the wand, chalice, blade, and pentacle is found in the Italian Tarot (the Cary-Vale Visconti deck dating from the mid-fifteenth century).

Chalice   **Pentacle**

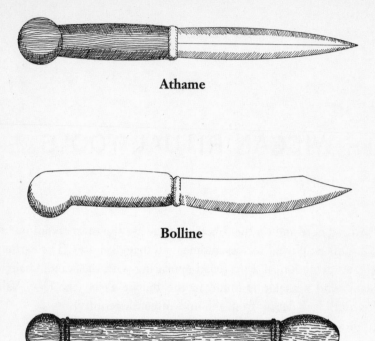

Athame

Bolline

Wand

THE ELEUSINIAN MYSTERIES

The Eleusinian Mysteries, originating in Greece, involve themes of descent and ascent, loss and regain, light and darkness, and the cycles of life and death. In the book *The Secret Teachings of All Ages*, by Manly Hall, the author relates that the rites associated with these Mysteries were performed at midnight during the Spring and Autumn Equinoxes. Hall reports that the Eleusinian Mysteries spread to Rome and then Britain. The Eleusinian Cult contained the *Greater Mysteries* and the *Lesser Mysteries*. The *Lesser* dealt with the abduction of Persephone by the Underworld God, a classic descent myth. The *Greater* Mysteries dealt with the Quest for the return of the Goddess, and the rites were performed in honor of Ceres (an agricultural goddess who was Patron of the Mysteries). This would account for many of the Wiccan concepts found in the mythos concerning the Descent and return of the Goddess, as well as many themes connected to the Equinox rites.

In the general mythos, Persephone descends into the Underworld and encounters its Lord. The life of the world disappears with Her and the first autumn and winter befalls the earth. The Lord of the Underworld falls in love with the Goddess and wants to keep Her in His realm. Ceres intervenes on Her behalf and pleads with the Underworld Lord to release Persephone. At first He refuses because Persephone has eaten the seeds of the pomegranate, an ancient symbol of the male seed (as we see in the Wiccan Descent Legend *they loved and were One*). Eventually He agrees on the condition that She return again to His realm for half of each year (cycle of the seasons). It is interesting to note that in the *Essay on the Mysteries of Eleusis*, by M. Ouvaroff, we find passages from the ancient philosopher Porphyry who reveals that the symbols of the Eleusinsian Mysteries included the circle, triangle and cone (all aspects of Wiccan rites).

In the Orphic Mysteries we find some very interesting connections to Celtic Wiccan beliefs. Orpheus, the Thracian Bard, was initiated into the Egyptian Mysteries where he gained a vast knowledge of magick, astrology, and medicine. He was also an initiate of the Mysteries of the Cabiri at Samothrace which is where the Pelasgians were also schooled in the Mysteries. We noted earlier that the Pelasgians of Greece were most likely the source of the Tuatha de Danaan legends. In the legends that sprang up around him we find that he was decapitated and that his head continued to live, becoming an oracle (a common myth seen later in Celtic legends). The ancients believed that he was the son of the God Apollo and a Muse. He was said to have played the lyre with such perfect harmonies that even the gods acknowledged his power. Legends say that through his music he conveyed divine secrets to humankind and we see in him many solar connections related also in Celtic legends not unlike those of the Celtic Bard Taliesin.

BIBLIOGRAPHY

Adler, Margot. *Drawing Down the Moon*. New York: Viking Press, 1979.

Alexander, Marc. *British Folklore*. New York: Crescent Books, 1982.

Anderson, William. *The Green Man, The Archetype of Our Oneness with the Earth*. New York: HarperCollins, 1990.

Ankarloo, Bengt, and Gustav Henningsen. *Early Modern European Witchcraft: Centres & Peripheries*. London: Oxford University Press, 1990.

Bardon, Franz. *Initiation into Hermetics*. Wuttertal, West Germany: Dieter Ruggeberg, 1971.

Bonfante, Larissa. *Etruscan*. London: Biritsh Museum Publications Ltd., 1990.

Bonnefoy, Yves (compiled by). *Roman and European Mythologies*. Chicago: University of Chicago Press, 1992.

Brennan, J. H. *Astral Doorways*. York Beach, ME: Samuel Weiser, 1971.

Briggs, K. M. *The Fairies in English Tradition and Literature*. Chicago: The University of Chicago Press, 1967.

Buckland, Ray. *Witchcraft from the Inside*. St. Paul: Llewellyn Publications, 1995.

Campbell, Joseph, Ed. "The Mysteries," papers from the *Eranos Yearbooks*. Princeton: Princeton University Press, 1978.

Campbell, Joseph. *Primitive Mythology*. New York: Penquin Books, 1969.

_____. *The Hero with a Thousand Faces*. Princeton: Princeton University Press, 1968.

_____. *The Masks of God: Primitive Mythology*. New York: Penquin Books, 1968.

Cavendish, Richard. *The Powers of Evil*. New York: Putnam, 1975.

Collingwood, R. G. *Roman Britain*. New York: Barnes & Noble Books, 1994.

Cowell, F. R. *Life in Ancient Rome*. New York: A Perigee Book, 1961.

Crowther, Arnold and Patricia. *The Secrets of Ancient Witchcraft, with the Witches Tarot*. Secaucus: University Book, Inc., 1974.

Cunningham, Scott. *Living Wicca, A Further Guide for the Solitary Practitioner*. St. Paul: Llewellyn Publications, 1993.

Davidson, Gustav. *A Dictionary of Angels: Including the Fallen.* New York: The Free Press, 1967.

Devereux, Paul. *Shamanism and the Mystery Lines.* St. Paul, MN: Llewellyn Publications, 1993.

Dudley, Donald R. *The Romans: 850 B.C.–337 A.D.* New York: Barnes & Noble Books, 1970.

Eisler, Riane. *Sacred Pleasure—Sex, Myth, and the Politics of the Body.* New York: HarperCollins, 1995.

Evans-Wentz, W. Y. *The Fairy Faith in Celtic Countries.* New York: Citadel Press Book, 1990.

Farrar, Stewart. *What Witches Do.* London: Peter Davies LTD, 1971.

Farrar, Janet and Stewart. *Eight Sabbats for Witches.* London: Robert Hale, 1981.

_____. *The Witches' Way.* London: Robert Hale, 1984.

_____. *The Witches' Goddess.* Custer: Phoenix Publishing Inc., 1987.

_____. *The Witches' God.* London: Robert Hale, 1989.

Ford, Patrick K. *The Mabinogi and Other Medieval Welsh Tales.* Berkeley: University of California Press, 1977.

Fortune, Dion. *Aspects of Occultism.* Wellingborough, Northamptonshire: The Aquarian Press, 1973.

Francia, Luisa. *Dragontime, Mystery and Magic of Menstruation.* New York: Ash Tree Publishing, 1991.

Frazer, James. *The Golden Bough.* New York: Macmillan Company, 1922.

Gardner, Gerald. *Witchcraft Today.* Seraucus: The Citadel Press, 1973.

_____. *The Meaning of Witchcraft.* New York: Samuel Weiser, 1976.

George, Demetra. *Mysteries of the Dark Moon.* New York: HarperCollins Publishers, 1992.

Gimbutas, Marija. *The Goddesses and Gods of Old Europe.* Berkeley: University of California Press, 1982.

_____. *The Language of the Goddess.* New York: HarperCollins, 1991.

Ginzberg, Carlos. *Ecstasies: Deciphering the Witches' Sabbath.* New York: Pantheon/Random House Inc., 1991.

Godwin, Joscelyn. *Mystery Religions in the Ancient World.* San Francisco: Harper & Row Publishers, 1981.

Grant, Kenneth. *The Magical Revival.* New York: Samuel Weiser, 1973.

_____. *Cults of the Shadow.* New York: Samuel Wieser, 1976.

Graves, Robert. *The White Goddess.* New York: Farrar, Straus, and Giroux, 1974.

Gray, William G. *Seasonal Occult Rituals.* London: The Aquarian Press, 1970.

_____. *Inner Traditions of Magic*. New York: Samuel Weiser, 1970.

_____. *Magical Ritual Methods*. Cheltenham: Helios Books, 1971.

_____. *Western Inner Workings*. New York: Samuel Weiser, 1983.

Green, Miranda. *Symbol & Image in Celtic Religious Art*. London: Routledge, 1989.

Grimassi, Raven. *Ways of the Strega*. St. Paul, MN: Llewellyn Publications, 1995.

Hackford, R. *Plato's Phaedrus*. New York: Cambridge at the University Press, 1979.

Hall, Manly. *Death to Rebirth*. Los Angeles: Philosophical Research Society, 1979.

_____. *Secret Teachings of All Ages*. Los Angeles: Philosophical Research Society, 1979.

Harding, Esther. *Woman's Mysteries: Ancient and Modern*. New York: Harper Colophon Books, 1976.

Hendricks, Rhoda A. *Classical Gods and Heroes—Myths as Told by the Ancient Authors*. New York: Morrow Quill Paperbacks, 1974.

Herm, Gerhard. *The Celts—The People Who Came Out of the Darkness*. New York: Barnes & Noble Books, 1976.

Holme, Bryan. *Myths of Greece and Rome*. New York: Penquin Books, 1979.

Jones, Prudence and Pennick, Nigel. *A History of Pagan Europe*. London: Routledge, 1995.

Knight, Chris. *Blood Relations—Menstruation and the Origins of Culture*. New London: Yale University Press, 1991.

Leland, Charles. *Aradia—Gospel of the Witches*. New York: University Books, 1963.

_____. *Etruscan Magick & Occult Remedies*. New York: University Books, 1963.

Luck, Georg. *Arcana Mundi, Magic and the Occult in the Greek and Roman Worlds*. Baltimore: Johns Hopkins University Press, 1985.

Macnamara, Ellen. *The Etruscans*. London: British Museum Press, 1993.

Mallory, J. P. *In Search of the Indo-Europeans*. London: Thames and Hudson, 1991.

Markale, Jean. *The Celts—Uncovering the Mythic and Historic Origins of Western Culture*. Rochester, VT: Inner Traditions International, 1978.

Matthews, Caitlin. *Elements of the Celtic Tradition*. London: Element Books, 1989.

Matthews, John & Caitlin. *Ladies of the Lake*. London: The Aquarian Press, 1992.

Matthews, John, ed. *The Celtic Reader*. London: The Aquarian Press, 1992.

Meyer, Marvin W., ed. *The Ancient Mysteries, a Sourcebook*. New York: Harper Collins, 1987.

Morris, John. *The Age of Arthur: A History of the British Isles from 350 to 650*. New York: Barnes & Noble Books, 1996.

Neumann, Erich. *The Great Mother*. Princeton: Princeton University Press, 1972.

Paine, Lauran. *Witchcraft and the Mysteries*. New York: Taplinger Publishing, 1975.

Picard, Gilbert. *The Ancient Civilization of Rome*. New York: Cowles Book Company, 1969.

Piggot, Stuart. *The Druids*. New York: Thames and Hudson, 1985.

RavenWolf, Silver. *To Ride a Silver Broomstick*. St. Paul: Llewellyn Publications, 1993.

Reich, William. *The Function of Orgasm*. New York: Orgone Institute, 1942.

Rutherford, Ward. *The Druids*. London: Gordon & Cremonesi, 1978.

Scullard, H. H. *Roman Britain—Outposts of the Empire*. London: Thames and Hudson, 1979.

Seznec, Jean. *The Survival of the Pagan Gods: The Mythological Tradition and Its Place in Renaissance Humanism and Art*. Princeton: Princeton University Press, 1981.

Spare, Austin O. *The Book of Pleasure (Self Love): The Psychology of Ecstasy*. Montreal: 93 Publishing, 1975 reprint of 1913 original.

Spence, Lewis. *The Mysteries of Britain*. North Hollywood: Newcastle Publishing, 1993.

_____. *The History and Origins of Druidism*. Van Nuys: Newcastle Publishing, 1995.

_____. *Magic Arts in Celtic Britain*. London: Aquarian Press, 1970.

Squires, Charles. *Celtic Myth and Legend*. Hollywood: Newcastle Publishing Co. Inc., 1975.

Stepanich, Kisma. *Sister Moon Lodge, The Power & Mystery of Menstruation*. St. Paul: Llewellyn Publications, 1991.

Stewart, R. J. *Celebrating the Male Mysteries*. Bath: Arcania Press, 1991.

Thwaite, Anthony. *Beyond the Inhabited World—Roman Britain*. New York: A Clarion Book, 1976.

Valiente, Doreen. *The Rebirth of Witchcraft*. London: Robert Hale, 1989.

_____. *Witchcraft for Tomorrow*. New York: St. Martin's Press, 1978.

Vaughan, Agnes Carr. *The Etruscans*. New York: Barnes & Noble Books, 1964.

INDEX

Stay in Touch ...

Llewellyn publishes hundreds of books on your favorite subjects!

To find the book you've been looking for, just call or write for a FREE copy of our full-color catalog, *New Worlds of Mind & Spirit. New Worlds* is brimming with books and other resources to help you develop your magical and spiritual potential to the fullest! Explore over 80 exciting pages that include:

- Exclusive interviews, articles and "how-to's" by Llewellyn's expert authors

- Features on classic Llewellyn books

- Previews of Llewellyn's latest books on astrology, tarot, Wicca, shamanism, magick, the paranormal, religion, mythology, alternative health and more

- Monthly horoscopes by Gloria Star

- Plus special offers available only to *New Worlds* readers

To get your free *New Worlds* catalog, call **1-800-THE-MOON**

or send your name and address to

Llewellyn, P.O. Box 64383, St. Paul, MN 55164-0383

Many bookstores carry New Worlds—ask for it! Visit our website at www.llewellyn.com.